# The Little, Brown ESL Workbook

**JOE DOWLING**

Nassau Community College

 HarperCollinsCollege*Publishers*

Sponsoring Editor: Patricia Rossi
Project Editor: Brigitte Pelner
Assistant Art Director: Dorothy Bungert
Production Administrator: Kathleen Donnelly
Compositor: Ruttle, Shaw & Wetherill, Inc.
Printer and Binder: R. R. Donnelley & Sons Company
Cover Printer: The Lehigh Press, Inc.

Page 254: William Carlos Williams: *The Collected Poems of William Carlos Williams 1909–1939, vol. I.* Copyright 1938 by New Directions Publishing Corporation. Reprinted by permission of New Directions Publishing Corporation.

The Little, Brown ESL Workbook

ISBN-0-673-52145-1

92 93 94 95  9 8 7 6 5 4 3 2 1

# Contents

## Chapter 6   Verb Tenses   115

# Chapter 9    Pronouns and Existentials    255

**Contents**  **xi**

# Chapter 16 Pronunciation 506

# Preface

*The Little, Brown ESL Workbook* is written for students who are in language transition. It is for all students who, for whatever reason, have left their native countries and are now seeking to be educated in an English-speaking educational environment. It is for those who were born in the United States but who acquired another language as their first language. It is for those many people around the world who want to review the basics and then master the subtleties of college-level English. It is intended as a supplement to, or precursor for, *The Little, Brown Handbook*, which is a comprehensive grammar, mechanics, and writing guide aimed primarily at native speakers of English.

*The Little, Brown ESL Workbook* is designed for college-bound students and others who are studying English as a second language at the intermediate and advanced level (TOEFL range 400 to 600). Students who use this book should already have a grasp of basic sentence structure and word order in English. This text is designed so that anyone who masters its content will be able to integrate with full confidence into the mainstream of higher education in English.

Though this text avoids needless technical jargon and terminology, it does use the vocabulary of linguistics wherever appropriate. By mastering English grammar and syntax, university-bound ESL students are, in effect, becoming experts in the field of applied linguistics. So, for example, instead of simply using the term *article* for *a/an* and *the*, the linguistic term *determiner* is used (and defined) to provide a more meaningful and understandable context for the student.

*The Little, Brown ESL Workbook* is a developmental skills text containing a full explanation of grammar, syntax, word order, and sentence structure in English. It begins with a review of the basics and leads to higher-level grammar and complex sentence structures. An intermediate student should master at least the first ten chapters. An advanced student should review these and then master the entire book. To a great extent, chapters are organized developmentally. But each chapter is separate, and the chapters may be reviewed in any order, as the instructor sees fit. This text may also be used in college English composition courses as an ancillary text for students with English as a Second Language who need in-depth work in specific areas not covered by the main curriculum.

A key feature of *The Little, Brown ESL Workbook* is that it gives full review and explanation of the five most common and persistent ESL writing errors.

1. It features a complete chapter on prepositions, the single most difficult area for most ESL students.
2. It provides a full treatment of articles and other determiners in English, the other area of most persistent error in ESL writing.
3. It contains a separate chapter on phrasal verbs and other idioms, including an extensive master list with definitions and exercises.
4. It has a complete, linguistically sound chapter on infinitives and gerunds, with a concluding section on *that* complements.
5. It examines the problem of conditional sentences, with a long section devoted to explaining the complex grammar of verb tenses in conditionals.

*The Little, Brown ESL Workbook* also includes many helpful tables and comprehensive lists of the most important English function words, irregular verbs, phrasal verbs and other idioms, verb + infinitive and verb + gerund combinations, plus complete vowel and consonant charts. It has sections devoted to the pronunciation of the most common word endings in English and a complete chapter on pronunciation with an overall review of the basic sounds, practice sections, and a bibliography.

### Acknowledgments

First I have to acknowledge all of my many ESL students over the years, whose motivation and hard work have inspired me. I also acknowledge the many fine teachers I have met and worked with throughout the years, especially Marie Ponsot. I want to thank two HarperCollins editors, Otis Taylor for initiating the project and Patricia Rossi for prodding this text along. Finally, I want to thank my family for supporting me and putting up with me throughout the entire project, especially Anne Delaney Dowling, whose support is so necessary for me.

Joe Dowling

# CHAPTER 1

# An International Study Group

## 1a  Student interview

Let's begin by getting to know one another first in pairs and then as a group. This text will assume that it is the goal of the class to practice English language skills while sharing ideas. Together, group members will increase their personal benefits and help educate each other.

Students with different native-language backgrounds bring richness to the learning of English as a second language (ESL). The various languages and their contrasts with English provide direct examples of human language and its variety. Each native language represented in the classroom and each accent will be respected in recognition of its contribution to the collective effort—a better understanding of the role of language in human interaction.

The power of a group of minds using skills learned from a variety of languages and cultures is expansive, and things may be learned more quickly and more intensely in such a group. Our initial writing exercise, the student interview, is designed to begin the process of forming an international study group.

First, fill out one copy of the Student Data Form, and give it to the teacher. Then, working in pairs, each student will interview another student, preferably from a different country of origin and a different language background.

Ask the other student all of the questions on the Student Data Form. If some of the questions do not seem relevant because you are a native speaker or for any other reason, just leave those questions blank and move on to the next.

STUDENT DATA FORM


Name:


**A. Personal History/Biographical Data**

Date of birth:


Country of birth:


Native language(s):


Other languages spoken:


Information about family:


Where have you lived?


Name all the cities and towns in which you lived in your native country.


When did you come to the United States?

Name all the cities and towns in which you've lived in the United States.

Where do you live now?

How do you get to school?

## B. Educational Background

Where did you go to grammar school, and when did you graduate?

Where did you go to high school (secondary school), and when did you graduate?

Do you have any college degrees? When did you receive them?

When did you begin to study English?

Where have you studied English?

When did you start college?

What courses have you taken?

What is your major?

What are your career goals?

What other schools do you plan to attend?

Do you plan to go to graduate school?

## C. Other Information

Do you have a job now? How many hours a week do you work?

Have you ever had any other jobs?

What do you do when you have free time?

What are your hobbies?

What kinds of books do you like?

What kinds of movies?

What kinds of music?

What kinds of food?

What kinds of people?

Do you play any sports?

What is your favorite book?

Your favorite movie?

Your favorite song or performer?

Your favorite color?

What places (cities, parks, and so on) have you visited in the United States and elsewhere in the world?

What places do you want to visit?

Is there anything you would like to add?

## STUDENT DATA FORM

Name:

**A. Personal History/Biographical Data**

Date of birth:

Country of birth:

Native language(s):

Other languages spoken:

Information about family:

Where have you lived?

Name all the cities and towns in which you lived in your native country.

When did you come to the United States?

Name all the cities and towns in which you've lived in the United States.

Where do you live now?

How do you get to school?

**B. Educational Background**

Where did you go to grammar school, and when did you graduate?

Where did you go to high school (secondary school), and when did you graduate?

Do you have any college degrees? When did you receive them?

When did you begin to study English?

Where have you studied English?

When did you start college?

What courses have you taken?

What is your major?

What are your career goals?

What other schools do you plan to attend?

Do you plan to go to graduate school?

## C. Other Information

Do you have a job now? How many hours a week do you work?

Have you ever had any other jobs?

What do you do when you have free time?

What are your hobbies?

What kinds of books do you like?

What kinds of movies?

What kinds of music?

What kinds of food?

What kinds of people?

Do you play any sports?

What is your favorite book?

Your favorite movie?

Your favorite song or performer?

Your favorite color?

What places (cities, parks, and so on) have you visited in the United States and elsewhere in the world?

What places do you want to visit?

Is there anything you would like to add?

# EXERCISE 1.1

## STUDENT INTERVIEW

Use the information furnished by the Student Data Form, plus any personal observations, to write an essay in your notebook introducing your classmate to the study group.

If you would like, you may write your interview essay using the following suggested format.

   I. Introduction
  II. Body
     A. Personal history
     B. Educational background
     C. Job, hobbies, interests, and other information
 III. Conclusion

In the introduction, identify yourself and the person you interviewed, and make a general statement, for example:

Good morning. My name is _____, and today I had

the pleasure of interviewing _____, a student from

_____ whose native language is _____.

We had a friendly chat and exchanged some information.

This may be followed by three body paragraphs about personal history, education, and job, hobbies, interests, and other information. A final paragraph—a conclusion—could read:

In conclusion, I want to thank _____ for such a pleas-

ant interview. I wish _____ all the success in the world.

Good luck, _____!

# EXERCISE 1.2

## MAP AND LANGUAGES OF THE WORLD

Using the following map and chart, locate your native country and the home country of the student you interviewed. Then indicate the languages spoken by you and the student you interviewed by checking them off on the Languages of the World chart.

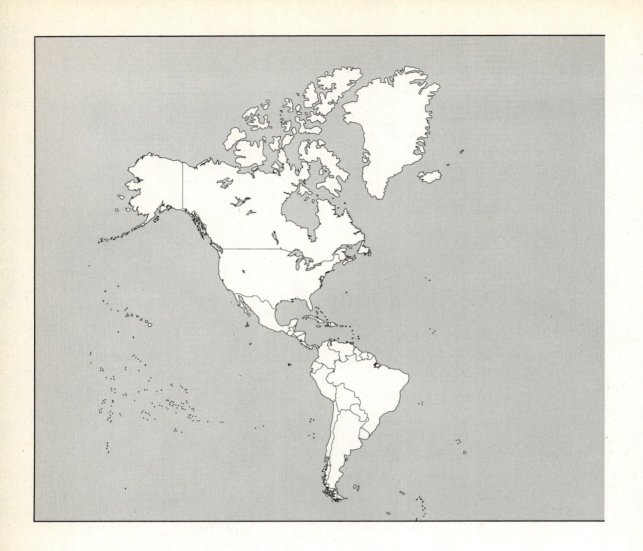

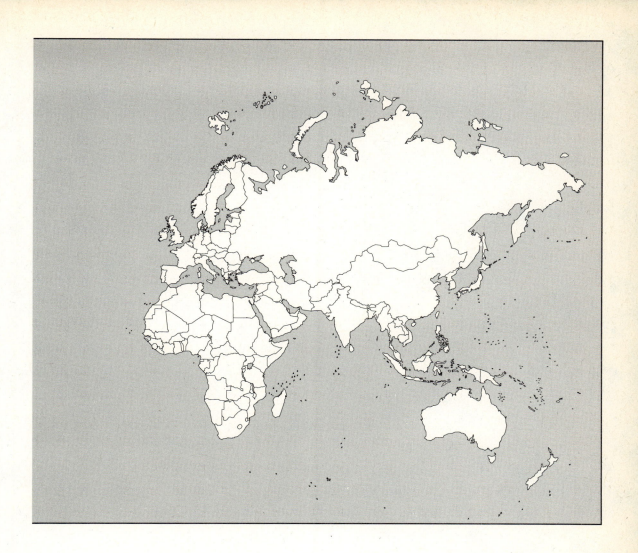

## Languages of the World

| | |
|---|---|
| _____ Afghani | _____ Gaelic |
| _____ Afrikaans | _____ German |
| _____ Albanian | _____ Greek |
| _____ American Sign Language | _____ Guarani |
| _____ Amharic | _____ Gujarati |
| _____ Arabic | _____ Haitian Creole |
| _____ Armenian | _____ Hebrew |
| Austronesian: _____ Indonesian | _____ Hmong |
| _____ Melanesian | _____ Hungarian |
| _____ Micronesian | _____ Ibo |
| _____ Polynesian | _____ Icelandic |
| _____ Other | _____ Invit |
| _____ Basque | _____ Hindi |
| _____ Bengali | _____ Iranian |
| _____ Bulgarian | _____ Italian |
| _____ Burmese | _____ Japanese |
| _____ Cambodian | _____ Kannada |
| Chinese: _____ Cantonese | _____ Korean |
| _____ Mandarin | _____ Kurdish |
| _____ Other | _____ Lakota |
| _____ Cree | _____ Lao |
| _____ Czech | _____ Latin |
| _____ Danish | _____ Lithuanian |
| _____ Dutch | _____ Malay |
| _____ English | _____ Malayalam |
| _____ Faeroese | _____ Marathi |
| _____ Farsi | _____ Mongolian |
| _____ Finnish | _____ Nahuatl |
| _____ French | _____ Navaho |
| _____ Frisian | _____ Nepali |

| | | | |
|---|---|---|---|
| _____ Norwegian | | _____ Swazi |
| _____ Other sign language | | _____ Swedish |
| _____ Papuan | | _____ Tagalog |
| _____ Persian | | _____ Tamil |
| _____ Polish | | _____ Telugu |
| _____ Portuguese | | _____ Thai |
| _____ Punjabi | | _____ Tibetan |
| _____ Quechua | | _____ Turkish |
| _____ Rumanian | | _____ Urdu |
| _____ Russian | | _____ Vietnamese |
| _____ Samoan | | _____ Welsh |
| _____ Sanskrit | | _____ Xhosa |
| _____ Serbo-Croatian | | _____ Yoruba |
| _____ Sesotho | | _____ Zulu |
| _____ Sinhalese | | |
| _____ Slovak | | _____ Other |
| _____ Slovene | | _____ |
| _____ Spanish | | _____ |
| _____ Swahili | | |

## EXERCISE 1.3

## CLASS SURVEY

Share the information from the student interviews and essays by reading each of them around the room.

In your own book, check off each language spoken by your classmates, and mark their countries of origin on the map.

**1a/Student Interview**     **15**

## EXERCISE 1.4

## FREEWRITING

1. Spend ten minutes writing about anything. Any topic is acceptable; just stick to one topic and write nonstop. If you feel yourself stopping, write your first name over and over until you begin to have some ideas about the topic again.

    After finishing, read all the freewriting aloud, listening to each others' ideas and sentences.
2. Continue to freewrite in your notebook, and share your writing with the group throughout the semester.
3. After a while, you will have four or five freewrites. In consultation with your instructor, select one of the freewrites, and do further research in the library on that topic. Then prepare a speech based on your research. Make it three minutes long if you can.
4. A long-range writing goal is to prepare a typed paper based on this or some other topic that you have researched. Ask your instructor about notation form.

### A note about writing and grammar

This text suggests some written exercises. This is only a beginning. Grammar is most efficiently learned in connection with writing. Each instructor and class will have to decide how much writing will be structured into the activities of the class. The freewriting described in this chapter is just the weekly minimum. Throughout the text it is suggested that student writing serve as a springboard for contextualized grammar study.

# CHAPTER 2

# Sentence Grammar and Structure

## 2a Parts of speech

Grammar is a way of describing how words work in relation to one another. Grammar helps in discussing and analyzing sentences, a practical ESL skill. For fruitful discussion and analysis, a common understanding of the vocabulary of grammar is necessary. Study the parts of speech as a first step.

---

### THE EIGHT MAJOR PARTS OF SPEECH

(For more information, see the chapters indicated in parentheses.)

**SUBSTANTIVES**

1. **Noun.** A noun names a person, place, thing or idea: *John, woman, Taft High School, river, Koran, chair, democracy, love.* (See Chapter 3.)
2. **Verb.** A verb expresses an action, occurrence, or state of being: *run, speak, become, be, seem.* (See Chapters 5 and 6.)
3. **Pronoun.** A pronoun substitutes for a noun and usually names a person, place, thing, or idea: *he, they, that, what.* (See Chapter 9.)
4. **Adjective.** An adjective modifies a noun or a pronoun: *blue, small, gentle, sad.* (See Chapter 10.)
5. **Adverb.** Adverbs modify verbs, adjectives, other adverbs, or whole clauses: *gently, helpfully, almost.* (See Chapter 10.)

**FUNCTIONAL WORDS**

6. **Preposition.** Prepositions relate nouns or pronouns to other words in a sentence: *about, by, to, in.* (See Chapter 8.)
7. **Conjunction.** Conjunctions connect words, phrases, or clauses: *and, but, or.* (See Chapter 4.)
8. **Determiner.** Determiners are modifying words that come before nouns and signal that a noun is coming. Functioning like adjectives, determiners identify or tell which instance of the noun is being talked about: *the, a/an, her, this, those.* (See Chapter 7.)

---

### A note on form and function

A word may serve different functions in different sentences. *Help* is a noun in "I need your help," but it is a verb in "Can you help me?" In

"I like your brown coat," *brown* is an adjective; in "Brown is my favorite color," it is a noun.

To determine a word's part of speech, you must examine its function in a sentence.

## EXERCISE 2.1

## PARTS OF SPEECH

A. Identify the part of speech of each word in the following sentences, using the abbreviations *N* (noun), *V* (verb), *P* (pronoun), *ADJ* (adjective), *ADV* (adverb), *PREP* (preposition), *C* (conjunction), and *D* (determiner).

*Example:*
    D ADJ N  V PREP D N
   The dark clouds came over the field.

1. Charles walked to school yesterday.

2. He saw a few birds.

3. I can do it for you.

4. That man is the teacher.

5. I wore a green scarf and a blue hat.

6. A gallon of gas and a pack of cigarettes cost almost the same amount of money.

7. Jose and Maria are from the same country.

8. When you give the speech, you should refer to the map of the world.

9. Her speech mentioned Taiwan but not Hong Kong.

10. It is difficult for her to hear the music because she is so far away.

11. The embassy is located in front of the train station.

12. The students had breakfast at home.

13. Those women are always reading books.

14. Of the group, he is the most prepared for the test.

15. When winter comes, Steve goes to Florida.

16. Last year, the company moved to South America.

17. Her father is in the import business.

18. We left the bags at the station.

19. The cab to the station cost a lot of money.

20. She cried when she fell off the bicycle.

**B.** Freewrite for ten minutes. After sharing your writing with the group, take each word in the first paragraph and tell what part of speech it is. Use the same abbreviations as in part A.

**C.** Discuss how it helps to know the part of speech of a word.

## 2b  Sentence structure

Word order—the position of the words in a sentence—is important in English. Most of the meaning of a sentence in English is determined by word order.

### 1  Basic pattern: subject and predicate

A sentence makes an assertion (the **predicate**) about something (the **subject**).

| SUBJECT | PREDICATE |
|---------|-----------|
| She | walked to school. |
| The man | has a large hat. |
| The boy | gave the book to his mother. |
| That man | is a teacher. |

The **subject** is a noun or pronoun (or words that function as a noun or pronoun) that performs the action of the sentence; it normally precedes the predicate. The **predicate** can have two parts: the **verb** and the **complement**. The **verb** is the word stating an action, occurrence, or state of being. The **complement** is usually a noun or pronoun (or words that function as a noun or pronoun) that receives the action of the verb or expresses something about the subject.

| SUBJECT | PREDICATE | |
|---------|-----------|---|
| | *Verb* | *Complement* |
| The man | has | a large hat. |
| The boy | gave | the book to his mother. |

## EXERCISE 2.2

## SUBJECTS AND PREDICATES

Draw a vertical line to divide each of the following sentences into subject (*S*) and predicate (*P*).

*Example:*   Jose | works in a bakery.

1. The stars are shining on my house.

2. Esperanza talked to her friend on the phone.

3. Our house needs a lot of repairs.

4. The classroom has a chalkboard and some chairs.

5. Xiao Li wanted to go back to his home in China.

6. New York is the home of the United Nations.

7. The store was closed when we got there.

8. I should have called her yesterday.

9. The red flowers over there are tulips.

10. The doctor sent Elmer directly to the emergency room.

11. That bag contains nothing but old rags.

12. She forgot to do her homework.

13. The decaffeinated coffee should be over in that corner of the store.

14. His two base hits won the big game for his school.

15. Colorful clothing was the style during the 1960s.

# EXERCISE 2.3

## SUBJECTS, VERBS, AND COMPLEMENTS

Underline the main parts of the following sentences. Underline the subject once, the verb twice, and the complement three times.

*Example:*   Some <u>athletes</u> <u>are</u> heroes in high school.

1. The teacher called his name.

2. I bought the bread at the bakery.

3. Mr. Smith walked home.

4. Some people have become well known in their lifetimes.

5. Chinese customs call for reverence of the elders.

6. That machine does all of the work.

7. No one has proved the existence of ghosts.

8. A few people there are good translators.

9. His class ended a long semester.

10. She became a saleswoman for a computer company.

11. The telephone operator will help you with that call.

12. The first president of our club was Jose.

13. My sister looks tired today.

14. That team plays Irish football.

15. His band plays rock music.

## 2 Special patterns

### Questions

The normal subject-verb-complement sentence order is changed for questions. Usually, the pattern involves the inversion of the subject and part of the verb. (See Chapter 5 for more on question formation.)

Is he a language student?

Do drivers need a special license?

Can students use the pool?

### Existentials

The normal subject-verb-complement sentence order is also varied for sentences beginning with *it* or *there*. (See Chapter 9.)

There is an award-winning teacher at the school.

It is sad that they have moved to another town.

In sentences like this, the words *it* and *there* do not function as a normal sentence part.

### Commands and directions

The normal sentence pattern is also varied for commands. There is no apparent subject; usually, it is understood to be *you*.

Explain it, please.

Stop the car.

## EXERCISE 2.4

## SPECIAL PATTERNS

A. In each of the following sentences, underline the subject once, the verb twice, and the complement three times. Mark each sentence *N* (normal pattern) or *S* (special pattern) in the space provided. If the sentence has a special pattern, indicate whether it is a question (*Q*), an existential (*E*), or a command (*C*).

*Example:*   <u>*N*</u>   He took a pen from the drawer.

         <u>*S-Q*</u>   Is this a map of Europe?

_____   1. Drop the car off at five o'clock.

_____   2. There are many forms of energy.

_____   3. Cheryl is the president of the club.

_____   4. Can someone help me?

_____   5. Is he mad at us now?

_____   6. Maria goes to school three days a week.

_____   7. It is often said that saving energy is important.

_____   8. Eat all the vegetables, please.

_____   9. People often misinterpret a foreign accent.

_____  10. What kind of car do you have?

**B.** Now write three versions of each of the special patterns.

**Questions**

1.


2.


3.

**Existentials**

4.


5.


6.


**Commands**

7.


8.


9.


**C.** Take a look at some freewriting you have done. How many special-pattern sentences—questions, commands, and existentials—can you find? Copy them in the space below, and share them with your group.

### 3 The five basic sentence patterns

Although infinite sentence variations are possible, there are only five basic sentence patterns.

1. SUBJECT + VERB (INTRANSITIVE)

    The car    stopped.

2. SUBJECT + VERB (TRANSITIVE) + DIRECT OBJECT

    Maria    speaks    French.

3. SUBJECT + VERB (LINKING) + SUBJECT COMPLEMENT

    Jose    is    tall.

| 4. SUBJECT + | VERB (TRANSITIVE) + | INDIRECT OBJECT + | DIRECT OBJECT |
|---|---|---|---|
| She | gave | him | a drink. |

| 5. SUBJECT + | VERB (TRANSITIVE) + | DIRECT OBJECT + | OBJECT COMPLEMENT |
|---|---|---|---|
| Students | consider | her | popular. |

**Transitive verbs** (patterns 2, 4, and 5) transfer the action from the subject to the object. If the object is a pronoun, it must be in the objective form. **Intransitive verbs** (pattern 1) do not pass action to a complement. These verbs are complete by themselves. **Linking verbs** (pattern 3) link the subject with a complement that describes or names the subject. Linking verbs include forms of the verb *be* and some other verbs that serve to describe the subject, such as *remain, appear, seem, feel, smell, look, sound,* and *taste.*

**NAMING**

Jose is a student of English.

These people were immigrants from Bolivia.

**DESCRIBING**

The sea seems calm today.

Lemons taste sweet.

## EXERCISE 2.5

## TRANSITIVE AND INTRANSITIVE VERBS

**A.** Use your dictionary to look up each of the following verbs. In the blank, indicate whether the verb is transitive (*T*) or intransitive (*I*). Then use it in a sentence.

*Example:* ___*I*___ tremble

*The earth trembled.*

_____ 1. sit

_____ 2. drive

_____ 3. talk

_____ 4. run

_____ 5. live

_____ 6. leave

_____ 7. buy

_____ 8. prepare

_____ 9. fall

_____ 10. learn

_____ 11. shine

_____ 12. wait

_____ 13. take

_____ 14. give

_____ 15. write

**B.** Read over some of your freewriting. Analyze the verbs. Underline the main verb in each sentence. Then list each of these verbs as transitive or intransitive. Count the totals. Share your statistics with the group.

## EXERCISE 2.6

## SUBJECT COMPLEMENTS

Supply an appropriate subject complement (noun or adjective) for the following sentences, which have linking verbs.

*Examples:* Jose is ___*a senior*___.

The air smells ___*delightful*___.

1. They are _____.

2. Maria appears _____.

3. That sandwich tastes _____.

4. My new sweater feels _____.

5. The teacher became _____.

6. The house smells _____.

7. She was _____.

8. The school appears _____.

9. Alberto has been _____.

10. That band sounds _____.


## EXERCISE 2.7

## SENTENCE PATTERNS

A. The following sentences are grouped by pattern. Within each group, identify the subjects (*S*), verbs (*V*), objects (*DO, IO*), and complements (*SC, OC*).

*Examples:*
   1. The man trembled uncontrollably.
        *S*    *V*

   2. Some people provide help to others.
        *S*    *V*  *DO*

   3. Yoga is a very ancient science.
        *S* *V*       *SC*

   4. Julia told him the news.
        *S*  *V* *IO*  *DO*

   5. The teacher declared him the winner.
        *S*    *V*  *DO*  *OC*


**Pattern 1: S-V**

1. Cats love to take naps.

2. Some plants grow to a great height.

3. The stars shine all night long.

4. The train travels best at top speed.

5. Some leftover food from the party still remains.

**Pattern 2: S-V-DO**

1. Some people may enjoy French food.

2. The company offered a steady job to every employee.

3. The guests ate the dessert.

4. I provided three big envelopes for all the papers.

5. We recognized the house right away.

**Pattern 3: S-V-SC**

1. Soccer is a sport that is played all over the world.

2. Nitrogen is an element that is needed for plant growth.

3. The word *phonetics* means the study of word sounds.

4. A permanent resident is a person who has a green card.

5. The tide is highest at midnight.

**Pattern 4: S-V-IO-DO**

1. I gave him the videotape of the race.

2. He bought me a piece of cake.

3. Parents feed their babies milk all day long.

4. The airplane pilot sent the airport a message.

5. The teacher in that class never gave the students much homework.

**Pattern 5: S-V-DO-OC**

1. The people call that man a hero.

2. The boss has declared tomorrow a holiday.

3. The driver made the passengers angry.

4. The board of trustee elected Pat Smith chairperson.

5. The bus driver considered the question fair.


**B.** Using the verbs given, write sentences that imitate the pattern of the model sentences. Identify the sentence parts.

    *Example:* bought

*She bought me a new bicycle.*

**Pattern 1: S-V**

  1. remain


  2. sit


  3. fall


**Pattern 2: S-V-DO**

  4. think


  5. collect


  6. throw

**Pattern 3: S-V-SC**

7. taste

8. feel

9. are

**Pattern 4: S-V-IO-DO**

10. write

11. send

12. give

**Pattern 5: S-V-DO-OC**

13. make

14. name

15. declare

**C.** Select a piece of your freewriting. Note which of the five basic sentence patterns each sentence in it uses. Count how many sentences you have of each pattern. Share the statistics with the group.

## 2c The objective case of pronouns

Personal pronouns used as direct objects, indirect objects, or objects of prepositions are in the objective case (see Chapter 9). Listed here are the personal pronouns in the subjective and objective cases.

| Subjective case | Objective case |
| --- | --- |
| I | me |
| you | you |
| it | it |
| he | him |
| she | her |
| we | us |
| they | them |

Maria saw *him* (objective case) at the movies.

*We* (subjective case) surprised *them* (objective case) with a present.

## 1 Types of complements

**Direct objects** (DO), patterns 2, 4, and 5, receive the action of the verb and answer the questions *what?* or *whom?* after the verb.

    S    V      DO
Elmer bought a book.

    S    V        DO
Carlos wears a school jacket.

**Indirect objects** (IO), pattern 4, can come before or after direct objects and indicate to or for whom or what the action of the verb is directed.

    S   V   IO    DO
He gave me the car.

    S   V     DO    IO
Maria sold the book to me.

**Subject complements** (SC), pattern 3, are nouns or adjectives following the linking verb that do not receive the action but refer to the subject. They rename or complete the subject.

    S   V    SC
Jose was the winner.

    S   V     SC
Maria seems well qualified.

**Object complements** (OC), pattern 5, are nouns or adjectives following the direct object that rename or describe the direct object. They complete the direct object.

       S   V    DO      OC
The storm made the city a disaster area.

    S   V   DO  OC
He makes me angry.

## EXERCISE 2.8

## COMPLEMENTS

Underline the objects and complements in the following sentences. Indicate whether they are direct objects (DO), indirect objects (IO), subject complements (SC), or object complements (OC).

*Examples:*   He gave him a book.

That man is very old.

Their behavior made me angry.

1. Clarita started a business on Hempstead Turnpike.

2. We visited Disneyland when we were in California.

3. Louisa knew Jose from her hometown.

4. She is the teacher.

5. The doctor seemed well qualified.

6. The worker told his boss the story.

7. The snowstorm left the city a mess.

8. Something tastes funny.

9. Johanna considered the test difficult.

10. That student has been late every day.

11. Maria became the chairperson of the group.

12. The salesperson showed us the car.

13. The little boy gave himself a black eye by falling down the stairs.

14. Dense jungles cover more than half of the country.

15. Mother was surprised by the party in her honor.

## EXERCISE 2.9

## OBJECTIVE PRONOUNS

**A.** Here are some sentences with the objective pronoun underlined. Circle the verb that each pronoun completes.

*Example:* She did not (recognize) him.

1. Tamara provided <u>me</u> with a letter of recommendation.

2. They insulted <u>us</u> with their behavior.

3. The whole family visited <u>them</u> when we went to Florida.

4. Will you invite <u>him</u> to your party?

5. Benita found <u>her</u> waiting for the bus.

**B.** Fill in the correct form of the pronoun in each of the following sentences.

*Example:* When I went to the movies, I could not avoid *them* (they).

1. I told _____ (you) about the meeting a week ago.

2. Carlos visited _____ (he) when he was in Guatemala.

3. He found _____ (we) at the restaurant.

4. The loud noise startled _____ (I).

5. They located _____ (she) in the library.

6. Jose told _____ (they) he was sorry.

7. Alberto called _____ (I) to say he had the tickets.

8. The teacher told _____ (you) to be quiet.

9. Our mother loves _____ (we).

10. The librarian checked the book out for _____ (she).

**2c/The Objective Case of Pronouns**    **33**

## 2 The order of direct and indirect objects

The order of the direct and indirect object depends on the verb you choose. There are four main possibilities.

### Verbs taking indirect object movement with *to*

FIRST PATTERN

```
S   V    DO        IO
He sold the book to Mr. Lopez.
```

SECOND PATTERN

```
S   V    IO      DO
He sold Mr. Lopez the book.
```

If the indirect object is a pronoun, we usually follow the second pattern.

```
     S     V   IO   DO
Herman gave him a present.
```

If the direct object is a pronoun, we always follow the first pattern.

```
     S     V  DO    IO
Herman gave it to Mr. Lopez.
```

The following verbs may have indirect object movement with *to*.

| | | | | |
|---|---|---|---|---|
| bring | offer | read | show | tell |
| give | owe | sell | sing | write |
| hand | pass | send | take | |
| lend | pay | serve | teach | |

### Verbs that call for an indirect object with *to* but do not permit indirect object movement

```
  S    V      DO       IO
We suggested changes to the man.
```

This cannot be written:

*We suggested the man changes.

The following verbs take an indirect object with *to* but do not permit indirect object movement.

| | | |
|---|---|---|
| admit | mention | report |
| announce | prove | say |
| describe | recommend | speak |
| explain | repeat | suggest |
| introduce | | |

* An asterisk preceding a sentence indicates incorrect usage.

**Verbs taking indirect object movement with *for***

**FIRST PATTERN**

> S     V     DO        IO
> Mr. Lopez built a house for them.

**SECOND PATTERN**

> S     V    IO    DO
> Mr. Lopez built them a house.

If the indirect object is a pronoun, we usually follow the second pattern.

> S   V   IO   DO
> She drew him a picture.

If the direct object is a pronoun, we always follow the first pattern.

> S    V    DO    IO
> Xiao Li made it for Chen.

These verbs use both patterns:

| | | |
|---|---|---|
| bake | draw | knit |
| build | find | make |
| buy | get | reserve |
| do | | |

**Verbs that can have an indirect object with *for* but do not permit indirect object movement**

> S   V       DO       IO
> He answered questions for us.

This cannot be changed to:

> *He answered us the questions.

The following verbs take an indirect object with *for* but do not permit indirect object movement.

| | | |
|---|---|---|
| answer | close | prepare |
| cash | design | prescribe |
| change | open | pronounce |

# EXERCISE 2.10

## INDIRECT OBJECT MOVEMENT WITH *TO* AND *FOR*

---

**A.** Change these sentences by putting the indirect object before the direct object.

*Examples:*　　The bank lends money to customers.

*The bank lends customers money.*

　　　　　　　She baked some bread for us.

*She baked us some bread.*

1. They will bring the book to us.

2. Mario cashed the check for me.

3. His wife handed the baby to him.

4. Alberto owes the money to the bank.

5. She found an apartment for us.

6. Mother knitted that sweater for Kevin.

7. He wrote a letter to the teacher.

8. The agent reserved three seats for them.

9. Atsushi drew a map for Naoko.

10. The substitute teacher taught the lesson to the class.

**B.** Underline the direct object once and the indirect object twice. Some sentences do not have both.

*Example:*　　The clerk showed me a coat.

1. I asked him a lot of questions about the class.

2. She answered the phone for us.

3. He suggested a plan to them.

4. They signed a contract.

5. The new fan will cost us $500.

6. The owner of the store gave me a price.

7. I made her a cup of coffee.

8. I handed her a book with all the pictures.

9. The bank lent them the money they needed.

10. The finance company charged me ten percent interest.

11. He mentioned the assignment to me.

12. The waiter added up the check.

13. He made me a lower offer.

14. She is keeping my car for me.

15. They signed an agreement with the banker.

# CHAPTER 3

# Nouns

**Nouns** name people, places, things, and concepts: *child, school, refrigerator, democracy.* **Proper nouns** name specific people, places, or things. They show this by using capital letters: *Roberto Clemente, Yale University, Toyota.*

## EXERCISE 3.1

## PROPER NOUNS

Read the following paragraphs. Underline the proper nouns. List these nouns under the three headings, depending on whether they stand for people, places, and things.

My grandfather said that when he came to this country, he wanted three things: a job, a home, and a Cadillac. He said he thought the United States was a land of unlimited opportunity. Grandfather's name was Giovanni, and in his native Italy he had heard of Abraham Lincoln, George Washington, and the Statue of Liberty. He said he decided to visit a cousin in New York after receiving a letter from her. She wrote about the Empire State Building, the Brooklyn Bridge, and her favorite baseball team, the New York Yankees.

After he came here, my grandfather decided to stay. He got a job on Wall Street, and he found a home in the Bronx with his wife, Annette, and later three children, Dominic, Ralph, and Maria. He never owned a Cadillac, but he did drive a few Fords and Chevrolets.

## 3a Count and noncount nouns

Measuring and counting account for most of the grammar about nouns. Nouns are distinguished as count, noncount, and mass nouns.

### 1 Count nouns

The most common nouns in English are **count nouns.** A count noun has a shape or limit. A single unit is easy to discern, and units are therefore separable and countable.

This is a *chair*.

This is a *person*.

This is a *car*.

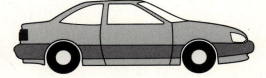

These are *chairs*.

These are *people*.

These are *cars*.

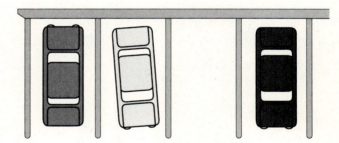

### Singular and plural

A **singular count noun** is always used with the singular verb form and requires an article (*a, an, the*) or some other determiner, even if a descriptive adjective precedes it.

The blue *hat* is on the chair.

He owns a blue *car*.

A *cow* walks slowly.

**Plural count nouns** are formed by adding *-s* or *-es* to the singular noun and are used with the plural verb form.

A few *hats* are on the chair.

He owns two *cars*.

*Cows* walk slowly.

*Spelling:* to make a plural, most nouns add *-s*. This includes nouns that end in a vowel + *o*.

| SINGULAR | PLURAL |
|---|---|
| pen | pens |
| cow | cows |
| cat | cats |
| dog | dogs |
| zoo | zoos |

Words ending in *ss, sh, ch, x*, or *z* add *-es* to make them plural. This also applies to nouns that end in a consonant +*o*.

| SINGULAR | PLURAL |
|---|---|
| kiss | kisses |
| wish | wishes |
| match | matches |
| fox | foxes |
| tomato | tomatoes |

If a noun ends in a consonant + *y*, we change the *y* to *i* and add *-es*.

| SINGULAR | PLURAL |
|---|---|
| baby | babies |
| city | cities |

If a noun ends in a vowel + *y*, we simply add *-s* to make it plural.

| SINGULAR | PLURAL |
|---|---|
| toy | toys |
| key | keys |

If a noun ends in *f* or *fe*, we change the *f* or *fe* to *v* and add *es*.

| SINGULAR | PLURAL |
|---|---|
| wife | wives |
| thief | thieves |

## FORMING THE PLURALS OF REGULAR NOUNS

|  | NOUN ENDING | SINGULAR | PLURAL |
|---|---|---|---|
| ADD -s | vowel | bee | bees |
|  |  | shoe | shoes |
|  | consonant | park | parks |
|  |  | cat | cats |
|  | vowel + *y* | toy | toys |
|  |  | play | plays |
|  | vowel + *o* | patio | patios |
|  |  | rodeo | rodeos |
| ADD -es | *ss, sh,* | kiss | kisses |
|  | *ch, x, z* | church | churches |
|  | consonant + *o* | potato | potatoes |
|  |  | mosquito | mosquitoes |
| ADD -ies | consonant + *y* | lady | ladies |
|  |  | story | stories |
| ADD -ves | *f* or *fe* | life | lives |
|  |  | leaf | leaves |

## EXERCISE 3.2

## MAKING NOUNS PLURAL

Make each of the following words plural, and then use it in a sentence.

*Example:* baby _babies_

There are two babies in that family.

1. couch _____

2. boy _____

3. knife _____

4. leaf _____

**3a/Count and Noncount Nouns**    43

5. city _____

6. tray _____

7. country _____

8. life _____

9. thief _____

10. cowboy _____

11. lady _____

12. dictionary _____

13. wife _____

14. key _____

15. party _____

16. bush _____

17. potato _____

18. tax _____

19. dish _____

20. class _____

### Pronouncing the -s/-es ending

The plural marker -s/-es has three different pronunciations (see also Chapter 16). After voiceless sounds /p, t, k, f, θ/, -s sounds like /s/.

| | | |
|---|---|---|
| trap*s* | crack*s* | month*s* |
| cat*s* | muff*s* | |

After voiced sounds /b, d, g, v, ð, m, n, ŋ, l, r/ and all vowels, -s sounds like /z/.

| | | |
|---|---|---|
| cab*s* | lathe*s* | hill*s* |
| seed*s* | ham*s* | car*s* |
| tag*s* | fan*s* | fee*s* |
| live*s* | thing*s* | |

After sibilant sounds /s, z, ʃ, tʃ, dʒ/, the -es sounds like /iz/ and is pronounced as a separate syllable.

| | | |
|---|---|---|
| nurs*es* | dish*es* | hunch*es* |
| phras*es* | garag*es* | ridg*es* |

## EXERCISE 3.3

## PRONUNCIATION of -s/-es

Fill in the blanks at the right with /s/, /z/, or /iz/ to indicate the correct pronunciation of these plural nouns. Say each plural aloud.

ages _____          purses _____

caps _____          bags _____

pads _____          sacks _____

buses _____         mills _____

hats _____          bees _____

fans _____          rings _____

causes _____        moths _____

bridges _____       lunches _____

cans _____          bushes _____

beaches _____       flaps _____

| stacks _____ | mirages _____ |
| naps _____ | robes _____ |
| slums _____ | rings _____ |
| fads _____ | liars _____ |
| bows _____ | sounds _____ |
| ploys _____ | stages _____ |
| oils _____ | ribs _____ |

## Irregular plurals

Some common nouns have irregular plural forms.

| SINGULAR | PLURAL |
|---|---|
| child | children |
| foot | feet |
| man | men |
| mouse | mice |
| tooth | teeth |
| woman | women |
| goose | geese |

Some nouns have the same form in the singular and in the plural.

| SINGULAR | PLURAL |
|---|---|
| fish | fish |
| sheep | sheep |
| deer | deer |

I have one sheep in the barn and ten sheep in the pasture.

Some nouns, such as *news*, *politics*, and *mathematics*, end in *s* but are singular.

Mathematics is not my favorite subject.

The news is bad tonight.

Finally, some nouns are always plural. They do not have a singular form.

| | | |
|---|---|---|
| eyeglasses | clothes | trousers |
| glasses | pants | scissors |
| pliers | slacks | people |
| pajamas | | |

## EXERCISE 3.4

## IRREGULAR PLURALS

Fill in the blank with the plural form of each noun. If there is no plural, put an *X*. Then write a complete sentence using each noun as the subject.

*Example:* fish _____*fish*_____

*Fish swim in the ocean.*

economics _____*X*_____

*Economics is my best subject.*

1. man _____

2. sheep _____

3. goose _____

4. mathematics _____

5. child _____

6. glasses _____

7. pants _____

8. deer _____

9. mouse _____

10. tooth _____

11. clothes _____

12. woman _____

13. news _____

14. politics _____

15. pajamas _____

16. foot _____

17. slacks _____

18. pliers _____

## 2 Noncount nouns

Since a count noun has a shape or limit, a single unit is easy to discern and is separable and hence countable. Plurals are possible.

A **noncount noun** is something we cannot count because it has no distinct shape; a single unit is difficult to discern because of size, shape, or definition.

### COMMON NONCOUNT NOUNS

| | | |
|---|---|---|
| advertising | fruit | pasta |
| advice | fun | pepper |
| air | furniture | petroleum |
| anger | gasoline (gas) | physics |
| bacon | gold | plastic |
| baggage | gravy | poetry |
| beauty | ham | politics |
| beef | happiness | pollution |
| beer | health | pork |
| biology | help | poverty |
| broccoli | homework | rain |
| butter | honesty | research |
| cabbage | ice | rice |
| candy | ice cream | salt |
| cauliflower | information | satisfaction |
| celery | intelligence | scenery |
| cement | jelly | silver |
| cereal | jewelry | snow |
| cheese | juice | soap |
| chicken | knowledge | soup |
| chocolate | lamb | spinach |
| clothing | love | steel |
| coal | luggage | sugar |
| coffee | lumber | tea |
| confidence | machinery | toast |
| corn | mail | transportation |
| courage | mathematics | truth |
| cream | meat | violence |
| dirt | milk | wealth |
| economics | money | weather |
| employment | music | wine |
| equipment | news | wood |
| fish | oil | wool |
| flour | oxygen | work |
| food | paper | yogurt |

# USING COUNT AND NONCOUNT NOUNS

**PLURALS**

Count nouns have a plural form and are used after numbers.

> He has three *books* with him.

> I own two *cars*.

Noncount nouns have no plural and cannot be used after numbers.

> *I have two furnitures.

> *Advices are good to get.

**ARTICLES**

Count nouns can take both definite and indefinite articles.

> I have *a* bottle.

> She has *the* keys.

Noncount nouns can use the definite article only.

> Mom made *the* bread and *the* gravy.

> I ate *the* food.

> *I have *a* furniture.

> *A* meal was delicious.

**SOME/A LOT OF**

Count nouns can use both *some* and *a lot of* with the plural.

> I have *some* books.

> I have *a lot of* books.

Noncount nouns can also use both.

> I have *some* water.

> He bought *a lot of* luggage.

**MANY/MUCH**

Count nouns can use *many*.

> I have *many* books.

> She has *many* shoes.

Noncount nouns use *much*.

> She has *much* information.

> We have had *much* rain this month.

**A FEW/A LITTLE**

Count nouns use *a few*.

>We have *a few* bottles left.

>He saved *a few* pennies.

Noncount nouns use *a little*.

>He has *a little* food.

>I ate *a little* bread.

Knowing if a noun is countable or noncountable is important for determining subject-verb agreement, the use of articles (*a, an, the*), and the use of quantifiers (*much, many*).

Nouns in the following categories are usually noncount nouns.

Liquids (*water, coffee*)

Gases (*oxygen, air*)

Solids (*wood, cement*)

Single groups made up of similar items (*furniture, clothing*)

Substances composed of minute particles (*sand, rice*)

Actions or states of being (*running, health*)

Emotions (*hatred, anger, love*)

Abstractions (*information, beauty*)

General topics (*pollution, politics*)

Fields of study and languages (*biology, economics, Chinese*)

General activities (*walking* and other gerunds)

Natural phenomena (*rain, gravity*)

## EXERCISE 3.5

## COUNT AND NONCOUNT NOUNS

**A.** Use *some* + the word in parentheses to complete these sentences. Make count nouns plural by adding *-s* or *-es*.

*Examples:*  (money) I need some ___money___.

(key) I have some ___keys___.

1. (gravy) I helped Mom make _____.

2. (elephant) He owned _____.

3. (cheese) Elmer ate _____.

4. (chair) We need to buy _____.

5. (flower) Carlos bought _____ for his mother.

6. (information) That tourist needs _____.

7. (furniture) Jesus bought _____.

8. (man, woman) My class includes _____ and

_____.

9. (child) The group includes _____.

10. (fruit) I would like _____.

11. (desk) He purchased _____.

12. (luggage) I lost _____ on the train.

13. (cookie) The children ate _____.

14. (rice) I always eat _____ with my meal.

15. (homework) She did _____ last night.

16. (blanket) He put _____ in the closet.

17. (pillow) I put _____ on the bed.

18. (gasoline) Jose stopped to get _____.

19. (book) He was carrying _____.

20. (traffic) We always have _____ on that road.


**B.** Use *a/an* and *some* to complete these sentences.

*Example:* Joe is making _____*a*_____ sandwich. He will eat

_____*some*_____ ham and _____*some*_____ cheese.

1. Joe will also have _____ soup and _____ coffee.

2. Maria is hungry. She would like _____ food. She'll have

   _____ sandwich with _____ milk. For dessert

   she will have _____ apple and _____ ice cream.

3. Janis is cooking _____ meat for supper. She is cooking

   _____ chicken for herself and _____ lamb for

   her children. They will also have _____ bread

and _____ vegetable. For dessert she is making

_____ cookies; the family will eat these with

_____ milk.

4. The reporter asked me for _____ information about the

weather that night. I told him there was _____ heavy

traffic and _____ rain.

5. At the grocery I bought _____ soup, _____

apple, and _____ tea.

6. For breakfast I always drink _____ water first. Then I have

_____ cup of coffee. I put _____ sugar in my

coffee. Sometimes I have _____ bowl of cereal or

_____ egg.

## EXERCISE 3.6

### MANY/MUCH, A FEW//A LITTLE

Underline the correct choices in these paragraphs.

*Example:* (Many, *much*) schools have laboratories where students may
conduct (*a few*, *a little*) scientific experiments.

Professor Delaney's laboratory has (*many, much*) different liquids, gases, and chemicals and (*a few, a little*) dust. (*Many, much*) students come to see him seeking (*a few, a little*) information about their experiments.

Professor Delaney does (*many, much*) simple experiments with the students. He says, "It only takes (*a few, a little*) observation to do a good job." One experiment is to take a big pot and boil as (*many, much*) water as possible for (*a few, a little*) minutes. Observing the surface of the water, at first you see (*a few, a little*) gas rising up; this gas soon turns into (*many, much*) steam and (*a few, a little*) bubbles. After covering the pot with a plate for (*a few, a little*) minutes, look under the plate and you will see (*many, much*) condensation.

## 3  Measure words

Since noncount nouns have no definite shape or limits, when we want to count or measure these things, we must define shape or limit for them or we must put them into something with a definite shape or limits.

She ate *a bowl of* rice.

I drank *a bottle of* water.

I ordered *a roomful of* furniture.

These are the most common counters and mass nouns:

| | | | |
|---|---|---|---|
| bar of | gallon of | a lot of | quart of |
| bottle of | glass of | pat of | some |
| bowl of | head of | piece of | spoonful of |
| cube of | jar of | pint of | stick of |
| cup of | a little (bit of) | pound of | tankful of |
| dish of | loaf of | | |

## EXERCISE 3.7

## MEASURE WORDS

In the space below, write a three-paragraph narrative of a trip to the grocery store. Be sure to include a shopping list and to use the correct measure words; for example, *I bought a loaf of bread.*

Though they appear to have a group connotation, grammatically, noncount nouns are considered singular. Thus -s/-es is never added, and a singular verb form is used.

Advice is good to get.

Beef is expensive this week.

Information is now a commodity.

Some nouns are countable when they have one meaning and non-countable when they have another meaning.

COUNTABLE

He made some changes in his business.

Many lives were lost in the disaster.

He had many chickens on his farm.

NONCOUNTABLE

Change is inevitable.

Life is short.

I didn't eat much chicken last night.

## EXERCISE 3.8

### DICTIONARY EXERCISE

Using the list of common noncount nouns, make a list of ten of the words that pertain to food (including fruits and vegetables). Look them up in the dictionary, and note that they have both count and non-count noun definitions. Write a sentence using both definitions for each word.

*Example:*      <u>*lamb*</u>

(count) *The farmer has three lambs in the pasture.*

(noncount) *I ate a lot of lamb at dinner last night.*

1. _____

    (*count*)

    (*noncount*)

2. _____

    (*count*)

    (*noncount*)

3. _____

    (*count*)

    (*noncount*)

4. _____

    (*count*)

    (*noncount*)

5. _____

    (*count*)

    (*noncount*)

6. _____

    (*count*)

    (*noncount*)

7. _____

    (*count*)

    (*noncount*)

8. _____

   (*count*)

   (*noncount*)

9. _____

   (*count*)

   (*noncount*)

10. _____

   (*count*)

   (*noncount*)

## CHAPTER 4

# Expanding the Basic Sentence Pattern

Most sentences are longer and more complicated than the basic subject-verb-complement pattern. This basic pattern is regularly expanded. There are three main ways to expand the basic sentence pattern:

1. Add modifiers.
2. Compound one or more parts of the basic pattern.
3. Compound the entire basic sentence through coordination and subordination.

## 4a Modifiers

A **modifier** is a word (or group of words) that describes or qualifies and makes more exact the meaning of one of the main sentence parts or another modifier.

### 1 Single-word modifiers: adjectives, adverbs, and determiners

The simplest way to expand sentences is to add details with single modifying words: adjectives, adverbs, and determiners.

**Adjectives** (see Chapter 10) limit or describe subjects and noun and pronoun complements.

| | |
|---|---|
| *blue* car | *beautiful* child |
| *different* kinds | *huge* surplus |

Adjectives usually come before the words they modify, but sometimes they follow. Adjectives may also serve as subject complements after linking verbs and as object complements.

**Adverbs** (see Chapter 10) limit or describe verbs, adjective complements, or other adverbs. An adverb indicates intensity (*very*) or explains how, why, where, or when.

| | |
|---|---|
| walked *quickly* | eat *very slowly* |
| *not* allowed | *never* seen |

Adverbs often end in *-ly*, but not always. When they modify verbs, adverbs are usually movable; when they modify adjectives or other adverbs, they usually come before the word they modify.

**Determiners** (see Chapter 7) are also modifying words. They signal that a noun is to follow and tell something about the noun.

*the* book        *an* apple
*her* school      *that* man


## EXERCISE 4.1

## ADJECTIVES, ADVERBS, AND DETERMINERS

**A.** In the following sentences, underline each word according to function: underline an adjective once, an adverb twice, and a determiner three times. Then draw an arrow to the word that each underlined word modifies.

*Examples:*  The tall man got into his car quickly.

We left the room quietly and got into the black car at the curb.

1. Rosa usually wears a leather jacket.

2. The students worked silently at a big wooden desk.

3. The police officer politely asked the older woman to show her license.

4. We saw a very boring movie.

5. They go to the big white church often.

6. The first big party was discreetly held in the gym.

7. An enormous truck hit the pole most powerfully.

8. That group enthusiastically says she is the best teacher in the school.

9. Eduardo always travels to school by bus.

10. A long holiday is often anticipated with some excitement.

B. Insert an appropriate adjective (*adj*) or adverb (*adv*) in each blank.

   *Example:* The _____*heavy*_____ (adj) rain _____*quickly*_____ (adv) washed the _____*old*_____ (adj) dam away.

1. Behind the _____ (adj) garage you will find a _____ (adv) old car.

2. The _____ (adj) people _____ (adv) took cover in their houses.

3. The moon _____ (adv) shone on the _____ (adj) water.

4. The most _____ (adj) thing I ever saw was a _____ (adj) roach.

5. She _____ (adv) cooks a _____ (adj) chicken dinner for me.

### 2 Phrase and clause modifiers

A **phrase** is a group of related words lacking a subject or a predicate and functioning as a single part of speech. A **clause** is a group of related words that contains both a subject and a predicate.

#### Prepositional phrases

A **preposition** is a function word that links one word or group of words to another (see Chapter 8). Prepositions never change form and always take an object. If the object is a pronoun, it is in the objective form.

**Prepositional phrases** are used quite often to expand the basic sentence pattern, and they often ride "piggyback" on a preceding prepositional phrase.

The oasis was on a hill in the desert by a cool pond.

Prepositional phrases may be used as adjectives or adverbs.

The men in the army must wear uniforms. (adjective phrase telling which men)

Many games are played in the evening. (adverb phrase telling when the games are played)

## EXERCISE 4.2

## PREPOSITIONAL PHRASES

Underline the prepositional phrases in each of the following sentences; then draw an arrow from each phrase to the words the phrase modifies.

*Example:* The house was built on top of a hill.

1. The speaker seemed inconsistent in his ideas.

2. The boat was sailing against the tide.

3. The magician has entertained many people with his tricks.

4. After lunch, we went for a ride in the car.

5. We are studying a book about the ancient ruins.

6. The award was given to the speaker with the best ideas.

7. Yesterday, she enrolled in the cooking course.

8. The coffee in the urn is cold.

9. The offices in this building are closed after six o'clock.

10. Aldelberto prefers going against the opinion of everyone.

11. In summer, you can swim for hours with no problem.

12. By the third hour, I was on the last part of the exam.

13. He is planning a tour of the parks in Virginia.

14. After breakfast, we hiked to the top of the trail.

15. Jose was late for his appointment with the teacher.

### Verbal phrases

**Verbals** include participles, gerunds, and infinitives (see Chapters 6 and 13). **Participles** function as adjectives modifying nouns and pronouns. **Gerunds** function as nouns. **Infinitives** can function as nouns, adjectives, and adverbs. These verbals may take objects, complements, and modifiers to make up verbal phrases.

**Infinitive phrases** and **participle phrases** may also be used as modifiers.

Pushing against the wind, the runner struggled to the finish line. (participle phrase as adjective modifying the noun *runner*; participle *pushing* modified by prepositional phrase)

Joe ate pizza to satisfy his hunger. (infinitive phrase as adjective modifying noun; infinitive has object: *hunger*)

We rushed to complete the job. (infinitive phrase as adverb modifying verb; infinitive has object: *job*)

# EXERCISE 4.3

## VERBALS

Underline the verbals in these sentences. Indicate in the blank whether each is a participle (*P*), an infinitive (*I*), or a gerund (*G*).

*Examples:*　　_I_　　 To be a new recruit is not easy.

　　　　　　　_G_　　 Mother has never complained about my dating.

　　　　　　　_P_　　 Crying in pain, the man was helped into the ambulance.

_____　　 1. After running two miles, she came home and rested.

_____　　 2. The restaurant was closed for the evening.

_____　　 3. You can twist the cap off to remove the top.

_____　　 4. Running each day is good for the health.

_____　　 5. Buying a new car can cost a lot of money.

_____　　 6. Her friends enjoy playing the piano.

_____　　 7. To drive a truck is hard work.

_____　　 8. It is difficult for old people to remain healthy and active.

_____　　 9. His job requires him to carry two bags.

_____　　 10. The general commanded his troops to march into the battle.

_____　　 11. The frame is for the picture painted by my wife.

_____　　 12. Waving the flag, the workman warned us of the work site.

_____ 13. Ting completed his plan to visit China.

_____ 14. He followed my suggestion to take the tunnel to New Jersey.

_____ 15. The old man's need to talk with someone was obvious.

_____ 16. The mail carrier hurried to deliver the special letter on time.

_____ 17. The teacher is planning to announce the winner.

_____ 18. Boxing is not my favorite sport.

_____ 19. Esperanza says she likes swimming the best.

_____ 20. He has wanted to find a new job for a while.

### Clause modifiers: independent and dependent clauses

A **main** or **independent clause** states a complete idea and forms a sentence.

A **subordinate** or **dependent clause** is like a phrase, functioning as a single part of speech. A subordinate clause cannot stand alone as a sentence since it is not a complete idea.

Subordinate clauses are connected to main clauses by **subordinating** conjunctions such as _because, since, if, when, unless,_ and _while_ or by relative pronouns.

| RELATIVE PRONOUNS | | |
|---|---|---|
| which | what | who (whose, whom) |
| that | whatever | whoever (whomever) |

Many cars pass over the bridge. The traffic is heavy. (two independent clauses; two complete sentences)

Many cars pass over the bridge _when_ the traffic is heavy. (one independent clause; second clause subordinated, adverbial)

Many cars pass over the bridge, _which_ is heavy with traffic. (one independent clause; second clause subordinated, adjectival)

# EXERCISE 4.4
## CLAUSE MODIFIERS

Underline the subordinate clause in the following sentences.

*Examples:*  She told him <u>what she thought</u>.

He was late <u>because of the traffic</u>.

1. Unless he pays the rent, he will be evicted.

2. In my family, we do whatever we can for each other.

3. Elmer passed the test, which was on Tuesday.

4. George always gets mad if he doesn't win the game.

5. He threw his helmet down as he walked back to the bench.

6. He caught the ball that I tossed to him.

7. The teacher asked us whose book this is.

8. We wrote a story about a man who is a hero.

9. She drove the car that is parked in front of the house.

10. While I was waiting for the bus, Franz drove by and picked me up.

## 4b  Compound parts

Another way to expand the basic sentence pattern is to compound any part of a sentence—clauses, phrases, and any part of speech—by linking them, provided that the parts are equivalent in both grammar and meaning. Sentence parts may be compounded with individual **coordinating conjunctions** or with **correlative conjunctions**, which come in pairs.

| COORDINATING CONJUNCTIONS | | |
|---|---|---|
| and | but, yet | for |
| so, also | or, nor | |

but . . . and
not . . . but
neither . . . nor

not only . . . but also
either . . . or

COMPOUND SUBJECT    Mary and Esperanza studied together last night.

COMPOUND VERB    Elmer ate and studied at the same time.

COMPOUND ADJECTIVE The dazzling and beautiful sunset pleased all of us.

COMPOUND PREPOSITIONAL PHRASE The old car was not only without wheels but also without a windshield.

## EXERCISE 4.5

## COMPOUNDING

**A.** Underline the conjunction that is being used to coordinate two equal words, phrases, or clauses in each of these sentences.

*Example:* The teacher and the student arrived at the same time.

1. Carlos and Esperanza became good friends.

2. The leader was firm yet sensitive.

3. He refused to pay the rent, so he was evicted.

4. The red car and the white truck belong to our company.

5. She can't decide whether to go or to stay.

6. He had to go to the bank and to the grocery store before going home.

7. The test was very difficult, but Johelle did quite well on it.

8. The judges had to choose the winner, Pablo or Jose.

9. He likes to eat rice and beans.

10. We were late for the movie, so we missed the beginning.

**B.** Write an appropriate coordinating conjunction in the space.

*Example:* He used hard work _____*and*_____ intelligence to pass the course.

1. I missed the last bus, _____ I had to call my father to pick me up.

2. His tests are difficult _____ fair.

3. Jeanine invited Flavio _____ Carlos to her party.

4. Please pay the waiter _____ waitress when you are finished.

5. Jose is sad _____ relieved that the class is finished.

6. She was sick, _____ she went to the doctor.

7. He ate his dinner, _____ later he took a nap.

8. She asked him to come over, _____ he couldn't make it.

9. He was quite ill, _____ he had eaten spoiled meat.

10. I'm taking algebra _____ trigonometry this semester.

**C.** Underline the correlative conjunctions in the following sentences.

*Example:* She was <u>not only</u> smart <u>but also</u> beautiful.

1. Both Jose and Maria are from Colombia.

2. After studying, I feel not only better but also confident.

3. Either you do it, or I will have to do the work.

4. Neither the bad weather nor the low temperature discouraged us from going to the game.

5. He received either an A or a B in that course.

## 4c Compound sentences

A sentence makes an assertion (the predicate) about something (the subject). As we have seen, this basic formula may be expanded in various ways.

## 1 Coordination

The basic sentence pattern may be expanded by coordinating two or more complete assertions. We call this a **compound sentence**. Each assertion has its own subject and verb, and they are joined (or coordinated) by either a comma plus a coordinating conjunction or a semicolon.

Using a compound sentence shows that the two assertions are equal grammatically and logically. Both can stand alone as independent clauses, complete sentences.

### Coordinating conjunctions

The main coordinating conjunctions are as follows.

**and:** to add together two or more sentence parts or complete sentences

    S    V                S    V
Julia went to the market, and she bought some dinner for tonight.

**but/yet:** to express a contrary idea

            S      V             S  V
The female students all speak Spanish, but the men have different language backgrounds.

**or:** to express alternatives where one excludes the other

   S   V        S   V
You can take a bus, or you can walk.

**so:** to express the result of the preceding idea

    S   V         S V
My car ran out of gas, so I was late for class.

**for:** to express the reason for the preceding idea

    S   V               S  V
He spent his vacation at home, for he had no place else to go.

*Punctuation:* since compound sentences really are two complete sentences joined together, it is important to punctuate them correctly. If the sentences are coordinated by a conjunction, always put a comma before the conjunction. If there is no conjunction use a semicolon.

## EXERCISE 4.6

## COMPOUND SENTENCES

**A.** Put a comma (,) or a semicolon (;) where appropriate.

*Examples:* He was tired, but he kept on playing.

Elmer was first in line; he arrived the earliest.

1. She was late getting up so she missed the bus.

2. Liliane speaks well but her writing needs work.

3. The student knew he had to study hard or he would fail his final exam.

4. Blanca plays basketball she is very athletic.

5. Flavio works as a waiter he makes good money.

**B.** Each of the following items contains two sentences that can be joined by a coordinating conjunction. Write a conjunction in the space provided, and add a comma before the conjunction.

*Example:* Joe wanted to speak Japanese fluently ____*so*____ he took classes at the college.

1. She loved him _____ he was so sincere and patient.

2. He was late for work _____ he didn't skip his breakfast.

3. Pierre loves to sing _____ he remained silent during the song festival.

4. I am a student _____ I have a part-time job.

5. This summer, I will go to Spain _____ I will work to make some money.

### Conjunctive adverbs

A more formal way of coordinating two complete sentences is to use **conjunctive adverbs**. Like conjunctions, these words connect equal clauses, and they are used to relate the idea of one main clause to that of a preceding main clause. These words are adverbial because they modify groups of words, showing how their clauses relate to other clauses.

The car's engine was quite warm; *accordingly*, the temperature inside was comfortable.

Milton has a secure job; *besides*, he has very marketable skills.

She wanted to go home; *however*, she went to work.

| COMMON CONJUNCTIVE ADVERBS | | | |
| --- | --- | --- | --- |
| accordingly | furthermore | moreover | similarly |
| also | hence | namely | still |
| anyway | however | nevertheless | then |
| besides | incidently | next | thereafter |
| certainly | indeed | nonetheless | therefore |
| consequently | instead | now | thus |
| finally | likewise | otherwise | undoubtedly |
| further | meanwhile | | |

*Punctuation:* when using a conjunctive adverb to join two main clauses into one compound sentence, the proper punctuation at the end of the first main clause is a semicolon; the conjunctive adverb is usually followed by a comma.

Louis was successful; nonetheless, he had many problems.

They traveled for twelve hours; finally, they reached home.

The conjunctive adverb is often used in a secondary position, after the subject and before the verb. In that position, it may be set off with commas, or it may take no punctuation.

Jose was a full-time student; he, moreover, worked two jobs.

Linda studied last night; she therefore passed the exam easily.

# EXERCISE 4.7

## CONJUNCTIVE ADVERBS

**A.** Punctuate the following sentences appropriately.

*Example:*  He had the money; however, he forgot to send it.

1. She studied hard accordingly she passed the exam.

2. Joe loves to swim he doesn't however live near the ocean.

3. The temperature in winter is quite cold the residents consequently always dress warmly.

4. I won the last game nevertheless I lost the match.

5. We ran for twenty miles therefore when we got home we were tired and sweating.

6. He was a champion swimmer moreover he could sing well too.

7. Jose was not allowed to go to the movies besides he was forbidden to leave his room.

8. I am a little tired otherwise I am feeling fine.

9. Marne was declared the winner she undoubtedly had the best presentation.

10. Lana studied for hours hence she got a good grade.

**B.** Make two kinds of compound sentences by joining the following pairs of sentences twice, first with coordinating conjunctions and then with conjunctive adverbs. Remember that a coordinating conjunction should be preceded by a comma; a conjunctive adverb that begins a clause should be preceded by a semicolon. Note the more formal tone of the second version.

*Example:*  She missed the bus. She was late for class.
*She missed the bus, and she was late for class.*
*She missed the bus; consequently, she was late for class.*

1. He failed the written exam. He passed the course anyway.

2. Buffalo is located on Lake Erie. It is called the "Queen City of the Lakes."

3. In the spring, Washington is full of cherry blossoms. In the winter, it has a lot of snow.

4. Once New York had the world's largest population. Now Tokyo has the largest population.

5. Kansas City is situated in the center of the country. Many businesses have offices there.

6. Christopher Columbus was the first southern European to sail to the New World. He is said to be the discoverer of America.

7. A large number of different birds fly over this spot in the spring. Many bird watchers come here.

8. The weather in Haiti is warm and sunny. In Germany, the temperature and the weather are quite different.

9. Once he was a student. Now he is a teacher.

10. That neighborhood has many clothing manufacturers. It is called the garment center.

**C.** Review freewriting that you have done. Underline any compound sentences that you used. Circle any conjunctive adverbs.

## 4d  Subordination

One final way of expanding the basic sentence pattern to combine sentences and ideas is to relate one or more subordinate clauses to a main clause. This involves clarifying the relationship between ideas by placing a **subordinating conjunction** or a **relative pronoun** in front of one of them.

This kind of a sentence—one main clause with a subject and a verb and at least one dependent clause with a subordinated subject and a verb—is a **complex sentence**. Using dependent clauses clarifies the logical relationships between the ideas being expressed.

Whereas a compound sentence shows that the assertions are equal grammatically and logically, **subordination** is a structural gesture that signals unequal grammatical order between the ideas in the assertions. One clause is a grammatically complete idea, an independent clause; the other is not a complete idea but a dependent clause clarifying the relationship between the ideas.

### COMMON SUBORDINATING CONJUNCTIONS

| | | | |
|---|---|---|---|
| after | even if | since | when |
| although | even though | so that | whenever |
| as | if | than | where |
| as if | in order that | that | wherever |
| as though | once | though | whether |
| because | only if | unless | while |
| before | provided that | until | |

Subordinating conjunctions have no function other than to connect clauses to other clauses by showing relationships.

The relative pronouns *who, whom, which, that, whose, where,* and *when* can not only link two clauses but also serve as pronouns, adjectives, or adverbs within their own clauses. And relative clauses may follow any noun in a sentence.

Joe thinks he will visit cities *that have a lot of churches*.

Poison ivy is a weed *whose roots go very deep*.

## EXERCISE 4.8

## RELATIVE CLAUSES

Combine these sentences using relative pronouns.

*Example:* Tom saw a film. The film was two hours long.

*Tom saw a film that was two hours long.*

1. They watched the seals. The seals jumped for fish.

2. She saw the man. He was jogging in the park.

3. I saw a man. He was walking in the road.

4. I talked to the student. She didn't do her homework.

5. We went to the game. Susan ate four hot dogs.

6. She talked to the student. He didn't do his homework.

7. They live in a large building. The building is made of brick.

8. The woman had a yellow dress. She was the class monitor.

9. A man answered the phone. He said Esperanza was out.

10. She works in the post office. The post office is in the city.

### Noun clauses

Subordinate clauses function in a sentence as a single part of speech: noun, adjective, or adverb. When a subordinate clause is used in a noun position (subject, direct object, object of a preposition, or complement), it is called a **noun clause**.

*That we have arrived home* makes me feel much better. (noun clause as subject)

Maria told her why she came *to this country*. (noun clause as direct object)

He gave the package to *whoever opened the door*. (noun clause as indirect object)

The relative pronouns used to introduce noun clauses are *that, what, whatever, which, whichever, who, whoever, whom, whomever,* and *whose*. The subordinating conjunctions *how, when, where,* and *why* also often introduce noun clauses.

## EXERCISE 4.9

## NOUN CLAUSES

A. In each sentence, underline the noun clause. On the line at the left, indicate whether the clause is being used as a subject (*S*), an object (*O*), or a noun complement (*NC*).

*Example:* ___*S*___ <u>What I feel</u> is private.

_____ 1. She knows that the prices are higher.

_____ 2. Going for a swim is what I intend to do this evening.

_____ 3. Who caused the accident is not important; we should be helping the injured.

_____ 4. Jose wanted to know when Esperanza would arrive.

_____ 5. I asked which assignment was due.

_____ 6. Where she lives is a big secret.

_____ 7. Please give the money to whoever comes to pick it up.

_____ 8. Whoever is picked as the monitor will be honored.

_____ 9. The customers asked why the prices had doubled.

_____ 10. How the machine works is a mystery to me.

_____ 11. I told him what I thought.

_____ 12. I know whose books these are.

_____ 13. This is what I want.

_____ 14. Tonight is when the moon is full.

_____ 15. She is sorry for whatever pain she caused.

**B.** Answer the questions in the space provided. Use a noun clause in each answer.

*Examples:* Why are you crying?

*Why I am crying is a private matter.*

How did they get there?

*I don't know how they got there.*

1. Why was she late?


2. Where did you go?


3. Which train should I take?


4. How much is that camera?


5. What is his name?

6. Whose book is this?


7. Why are you crying?


8. When will the train arrive?


9. How long will it take to get there?


10. Which textbook should we buy?


### Adjective clauses

Sometimes a subordinate clause in a sentence is used to modify a noun or a pronoun. This is called an **adjective clause** and usually begins with one of these relative pronouns: *who, whom, whose, that, which, where,* or *when*.

The man *who lives in the green house* is a friend of mine.

The door *that leads to the attic* needs to be painted.

A complex sentence with an adjective clause is really a reduced sentence that is incorporated into another sentence. The combination is possible because the subordinating word substitutes for a noun or pronoun in the first clause and relates directly to the word being modified. Because of this, the relative word always begins an adjective clause and comes as close to the antecedent noun or pronoun as possible.

Note the substitutions and repetitions in the following examples of sentence combining.

This is a well-made car. The car will go a long way.
This is a well-made car *that* will go a long way.

Jay has a new friend. The friend works in a bookstore.
Jay has a new friend *who* works in a bookstore.

The department hired Julia. The chairperson knew Julia in graduate school.
The department hired Julia, *whom* the chairperson knew in graduate school.


**4d/Subordination**    **79**

# EXERCISE 4.10

## ADJECTIVE CLAUSES

**A.** Underline the adjective clause in each sentence. Then draw an arrow to the word the clause modifies.

*Example:*   The woman <u>who is the teacher</u> is standing on the left.

1. The man who wants to be mayor must get the most votes.

2. Frederick Douglass is a man who accomplished much.

3. I like the teacher whose name is Smith.

4. The race was won by Anna, who trained diligently.

5. New Jersey, which is known as the Garden State, borders on New York.

6. A person whose will is weak will be tempted by many things.

7. The tree we planted grew to quite a large size.

8. The prize will be given to the person who gets the most points.

9. She supported Mayor Smith, whose main issue was the environment.

10. The coat she bought is warm and comfortable.

**B.** Combine each pair of sentences by making them into a complex sentence with an adjective clause. Consult the list of relative words for appropriate subordinators.

*Example:* A mountain climber attempts to climb Mount Everest. He must be prepared for severe weather conditions.

*When a mountain climber attempts to climb Mount Everest, he must be prepared for severe weather conditions.*

1. Mount Everest is the tallest mountain in the world. Mount Everest is 29,028 feet tall.

2. Mount Everest is located on the border between Nepal and Tibet. It is in Asia.

3. Mount Everest's original name was Chomolungma. Mount Everest is part of the Himalayan mountain range.

4. Chomulungma means "mountain so high no bird can fly over it." Chomulungma was named by the ancient Tibetans.

5. Mountain climbers climb this great mountain. The mountain climbers need ropes, mountain boots, ice axes, and oxygen tanks.

6. Sir Edmund Hillary led an expedition to the top of Mount Everest. Sir Edmund Hillary was born in New Zealand.

7. Tenzing Norgay was a local villager. Tenzing Norgay was one of the first to climb to the top of Mount Everest.

8. At the top of the mountain, the air is very thin. At the top of the mountain, climbers cannot survive without a supply of oxygen.

9. The weather is characterized by blizzards, high winds, ice, and snow. The weather is more severe at higher elevations.

10. Many people attempt to climb Mount Everest. They should be in excellent physical condition.

**Reduced relative clauses**

Native speakers of English often omit certain words in an adjective clause.

In such a **reduced clause**, the missing words are understood even though they are not expressed.

An adjective clause may be reduced in the following ways.

1. You can omit the subject pronoun and a form of the verb *be*.

The man [who is] visiting me is my brother.
The man visiting me is my brother.

The book [that is] over there is mine.
The book over there is mine.

2. If there is no form of the verb *be* in the adjective clause, it is sometimes possible to omit the subject pronoun and change the verb to its *-ing* form.

Chinese uses characters *that consist* of many strokes.
Chinese uses characters *consisting* of many strokes.

Anyone *who wants* to visit is welcome.
Anyone *wanting* to visit is welcome.

3. The object pronouns (*whom, which, that*) are often omitted in the adjective clause.

The man [whom] you met is my brother.
The man you met is my brother.

I liked the noodles [that] we made yesterday.
I liked the noodles we made yesterday.

## EXERCISE 4.11

## REDUCED RELATIVE CLAUSES

Rewrite these sentences by reducing the relative clauses.

*Examples:*   The people who are coming for dinner are late.

*The people coming for dinner are late.*

I listened to everything that she said.

*I listened to everything she said.*

1. The door that is closing slowly is making a lot of noise.

2. The book, which was published in May, is a best seller.

3. They are looking for the animal that is hiding in the woods.

4. The books that were destroyed by the fire are valuable.

5. The people who live in the jungle are not familiar with jet planes.

6. The people who were teasing the animal soon left.

7. The trees that you always watered have grown tall.

8. He will have to sell the horses, which are running wild.

9. The experiment, which was conducted at the University of Miami, was a failure.

10. The orchestra that we listened to was not loud enough.

11. We all watched the man who was washing the windows.

12. The flowers that grew here are all gone.

13. The students who are studying every night are doing the best.

14. Did you get the message, which was about the meeting?

15. The physicist who is studying the properties of light is very quiet.

### Adverb clauses

Sometimes the subordinate clause functions as an adverb and modifies the verb. These **adverb clauses** answer the questions *how? where? when? why?* and *under what conditions?*

*How?:* She acted as if she owned the place.

*Where?:* They walked wherever they wanted to.

*When?:* They met before she graduated from college.

*Why?:* Jose was late because his car broke down.

*Under what conditions?:* I will not work unless you provide transportation.

Whereas a noun clause names and an adjective clause describes, an adverb clause explains. Each type of clause may combine with other ideas and clauses into a complex sentence. A sentence with an adverb clause has an embedded sentence that explains something about the main clause.

## EXERCISE 4.12

## ADVERB CLAUSES

**A.** Underline the adverb clause in each sentence. Then draw an arrow to the word the adverb clause modifies.

*Example:* You should not leave the class <u>until the instructor has finished the lecture.</u>

1. While I was speaking, the new student walked right by me.

2. The truck was out of control when it hit the other vehicle.

3. As long as he is the captain, his boat will sail this course.

4. John was absent from class because he had the flu.

5. Whether you want to or not, you still have to pay your taxes.

6. Although Elmer can sing well, he wasn't chosen for the choir.

7. The police found the money where the thief had left it.

8. Since the people stopped coming, the resort town has had a failing economy.

9. She drove as though she were heading for a fire.

10. Before we left on vacation, we paid all the bills.

B. In the space provided, write an adverb clause that completes each sentence. Refer to the list of common subordinating conjunctions for appropriate subordinators.

Example: He was late, *though not enough to miss the first number.*

1. She said that she couldn't leave _____

_____.

2. _____, he failed his driver's test.

3. The alarm always sounds _____

_____

4. Maria was afraid to go _____

_____ .

5. The car was on sale _____

_____ .

6. _____ , Joel still kept on trying.

7. The team was happy _____

_____ .

8. They decided to continue the trip _____

_____

9. _____ , they got married in May.

10. Don't hand in the work like that _____

_____

### Logical categories

A writer decides what is to be subordinated according to the intended meaning of the sentence. The relationship between an adverb clause and the main clause is shown by the subordinating conjunction that introduces the adverb clause. In general, subordinating conjunctions are used to explain details of *time, place, cause, condition, concession, purpose, manner,* and *comparison.*

Since the compound sentence is a gesture of balance, the coordinating conjunction can be omitted altogether and a mark of punctuation put in its place. We cannot, however, omit a subordinating conjunction. The subordinating conjunction indicates a balance that is missing or hidden, and it makes a difference in the meaning.

The team won the game yesterday, and it had a celebration.
The team won the game yesterday; it had a celebration.

These sentences mean exactly the same thing, and both are compound. But if we try to remove the subordinator, we wind up changing the meaning of the sentences—we remove the subordinating detail of cause.

He was late because his car broke down on the street.
He was late. His car broke down on the street.

# EXERCISE 4.13

## LOGICAL CATEGORIES OF SUBORDINATORS

**A.** Use the subordinators in parentheses to write complex sentences with adverbial clauses in each category. Use the dictionary for this exercise. The subordinators are useful and important words. Look each one up individually before writing your sentence. Note that some words, such as *as* and *since*, appear in more than one category.

*Examples:* TIME (*after*)

*He went to the film after he ate dinner.*

CONDITION (*if*)

*If it rains, they will not play.*

MANNER (*as though*)

*Maria felt as though they didn't like her.*

**TIME**

1. (*after*)

2. (*as*)

3. (*as soon as*)

4. (*before*)

5. (*since*)

6. (*until*)

7. (*when*)

8. (*whenever*)

9. (*while*)


**PLACE**

10. (*where*)

11. (*wherever*)


**CAUSE**

12. (*because*)

13. (*since*)


**CONDITION**

14. (*if*)

15. (*provided that*)

16. (*since*)

17. (*unless*)


**CONCESSION**

18. (*although*)

19. (*even if*)

20. (*even though*)

21. (*though*)

**MANNER**
22. (*as*)

23. (*as if*)

24. (*as though*)

**PURPOSE**
25. (*in order that*)

26. (*so that*)

27. (*that*)

**COMPARISON**
28. (*as*)

29. (*so*)

30. (*than*)

**B.** In the following paragraphs, combine sentences wherever possible by using the logical connectors to create adverb clauses.

1.    Maria went into town this morning. She had some things to do.

She took a bus. Her daughter needed the car. Maria went to the bank first. She needed some money. It was early. There were hardly any people in the bank. She wanted to buy some presents. It was her daughter Alice's birthday. The stores were just opening. It was ten o'clock. It had rained hard during the night. The streets were wet and muddy. Maria was wearing her boots. The puddles were no problem. She wanted to make lunch for her daughter at noon. She hurried to catch the early bus.

2.      Elmer is in college. He is working in a supermarket. He needs the money. Elmer usually travels to work by bus. He doesn't own a car. Elmer has coworkers. The coworkers are college students. Elmer works from 5 P.M. to 9 P.M. He goes to school during the day. The schedule is difficult. Elmer enjoys his life. He has many friends. He has many activities.

**C.**  Fill in the blanks with the appropriate subordinate conjunction from the following list: *after, although, because, before, even though, since, so that, though, when, while.*

      Christopher Columbus is known as the discoverer of the New

World, _____ Leif Erickson and possibly other European explorers made the journey before him.

In 1492, Columbus sailed west _____ he was convinced the earth was round. _____ he and his men had sailed for months, they sighted an island in what we now know as the Bahamas. A story is told that Columbus named the friendly local inhabitants Indians _____ he thought he had reached India. For a time, Columbus explored the local area. _____ he returned to Spain with some gold and a few local inhabitants, he established a settlement and left some of his men behind. _____ he returned in 1493, he found the settlement destroyed and all the men missing.

Columbus originally sailed _____ he would reap financial rewards. In reality, he encountered many struggles and hardships along with his discoveries. _____ on his third voyage, for example, he was arrested and sent back to Spain. _____ his dreams of success were not fulfilled, eventually he did become one of the most famous men in modern history. And we still celebrate Columbus Day, _____ he never became rich or found the elusive Northwest Passage to India.

**D.** Review some of your freewriting. Underline any complex sentences, circle the subordinating words.

CHAPTER 5

# Verbs: Parts and Forms

---

**Verbs** are words that describe action, thought, or state of being.

Esperanza *studies* English every day.

John *is running* to the train station.

The teacher *considered* the question.

Mary *felt* warm and comfortable.

Kim *is* the class president.

## 5a Principal parts

Every verb has four principal parts:

1. Base (dictionary) form
2. Present participle: base + *-ing*
3. Past participle: base + *-ed*
4. Infinitive: *to* + base

Along with the principal parts, every verb has an *-s* form (for the third-person singular) and a past *-ed* form. It's important to know these parts and forms since, often combined with auxiliary verbs, they form the very nucleus of the sentence.

### EXERCISE 5.1

### DICTIONARY USE

---

Using your dictionary, look up each verb. List the principal parts, the *-s* form, and the past *-ed* form.

*Example:*  base: *walk*

present participle: *walking*

past participle: *walked*

infinitive: *to walk*

-s: *walks*

-ed: *walked*

1. base: *talk*

   present participle:

   past participle:

   infinitive:

   -s:

   -ed:

2. base: *believe*

   present participle:

   past participle:

   infinitive:

   -s:

   -ed:

3. base: *relax*

   present participle:

   past participle:

   infinitive:

   -s:

   -ed:

4. base: *look*

   present participle:

   past participle:

   infinitive:

   *-s:*

   *-ed:*

5. base: *enjoy*

   present participle:

   past participle:

   infinitive:

   *-s:*

   *-ed:*

6. base: *taste*

   present participle:

   past participle:

   infinitive:

   *-s:*

   *-ed:*

7. base: *live*

   present participle:

   past participle:

   infinitive:

   *-s:*

   *-ed:*

8. base: *complain*

   present participle:

   past participle:

   infinitive:

   *-s:*

   *-ed:*

9. base: *argue*

   present participle:

   past participle:

   infinitive:

   *-s:*

   *-ed:*

10. base: *try*

    present participle:

    past participle:

    infinitive:

    *-s:*

    *-ed:*

## 5b Auxiliary verbs

Some sentences require only a one-word verb.

**SINGLE-WORD VERBS**

Jose *is* the student from El Salvador.

Maria *runs* a mile each day.

Other sentences require one or more **auxiliary** or **helping verbs**, making multiple-word verbs.

MULTIPLE-WORD VERBS

Jose *is living* in the United States.

Maria *has been running* a mile a day since she graduated from high school.

In English, the auxiliary verb shows agreement in number (subject-verb) and tense.

---

## COMMON AUXILIARY VERBS

STANDARD AUXILIARY VERBS

| *Infinitive* | *Present* | *Past* |
|---|---|---|
| to be | is, am, are | was, were |
| to have | have, has | had |
| to do | do, does | did |

MODAL AUXILIARIES

can, will, may, could, would, might, shall, must, should

---

## 5c Questions

In English, the question form of a sentence usually requires subject-verb inversion. With the verb *be* or a multiple-word verb, we put a form of *be* or the first auxiliary verb before the subject.

STATEMENT You are the teacher.
QUESTION   Are you the teacher?

STATEMENT She is the oldest daughter.
QUESTION   Is she the oldest daughter?

STATEMENT He has walked to school each day this week.
QUESTION   Has he walked to school each day this week?

STATEMENT They could have been driving for two hours.
QUESTION   Could they have been driving for two hours?

### 1 *Do* support

If there is no form of *be* in the verb or no auxiliary verb exists, we must substitute *do*. This is called *do* support. If the verb is in the simple present, use *does* (with *he, she, it*) or *do* (with *I, you, we, they*). If the verb is in the simple past, use *did*. The main verb is in the base form.

STATEMENT The cats cross the road to get home.
QUESTION    Do the cats cross the road to get home?

STATEMENT He ate all the cookies.
QUESTION    Did he eat all the cookies?

## 2 | Question types

There are a number of question types, including yes/no questions, information questions, and tag questions.

### Yes/no questions

A yes/no question invites a response of "yes" or "no," often followed by a short elaboration.

QUESTION Is she the new student?
ANSWER    No, she isn't.

QUESTION Does March have thirty-one days?
ANSWER    Yes, it does.

QUESTION Has he been here long?
ANSWER    Yes, he has.

QUESTION Did they arrive on time?
ANSWER    No, they didn't.

## EXERCISE 5.2

## QUESTION FORMATION

Transform each statement into a yes/no question; then write a short answer to it.

*Example:* Elmer writes to his mother often.

*Does Elmer write to his mother often?*
*Yes, he does.*

1. Esperanza speaks Spanish and English.

2. The students are happy with the class schedule.

3. The earthquakes damaged a lot of homes.

4. The power source is located outside the house.

5. The bed was covered with papers and books.

6. The sun is shining brightly today.

7. The street was quiet and dark.

8. They saw a raccoon on the back porch.

9. You have a new car.

10. You can have my ticket.

### Information questions

Information questions require more than a simple yes or no answer; they ask for information. Such questions begin with the words *who, whom, whose, what, which, when, where, why,* and *how;* hence they are sometimes referred to as the *wh-* questions.

There are two main *wh-* question patterns:

1. Questions about the subject of the sentence
2. Questions about objects or other parts of the predicate

SUBJECT QUESTION PATTERN: If the subject of the basic sentence pattern is human, simply substitute *who* for the complete subject. If the subject is nonhuman, substitute *what* for the complete subject. If the replaced subject is plural, change the auxiliary verb to its singular form. In this pattern, there is *no subject-verb inversion.*

STATEMENT Bruce is the boss.
QUESTION Who is the boss?

STATEMENT John gave his money to Maria.
QUESTION Who gave his money to Maria?

STATEMENT The boys at the corner were fooling around.
QUESTION Who was fooling around?

STATEMENT The high school went up in flames last night.
QUESTION What went up in flames last night?

STATEMENT The cows were eating all the grass.
QUESTION What was eating all the grass?

## EXERCISE 5.3

## INFORMATION QUESTIONS ABOUT THE SUBJECT

Form an information question by substituting *who* or *what* for the complete subject.

*Example:* The man caused the accident.

*Who caused the accident?*

1. Kelly lives in the city.

2. Jose can answer the question.

3. The dogs and cats live under the front porch.

4. The evening newspaper is full of horrible news.

5. Mary and Frank have three children.

6. Naoko ate pizza for dinner.

7. All the Haitian students are proud of their new president.

8. Maria has been working in the hospital for three years.

9. Iris went home to Puerto Rico to see her family.

10. The whole mountain seemed to move when the explosion happened.

11. The teachers played basketball with the students.

12. Chung Wai is from mainland China.

13. Three stories were assigned for homework.

14. Jose Chavez and Maria Calderon are from Colombia.

15. The large automobile caused all the damage.

**OBJECT-PREDICATE PATTERN:** In this pattern, the auxiliary word (or a form of *be* or *do*) is placed before the subject, the *wh-* word replaces the object or other part of the predicate, and the *wh-* word is placed in front of the auxiliary word. If the object is human, the *wh-* word is *whom*. If the object is nonhuman, we use *what*.

STATEMENT The principal addressed the students in the assembly.
QUESTION Whom did the principal address in the assembly?

STATEMENT The newspaper carried a story about the game on page one.
QUESTION What did the newspaper carry on page one?

Other *wh-* question words used as substitutes for parts of the predicate are as follows:

*where* for place

*when* for time

*why* for purpose or reason

*how* for manner (*how much/how many* for quantity)

*whose* for possessives (the accompanying noun is also moved to the front of the sentence)

*which* for choosing from a group of people or things (often followed by the word *of* and a plural noun)

*How* is often followed by other adjectives to ask special information questions (*how far* for distance, *how hot/cold* for temperature, *how old* for age, and so on).

STATEMENT The car is parked in front of the building.
QUESTION Where is the car parked?

STATEMENT Esperanza met Sonia after school.
QUESTION When did Esperanza meet Sonia?

STATEMENT John was late because his car broke down.
QUESTION Why was John late?

STATEMENT Fred quickly turned his car around.
QUESTION How did Fred turn his car around?

STATEMENT Ken gave Irma's books to Maria.
QUESTION Whose books did Ken give to Maria?

STATEMENT Here are some hats.
QUESTION Which of the hats do you prefer?

STATEMENT The house is five miles from here.
QUESTION How far is the house from here?

## EXERCISE 5.4

## OTHER INFORMATION QUESTIONS

Transform the following statements into information questions by replacing the words in italics.

*Example:* John is *at school* today.

*Where is John today?*

1. Sonia gave her books to Maria *in front of the library*.

2. She gave me the money *after school*.

3. Larry left early *because he had to work*.

4. The teacher gave *her book* to Adam.

5. Here are *some colors*.

6. That is *Maria's pencil*.

7. The student could not buy the book *because he had no money*.

8. The thief *quietly* entered the locked house.

9. She was quite tired *after lunch*.

10. The storm is coming *from Canada*.

11. Esperanza was hurt *by the flying glass*.

12. The weather is *very cold* today.

13. Here are *some pens*.

14. *Because he was angry*, Elmer didn't come to the party.

15. We met them *early in the evening*.

## EXERCISE 5.5

## QUESTION FORMATION

Make up an exam of twenty questions about the following passage by substituting *wh-* words for the italicized parts of the sentences.

*Frederick Douglass* (1) was born a slave *in Easton, Maryland* (2), *in 1818* (3). Douglass escaped from slavery *when he was 20* (4) *by using the underground railroad* (5) through Canada. He went *to Massachusetts* (6) and made speeches against *slavery* (7).

Douglass wrote **The Narrative of the Life of Frederick Douglass**. This was his own story about what it was like to be a slave. *Many people* (8) were affected by his book. He feared *that he would be captured and sent back to slavery* (9), so he went *to England* (10) and *stayed several years* (11). He earned money there, and when he came back to America, he bought *his freedom* (12).

He founded a newspaper called *The North Star* (13). This paper printed articles *against slavery and in favor of women's rights* (14). Douglass was the editor *for seventeen years* (15). *During the Civil War* (16), Douglass organized *two regiments of black soldiers* (17) to fight for the North.

After the war, he held many important jobs. *In 1889* (18), he was appointed minister *to Haiti* (19). Douglass died in 1895, when he was *seventy-eight years old* (20).

Examples:  3. *When was Frederick Douglass born?*
12. *What did he buy when he came back from England?*

1.

2.

3.

4.

5.

6.

7.

8.

9.

10.

11.

12.

13.

14.

15.

16.

17.

18.

19.

20.

### Tag questions

A tag question is a question added at the end of a sentence. Tag questions are used to make sure that information is correct or to seek agreement.

An affirmative sentence with a negative tag assumes that an affirmative answer is expected.

Esperanza can speak Spanish, can't she?

Yes, she can.

A negative sentence with an affirmative tag assumes that a negative answer is expected.

George can't speak French, can he?

No, he can't.

**Tag pronouns**

The tag pronoun for *this, that,* and *everything* is *it.*

That is your car, isn't it?

Everything is OK, isn't it?

The tag pronoun for *these* and *those* is *they.*

Those are yours, aren't they?

In sentences with *everyone, everybody, everything, someone, somebody, nobody,* and *no one, they* is also used in the tag.

Everybody came in, didn't they?

No one told the teacher, did they?

Someone was there, weren't they?

In sentences with *there* + a form of *be, there* is used in the tag.

There is a class tomorrow, isn't there?

## EXERCISE 5.6

## TAG QUESTIONS

Add a tag question to each sentence.

*Examples:*  You like coffee, _*don't you?*_

You don't like coffee, _*do you?*_

1. Jose is a student, _____

2. They want to go, _____

3. He won't arrive until ten, _____

4. They want to eat here, _____

5. Maria is a nurse, _____

6. They have all learned a lot in the past week, _____

7. She is invited, _____

8. He wasn't told, _____

9. Elmer isn't feeling well today, _____

10. Nothing is missing, _____

11. There is plenty of food, _____

12. This is your book, _____

13. He owns a bicycle, _____

14. He has never been to Haiti, _____

15. Everyone can take a turn, _____

16. Nobody looked at the answers, _____

17. They were warned, _____

18. Everything seems in order, _____

19. There is a class tonight, _____

20. Those are your boots, _____

## 5d Negatives

*Not* and other negative words are used to make negative statements in English.

To make a statement negative, *not* immediately follows the first auxiliary verb or *be*. If there is no form of *be* and no auxiliary, *do* support is necessary.

I cannot go to the movies.

She would not listen to reason.

Jose and Maria have not finished the project.

He is not an engineer.

They did not arrive until ten o'clock.

In addition to *not*, the following are negative adverbs.

| | | |
|---|---|---|
| never | rarely | scarcely ever |
| seldom | hardly ever | barely ever |

He never takes the dog for a walk.

They hardly ever go to see him.

*No* is also used to express negative ideas.

There's no food in the house.

### 1 Compare *not* and *no*

*Not* is used to make a verb negative. *No* is used as an adjective in front of a noun.

He does not have a car.

He has no car.

### 2 Avoid double negatives

Using two negatives in one clause within a sentence is confusing and grammatically incorrect. One clause should contain only one negative.

INCORRECT  I don't have no car.
CORRECT  I don't have a car.

INCORRECT  He didn't do no homework last night.
CORRECT  He did no homework last night.

Note that *some* is used to qualify nouns, and *any* is the negative form. (See also Section 7c3.)

## EXERCISE 5.7

## NEGATIVES

Change the following statements into negatives in two ways: Use *not . . . any* in one sentence and *no* in the other.

*Example:*  I have some books

*I don't have any books.*
*I have no books.*

1. There was some mail.

2. I need some food.

3. He saw someone.

4. They have some money to spend.

5. There was someone in the house.

6. I received some news from home.

7. She had some problems with her visa.

8. We have some cash.

9. She will find someone to help her.

10. You should have given the other student the answer.

## DOUBLE NEGATIVES: ERROR ANALYSIS

Correct the following sentences.

*Example:*   I don't have no money.

> *I have no money.*
> *I don't have any money.*

1. We don't need no help.

2. He never does no work.

3. I seldom do no homework.

4. He didn't eat no food.

5. We couldn't see nothing from the roof.

6. He couldn't hardly hear the speaker.

7. We didn't do nothing.

8. I can't never believe what he says.

9. He doesn't like neither jazz nor pop music.

10. When we looked, we didn't see nobody.

## **5e** Contractions in English

Contractions are quite common especially in informal and spoken English. Contractions of verb phrases (e.g., *don't* and *weren't*) and of pronoun–verb pairs (e.g., *I'll* and *you're*) are the most common.

An apostrophe is used to indicate that one or more letters have been removed.

---

### CONTRACTIONS IN ENGLISH

#### NEGATIVES

| | | | | |
|---|---|---|---|---|
| is not | = isn't | | have not | = haven't |
| are not | = aren't | | had not | = hadn't |
| was not | = wasn't | | | |
| were not | = weren't | | will not | = won't |
| | | | would not | = wouldn't |
| do not | = don't | | cannot | = can't |
| does not | = doesn't | | could not | = couldn't |
| did not | = didn't | | | |
| | | | should not | = shouldn't |

#### CONTRACTIONS WITH *TO BE*   CONTRACTIONS WITH *WILL*

| | | | | |
|---|---|---|---|---|
| I am | = I'm | | I will | = I'll |
| you are | = you're | | you will | = you'll |
| he is | = he's | | he will | = he'll |
| she is | = she's | | she will | = she'll |
| it is | = it's | | we will | = we'll |
| we are | = we're | | they will | = they'll |
| they are | = they're | | | |
| | | | | |
| there is | = there's | | | |

| CONTRACTIONS WITH *HAVE* | | CONTRACTIONS WITH *WOULD* | |
|---|---|---|---|
| I have | = I've | I would | = I'd |
| you have | = you've | you would | = you'd |
| he has | = he's | he would | = he'd |
| she has | = she's | she would | = she'd |
| we have | = we've | we would | = we'd |
| they have | = they've | they would | = they'd |

**CONTRACTIONS WITH QUESTION WORDS**

| where is | = where's |
|---|---|
| who is | = who's |
| where is | = where's |
| what is | = what's |
| how is | = how's |

Nouns sometimes combine with *is* and *has*. Sentences such as the following are very common in everyday speech.

> My car's in the shop. (car is)

> Maria's been late quite frequently. (Maria has)

Note: Be careful not to confuse the personal pronouns *its, their, your* and *whose* with the contractions *it's, they're, you're* and *who's*.


## EXERCISE 5.8

## USING CONTRACTIONS

**A.** Fill in the following dialogue with the appropriate contractions. One of the contractions listed is used twice.

*Example:* Hi Maria. (*What's*) your next class.

| she'd | it's | he's |
|---|---|---|
| where's | you're | I'm |
| we've | who's | I've |
| Mr. Blake's | I'll | |

*First Day of Class*

Maria: Hi Bob. _____ your next class?

Bob: _____ going to North Hall.

Maria: _____ your teacher?

Bob: _____ the teacher. _____ new in the department.

Maria: _____ the second person who told me that.

Bob: By the way, have you seen Mark and Monica lately?

Maria: Yes. _____ met in the library a few times. _____ been working in the lab, and _____ like to come back as a full-time student soon.

Bob: Well, _____ time for me to get to the bookstore; _____ got to buy my book. _____ see you soon.

Maria: Good-bye.

**B.** Answer the following questions using an appropriate contraction.

*Example:* What time is it?
*Answer:* It's 4 o'clock.

1. Who is that man?

2. Who are those students?

3. Who has been studying in this room?

4. What have you been reading?

5. Where are you studying?

6. Where am I sitting?

7. What would they like to eat?

8. What had you been doing before you came to school?

9. Who is your teacher?

10. What am I supposed to do?

# CHAPTER 6

# Verb Tenses

**6a** **Present continuous aspect**

The present continuous aspect (see Section 6i) is a verb tense commonly used to express current, repeated, or frequent action.

**1** **Form**

The form of the present continuous is *be* + present participle.

| SUBJECT | BE | VERB + ING |
|---------|-----|------------|
| I | am | reading. |
| You<br>We<br>They<br>Jose and Maria | are | reading. |
| He<br>She<br>It<br>Esperanza | is | reading.<br>studying.<br>sleeping.<br>talking. |

NEGATIVE

He is not reading.

They aren't studying.

I am not eating.

YES/NO QUESTIONS AND SHORT ANSWERS

Is he reading?
No, he isn't.

Are they studying?
Yes, they are.

INFORMATION QUESTIONS

What is he reading?

Why are they studying?

Who am I looking at?

## 2 Use

1. The present continuous expresses an action that is happening right now. We often use such expressions as *(right) now*, *at the moment*, and *at present* in these sentences.

   What are you doing now?
   I am eating my lunch.

   At this moment, what are they doing?
   They are studying English.

2. The present continuous expresses an action that is repeated or endures up to the present time, though the action is not necessarily happening right now. The present continuous is used in this way for a temporary activity. We often use such expressions as *these days, nowadays, today, this week,* and *this semester* with sentences of this sort.

   Jose is relaxing this week.

   Maria is temporarily working as a cook.

   I am learning about American customs this semester.

3. The present continuous is used for a frequent activity about which some emotion is felt. We use it with the adverbs *always, forever,* and *constantly.*

   They are constantly bothering the teacher.

   She is always complaining.

## 3 Spelling

1. When adding *-ing*, do not change a final *y*.

   | carry | carrying |
   |-------|----------|
   | worry | worrying |
   | study | studying |

2. For one-syllable verbs that end in consonant-vowel-consonant, double the final consonant and add *-ing*.

   | plan | planning |
   |------|----------|
   | sit  | sitting  |
   | stop | stopping |

   EXCEPTIONS: Do not double a final *-w, -x,* or *-y*.

   | mow  | mowing  |
   |------|---------|
   | fix  | fixing  |
   | stay | staying |

3. For two-syllable words that end in consonant-vowel-consonant, double the final consonant if the last syllable is stressed.

refer         referring
begin         beginning

4. With words ending in a consonant + -e, drop the -e before adding -ing.

type          typing
write        writing

## EXERCISE 6.1

## SPELLING

Write the present participle (-ing form) of the verb.

*Example:* grab *grabbing*

1. study

2. sit

3. pray

4. grow

5. marry

6. fix

7. happen

8. plan

9. begin

10. win

## EXERCISE 6.2

## PRESENT CONTINUOUS

**A.** Use the following verbs to write sentences using the present continuous to describe a person doing something.

*Example:* sleep

*She is sleeping in a bed.*

1. run

2. drop

3. carry

4. read

5. fish

6. write

7. dance

8. listen

9. eat

10. watch

**B.** Talk about a person in the class. Tell if he or she is or isn't wearing the item listed.

*Examples:* boots

*Naoko isn't wearing boots.*

glasses

*She isn't wearing glasses.*

1. a tie

2. a ring

3. earrings

4. socks

5. blue jeans

6. a dress

7. a sweater

8. a necklace

9. a skirt

10. a hat

**C.** Fill in the blanks with the present continuous tense of the verb in parentheses.

*Example:* Machines _are taking_ (take) over many jobs these days.

1. Many families _____ (buy) new cars this year.

2. The number of jobs in manufacturing _____ (decrease).

3. Children _____ (learn) more about everything each day.

4. Schools _____ (use) more computers in the classroom.

5. The principal _____ (look) for qualified teachers.

6. This month, I _____ (cook) the meals in my house.

7. This semester, she _____ (study) Spanish and French.

8. We _____ (travel) to school by bus this term.

9. This year, he _____ (advise) the students not to take chemistry.

10. The train _____ (leave) at ten o'clock.

**D.** Write an essay about the things you are doing this semester. When you have finished, go back through the essay and underline all the present participles (*-ing* forms of verbs).

**E.** Using the adverbs *forever, always,* and *constantly,* write two different sentences in the present continuous tense for each verb. These sentences should express an emotion.

*Examples:* talk

*She is forever talking on the phone.*
*He is constantly talking in class.*

1. complain


2. eat


3. bother


5. leave


6. make


7. cause


8. reveal

9. tell


10. do

## **6b** Noncontinuous verbs

Some verbs are not used in any of the continuous tenses. These verbs describe states or conditions that exist; they do not describe activities that are in progress. They are nonaction verbs.

---

### COMMON NONCONTINUOUS VERBS

**CONDITION**

| | | |
|---|---|---|
| be* | equal | owe |
| consist | fit* | resemble |
| cost | matter | weigh* |

**POSSESSION**

| | | |
|---|---|---|
| belong | have* | possess |
| contain | town | |

**PERCEPTION**

| | | |
|---|---|---|
| appear* | look* | smell* |
| feel* | see* | sound* |
| hear* | seem | taste* |

**EMOTIONAL STATE**

| | | |
|---|---|---|
| appreciate | hate | need |
| approve | imagine | prefer |
| believe | know | recognize |
| desire | like | remember |
| dislike | love | think* |
| doubt | mean* | understand |
| guess* | mind* | want |

The verbs marked with an asterisk (*) are also commonly used as continuous verbs, with a difference in meaning. Compare the following sentences.

---

**NONCONTINUOUS**

1. I think it's too late. (*think* = believe, have an opinion)
2. He has a bicycle. (*have* = possess)
3. The food tastes awful. (*taste* = have a taste, perceive involuntarily)
4. That smells nice. (*smell* = have a smell)
5. I see an eagle. (*see* = perceive with the eyes)
6. The boss feels it's a good plan. (*feel* = think, believe)
7. She looks happy. (*look* = seem)
8. The baby appears to be asleep. (*appear* = seem)
9. A car weighs at least two tons. (*weigh* = have weight)
10. George is foolish. (*be* expresses a permanent characteristic)

**CONTINUOUS**

1. Please wait, I'm thinking. (*think* = consider, reflect)
2. She is having lunch. (*have* = eat, drink)
3. She is tasting your cake right now. (*taste* = sample, try)
4. The dog is smelling the ground. (*smell* = sniff)
5. The doctor is seeing a patient. (*see* = meet with)
6. I'm feeling better now. (*feel* = experience an emotional or physical feeling)
7. He is looking out the window. (*look* = use the eyes)
8. Yuko is appearing on stage this week. (*appear* = perform)
9. She is weighing the meat. (*weigh* = put on a scale)
10. Jose is being foolish. (*be* expresses a momentary action)*

---

\* The verb *be* + an adjective is used to describe a temporary characteristic. A few adjectives are used with *be* in the continuous. Among them are *foolish, nice, kind, lazy, careful, patient, silly, rude, polite*, and *impolite*.

---

## EXERCISE 6.3

## NONCONTINUOUS VERBS

Write a yes/no question and a short answer for each of the following nonaction verbs.

*Example:*  need

*Do you need anything?*
*No, I don't.*

1. want

2. like

3. have

4. understand

5. possess

6. know

7. remember

8. have

9. prefer

10. seem

11. cost


12. hate


13. feel


14. mind


15. believe


## 6c  Simple present tense

### 1  Form

The simple present tense has two forms, the base form and the -s form. We use the base form with *I, you, we, they,* and plural nouns. We use the -s form with *he, she, it,* and singular nouns.

|  | SINGULAR | PLURAL |
|---|---|---|
| FIRST PERSON | I walk | we walk |
| SECOND PERSON | you walk | you walk |
| THIRD PERSON | he/she/it walks | they walk |

Some verbs have irregular -s forms.

| | |
|---|---|
| have | has |
| go | goes |
| do | does |

## 2 Use

1. The simple present tense is used to express habits, regular activity, or repeated action.

   The children always take a nap at two o'clock.

   The students usually do their homework.

   We meet here on Mondays and Wednesdays.

   She seldom comes to school.

2. The simple present tense is also used for statements of fact. We use the base form and the -s/-es form for affirmative statements.

   November has thirty days.

   Maria and George have a baby.

## 3 Spelling

For most verbs, the third-person singular in the present tense is formed by adding -s to the base form.

| | |
|---|---|
| like | likes |
| need | needs |
| dream | dreams |
| smile | smiles |

If the base form ends in -ss, -sh, -ch, or -x, we add -es.

| | |
|---|---|
| miss | misses |
| push | pushes |
| teach | teaches |
| fix | fixes |

If the base form of the verb ends in a consonant + y, we change the y to i and add -es.

| | |
|---|---|
| cry | cries |
| study | studies |

If the base form ends in a vowel + y, we simply add -s.

| | |
|---|---|
| pay | pays |
| buy | buys |

## 4 Pronunciation of -s/-es

The -s/-es that makes the third-person singular has three different pronunciations (see also Chapter 16).

After the voiceless sounds /k/, /p/, /t/, and /f/, the final -s/-es sounds like /s/.

| | |
|---|---|
| drink | drinks |
| sleep | sleeps |
| write | writes |
| laugh | laughs |

After the voiced sounds /b/, /d/, /g/, /v/, /m/, /n/, /ŋ/, /l/, /r/ and all vowels, the final -s/-es is pronounced /z/.

| | |
|---|---|
| rob | robs |
| hide | hides |
| tag | tags |
| wave | waves |
| dream | dreams |
| run | runs |
| long | longs |
| smile | smiles |
| wear | wears |
| pay | pays |
| snow | snows |

After verbs that end in ss, z, sh, ch, x, ge, ce, or se, the final -es is pronounced /iz/, as an extra syllable.

| | |
|---|---|
| miss | misses |
| buzz | buzzes |
| push | pushes |
| watch | watches |
| fix | fixes |
| use | uses |
| charge | charges |
| prance | prances |

A few verbs have a change in the vowel sound when they are put into the third-person singular present tense.

| | |
|---|---|
| say /sei/ | says /sɛz/ |
| do /du/ | does /dʌz/ |

## EXERCISE 6.4

## PRONUNCIATION of -s/-es

Fill in the blank with /s/, /z/, or /iz/ to indicate the correct pronunciation.

*Example:*  /z/  needs

| | | | | |
|---|---|---|---|---|
| 1. _____ | likes | | 21. _____ | uses |
| 2. _____ | flies | | 22. _____ | charges |
| 3. _____ | pushes | | 23. _____ | laughs |
| 4. _____ | hisses | | 24. _____ | clips |
| 5. _____ | raises | | 25. _____ | sees |
| 6. _____ | teaches | | 26. _____ | rains |
| 7. _____ | hits | | 27. _____ | trades |
| 8. _____ | begs | | 28. _____ | buzzes |
| 9. _____ | raves | | 29. _____ | fixes |
| 10. _____ | knows | | 30. _____ | goes |
| 11. _____ | has | | 31. _____ | cheats |
| 12. _____ | drinks | | 32. _____ | strokes |
| 13. _____ | watches | | 33. _____ | wears |
| 14. _____ | limps | | 34. _____ | lacks |
| 15. _____ | sags | | 35. _____ | buys |
| 16. _____ | seems | | 36. _____ | washes |
| 17. _____ | pays | | 37. _____ | wills |
| 18. _____ | huffs | | 38. _____ | hints |
| 19. _____ | kisses | | 39. _____ | carries |
| 20. _____ | studies | | 40. _____ | fixes |

**6c/Simple Present Tense**    **129**

# EXERCISE 6.5

## SPELLING AND PRONUNCIATION

Fill in each blank with the correct form of the verb or noun in parentheses. Between the slashes after each, put /s/, /z/, or /iz/ to indicate the correct pronunciation.

Every day, Emanuela (do) _does_ / z / the same (thing)

_____ / / . She (get) _____ / / up at 7:00 A.M.; she (wash)

_____ / / her face and (brush) _____ / / her teeth.

Then she (go) _____ / / into the kitchen and (eat) _____

/ / breakfast. She usually (have) _____ / / a bowl of cereal

with some (banana) _____ / / and (raisin) _____ / / .

She (drink) _____ / / two (glass) _____ / / of water

and (finish) _____ / / with a cup of coffee. After this, she

(dress) _____ / / for school; she often (have) _____ / /

trouble finding her (shoe) _____ / / . Usually, she (leave)

_____ / / the house at 8:15. She (have) _____ / / to

take two (bus) _____ / / to school. She (carry) _____

/ / two (bag) _____ / / with her—one for her lunch and the

other for her (book) _____ / / . Emanuela (like) _____

/ / riding both (bus) _____ / / because she usually (meet)

_____ / / a few of her (classmate) _____ / / and

(friend) _____ / / on the way.

At school, she (have) _____ / / five different (class) _____

/   /. Her (teacher) _____ /   / are friendly and helpful.

Emanuela (do) _____ /   / have a few (goal) _____

/   /. She (plan) _____ /   / to major in education and (want)

_____ /   / to work in bilingual education. Her (adviser) _____

/   / all urge her to complete the required (course) _____

/   / and (credit) _____ /   / so that she can achieve all her

(dream) _____ /   /.

<br>

**5**    **Frequency adverbs**

    The simple present tense expresses habitual or regular activity and repeated actions. *Frequency adverbs* tell how often the activity or action is repeated.

    The frequency words range from *always* (one hundred percent of the time) to *never* (zero percent of the time).

| *Percent of the time* | *Frequency adverbs* |
| --- | --- |
| 100 | always |
| 90 | usually, generally |
| 75 | often, frequently |
| 50 or less | sometimes, occasionally |
| 20 or less | seldom |
| 10 or less | rarely |
| 0 | never |

Frequency adverbs most often come between the subject and the main verb. *Often, sometimes*, and *usually* can come at the beginning of a sentence.

    The teacher always rides a bike.

    Liz usually pays her bills on time.

    The family often eats together.

    Sometimes Peter writes to his family.

    That student seldom wastes time.

    We rarely see her.

    He never walks to school.

## EXERCISE 6.6

## FREQUENCY ADVERBS

A.  Write a sentence based on each statement.

*Example:*  something you always do in the morning

*I always brush my teeth in the morning.*

1.  something you always do at night


2.  something you usually do every day


3.  something you usually do in the afternoon


4.  something you generally do every week


5.  something you often do in the evening


6.  something you frequently do each month


7.  something you sometimes do during the summer


8.  something you occasionally do during the school year


9.  something you seldom do during the school week


10.  something you rarely do when you are busy

**B.** Fill in the correct frequency adverb.

*Example:* I *often* go to the movies.

1. It _____ snows in the winter.

2. The weather is _____ mild in June.

3. It is _____ cold in February.

4. I _____ go to the pool; I can't swim.

5. He _____ does his homework because he is too busy.

6. I _____ visit my aunt—about once a month.

7. I _____ listen to the radio at night; I'm too tired.

8. I _____ drink tea with dinner.

9. I'm _____ late for dinner.

10. She _____ runs three miles.

**Frequency adverbs with be**

Frequency adverbs often follow the verb *be*.

I am seldom on time for anything.

She is often late.

They are always in the first row.

## EXERCISE 6.7

## FREQUENCY ADVERBS WITH *BE*

Write a complete sentence using the words given and a form of the verb *be* in the present tense.

*Example:*   I, usually

*I am usually on time for class.*

1. he, often

2. she, never

3. they, rarely

4. Mariko, occasionally

5. Marianne, sometimes

6. Loretta, generally

7. Esperanza, seldom

8. Maria, frequently

9. Kevin, occasionally

10. Harumi, always

### Frequency questions and answers

If we want a frequency answer, we use *ever* in a question.

Are you ever lonely?
Yes, I am sometimes lonely.

Does Jose ever come late?
Yes, he always comes late.


## EXERCISE 6.8

## FREQUENCY QUESTIONS AND ANSWERS

---

First, write a question using the word *ever*; then answer it using an adverb of frequency.

*Example:*  drive a car  *Does Hiroshi ever drive a car?*

        or          *Yes, he often drives a car.*

                          *No, he never drives a car.*

1. eat at the cafeteria


2. do the homework


3. repair the car


4. drink alcohol


5. smoke cigarettes


6. work until midnight

7. hurry to class

8. bring food for everyone

9. see the teacher after class

10. study Japanese

**6**  **Statements of fact**

The simple present tense is also used to express statements of fact.

The stars shine at night.

Traffic moves fast on this street.

Pandas live in China.

## EXERCISE 6.9

## STATEMENTS OF FACT

**A.**  Write a sentence stating a fact about each place.

*Example:*  a hospital

*A hospital has doctors, nurses, and patients.*

or  *A hospital is a place where sick people get well.*

1. a university

2. a prison

3. a church

4. a small town

5. a supermarket

6. a fast-food restaurant

7. a movie theater

8. a park

9. a beach

10. a library

**B.** Write one paragraph about the facts of your current life, a second about a friend's life, and a third about the life of a classmate. Use the simple present tense.

Examples:
1. *I am a student. I study English....*

2. *She is a student. She drives to school every day....*

3. *They are immigrants. They have permanent visas. They always study hard....*

1.

2.

3.

## 6d Simple past tense

### 1 Form (regular verbs)

Regular verbs form the simple past tense and the past participle by adding *-ed* to the base form.

| | |
|---|---|
| walk | walked |
| love | loved |

### 2 Spelling

If the base form of the verb ends in a consonant + *y*, change the *y* to *i* and add *-ed*.

| | |
|---|---|
| carry | carried |
| worry | worried |
| study | studied |
| hurry | hurried |

If the base form of the verb ends in a vowel + *y*, do not change the *y*.

| | |
|---|---|
| pray | prayed |
| convey | conveyed |
| annoy | annoyed |

If the verb has one syllable and the last three letters are consonant-vowel-consonant, double the final consonant and add *-ed*.

| | |
|---|---|
| stop | stopped |
| drop | dropped |

However, the letters *w* and *x* are never doubled in English.

Compare these:

| | |
|------|--------|
| curb | curbed |
| race | raced |
| sew | sewed |
| fix | fixed |

If the verb has two syllables and the final syllable is stressed, the consonant-vowel-consonant rule applies.

| | |
|-------|----------|
| defer | deferred |
| occur | occurred |

If the base form of the verb ends in *e* add *d* only.

| | |
|------|--------|
| move | moved |
| hate | hated |
| live | lived |
| love | loved |

## EXERCISE 6.10

## PAST TENSE

Change each verb into the past tense. Then use it in a complete sentence.

*Example:* study

*studied: He studied his math all night.*

1. play

2. love

3. carry

4. look

5. turn

6. decide

7. enjoy

8. prefer

9. want

10. stop

11. happen

12. grab

13. race

14. save

15. hurry

16. start

17. roar

18. wash

19. concur

20. charge

## 3 Pronunciation

The *-ed* past-tense marker may be pronounced in three different ways, depending on the final sound in the base form of the verb.

The *-ed* ending is pronounced /t/ when the final sound in the verb is one of the voiceless sounds /p/, /k/, /f/, /s/, /ʃ/, /tʃ/.

| | |
|---|---|
| pump | pumped |
| like | liked |
| puff | puffed |
| miss | missed |
| wash | washed |
| watch | watched |

The *-ed* ending is pronounced /d/ when the verb ends in one of the voiced sounds /b/, /g/, /v/, /ð/, /z/, /dʒ/, /m/, /n/, /ŋ/, /l/, or /r/.

| | |
|---|---|
| curb | curbed |
| tag | tagged |
| live | lived |
| bathe | bathed |
| use | used |
| charge | charged |
| tame | tamed |
| earn | earned |
| long | longed |
| pull | pulled |
| fire | fired |

The *-ed* ending is pronounced as the separate syllable /id/ when the final sound in the verb is /d/ or /t/.

| | |
|---|---|
| add | added |
| need | needed |
| wait | waited |
| taste | tasted |

## EXERCISE 6.11

## PRONUNCIATION OF *-ed*

**A.** Pronounce the following verbs, all of which end in voiceless sounds; the final *-ed* should sound like /t/.

| | |
|---|---|
| slap, slapped | jump, jumped |
| work, worked | stuff, stuffed |
| hatch, hatched | cease, ceased |
| crash, crashed | whip, whipped |

**B.** Pronounce the following verbs, all of which end in voiced or vowel sounds; the final *-ed* should sound like /d/.

| | |
|---|---|
| rob, robbed | snag, snagged |
| save, saved | breathe, breathed |
| use, used | arrange, arranged |
| tame, tamed | earn, earned |
| long, longed | dial, dialed |
| fire, fired | enjoy, enjoyed |

**C.** Pronounce the following verbs, all of which end in /d/ or /t/ sound; the final *-ed* should sound like the separate syllable /id/.

| | |
|---|---|
| want, wanted | decide, decided |
| hate, hated | add, added |
| seed, seeded | heat, heated |

**D.** In the blank, write /t/, /d/, or /id/ to indicate the correct pronunciation of the final *-ed*.

*Examples:*   __/d/__   lived

__/t/__   helped

| | | | | |
|---|---|---|---|---|
| 1. _____ | hurried | | 14. _____ | annoyed |
| 2. _____ | smoked | | 15. _____ | waxed |
| 3. _____ | bashed | | 16. _____ | stacked |
| 4. _____ | needed | | 17. _____ | placed |
| 5. _____ | picked | | 18. _____ | rushed |
| 6. _____ | wished | | 19. _____ | cracked |
| 7. _____ | filed | | 20. _____ | seated |
| 8. _____ | turned | | 21. _____ | wished |
| 9. _____ | roared | | 22. _____ | dropped |
| 10. _____ | entered | | 23. _____ | looked |
| 11. _____ | cashed | | 24. _____ | stored |
| 12. _____ | fussed | | 25. _____ | kissed |
| 13. _____ | whipped | | 26. _____ | crossed |

27. _____ clothed    29. _____ knocked

28. _____ stopped    30. _____ saved

## 6e Past continuous tense

### 1 Form

To form the past continuous, the past tense of *be* is followed by the present participle.

She was reading a book.

They were eating their dinner.

He wasn't listening to me.

Was he listening to me?

What was he doing last night?

### 2 Use

1. The past continuous tense describes an action that was in progress at a specific time in the past.

    He was studying math at nine o'clock last night.

    They were attending high school in 1989.

    The simple past may also be used for a continuous past event.

    He studied math at nine o'clock last night.

    They attended high school in 1989.

    The past continuous tense (*be* + present participle) emphasizes duration. The simple past emphasizes completion.

2. The past continuous and the past are often used in a complex sentence to show that one thing interrupted another. The subordinating conjunctions of time—*when* and *while*—are used. *While* + past continuous is used for events of longer duration.

    While I was studying last night, a friend called me.

    While I was driving to work, I saw my teacher.

    *When* + simple past is used for events of short or no duration.

The students were writing when the bell sounded.

We were walking to school when the bus went by.

## EXERCISE 6.12

### PAST CONTINUOUS

**A.** Fill in each blank with the past continuous of the verb.

*Example:* The man ___*was eating*___ (eat) his dinner.

1. Those people _____ (travel) for two weeks.

2. The tourists _____ (go) to see the Statue of Liberty.

3. We _____ (have) a wonderful time at the party.

4. The truck _____ (move) very fast.

5. While the children _____ (cross) the street, their mother walked up to them.

6. While the father _____ (park) the car, the mother took the children upstairs.

7. We _____ (play) tennis when the sun came out.

8. When he arrived, I _____ (cook) dinner.

9. While I _____ (read) last night, Nancy called.

10. I _____ (take) a shower when the lights went out.

**B.** Write a sentence that describes a specific time in the past when you were doing these things.

*Example:* go to high school

*I was going to high school last year.*

1. go to grammar school

2. study English

3. watch a movie

4. eat lunch

5. take a bath

6. live in my country

7. sleep

8. work

9. apply for a visa

10. visit my grandparents

**C.** Write a question about the time given and then an answer to it. Follow the example.

*Example:* at ten o'clock

*What were you doing at ten o'clock?
I was sleeping.*

1. at four o'clock this morning

2. before the meeting

3. yesterday afternoon

4. at this time yesterday

5. at 6 P.M.

**D.** Fill in the blanks with the past continuous and the simple past.

Example: I _was walking_ (walk) to school when I
_saw_ (see) my friends.

1. He _____ (eat) his dinner when the phone
_____ (ring).

2. They _____ (play) volleyball when it
_____ (begin) to rain.

3. She _____ (read) a book when her husband
_____ (arrive) home.

4. We _____ (try) to finish the project when the teacher
_____ (call) us back into the room.

5. Elmer _____ (work) when he _____
(attend) college.

**E.** Rewrite the sentences in D, changing *when* to *while*.

*Example:* I was walking to school when I saw my friends.

*While I was walking to school, I saw my friends.*

1.

2.

3.

4.

5.

**1** **Form**

*Will* or *be going to* plus the base form of the verb forms the future tense. *Will* is often contracted in combination with a pronoun.

| | |
|---|---|
| I will | I'll |
| They will | They'll |

*Will not* is contracted as *won't*.

I won't go to the dance.

Elmer won't arrive until tonight.

I will be there in a week.

She will cook dinner tonight.

Will you call me next week?

Maria won't go to the dance.

When will you be leaving?

## 2 Use

The future tense is used for something expected or planned at a later time. It is often used with a time clause (see Chapter 6) or an *if* clause (see Chapter 14).

I'll be there tonight.

She is going to be there tomorrow.

I'll see you after dinner.

When he arrives, we will leave for the game.

I'll be mad if he damages my car.

If you need me, I'm going to be at home tomorrow.


## EXERCISE 6.13

## FUTURE TENSE

**A.** Fill in each blank with *will* or a form of *be going to*.

*Example:* When summer is over, the youngsters _____*will go*_____ (go) back to school.

After classes are finished, Jose _____ (go) to work.

On the way there, he _____ (stop) off at the supermarket. He _____ (buy) some groceries for a late dinner.

He _____ (visit) his grandmother for a few minutes before getting to work. This evening _____ (be) very busy at work, so he _____ (have) a lot to do. Jose likes work, but during the whole work shift, he _____ (anticipate) getting home.

**B.** Write question and answer sentences to talk about the coming week. Use *be going to* or *will*.

*Example:*  next Tuesday

*What will you do next Tuesday?*
*I will work next Tuesday.*
or *I am going to work next Tuesday.*

1. next Monday evening

2. next Friday morning

3. next Sunday

4. next Tuesday night

5. next Saturday afternoon

**C.** Pretend that you are running for president of the student association. Use the following verbs and phrases, plus *be going to* or *will*, in sentences for your campaign speech.

*Examples:*   tuition increases (not vote)

*I won't vote to pass the tuition increases.*

student parking (seek)

*I will seek more student parking.*

1. lower tuition (demand)

2. more free books (ask for)

3. better food (promote)

4. classrooms (clean up)

5. higher tuition (not support)

**D.** Ask a question using *be going to* and the words given.

*Examples:*   we, have an exam

*Are we going to have an exam next week?*

when, we, have an exam

*When are we going to have an exam?*

1. we, finish this lesson

2. they, receive the assignment

3. how many students, the class, have

4. you, be in this class, next semester

5. when, you, finish the letter

**E.** Write two paragraphs. In one, make plans for a class party. In the other, make plans for a vacation.

*Example:*

*We are going to have a class party next week. I will bring some cupcakes. Jose will bring the ...*

1.

2.

## 6g Simple present tense with future meaning

1. The simple present tense can have a future meaning in subordinate clauses that express time and condition. The subordinate clause begins with one of the time words *when, whenever, while, as, until, before, after, as soon as,* or *by the time* or one of the condition words *if, unless,* or *in case* (see Chapters 4 and 14).

   When he gets here tomorrow, I'll be at work.

   Before you go to work, will you please call me?

   You will have a good time unless it rains.

2. The simple present tense may also have a future meaning with certain verbs that indicate a scheduled event. These include *start, begin, open, end, close, arrive, leave, take off, get to, land, rise,* and *set.*

The sun rises at 6 A.M. tomorrow.

That store closes at nine o'clock tonight.

The plane takes off tomorrow morning.

## EXERCISE 6.14

## SIMPLE PRESENT WITH FUTURE MEANING

A. Write a complex sentence using each of the following words. Use the simple present tense to convey a future meaning. You may put the subordinate clause at the beginning or the end of the sentence. Use proper punctuation.

*Examples:* while

*While he gets the car, I'll be waiting here.*

if

*If he wins the prize, he'll be very surprised.*

1. when

2. whenever

3. in case

4. as

5. until

6. before

7. after

8. as soon as

9. by the time

10. unless

**B.** Using these verbs, write a sentence expressing the future by using the simple present tense.

*Example:*  start

*The new semester starts tomorrow.*

1. rise

2. begin

3. open

4. end

5. close

6. arrive

7. leave

8. take off

9. get to

10. land

## 6h Irregular verbs

Most verbs in English are **regular**. The simple past tense of the verb is formed by adding *-ed* to the base form. The past participle is identical to the past form.

| BASE | PAST | PAST PARTICIPLE |
|------|------|-----------------|
| walk | walked | walked |

There are, however, a number of verbs in English that are **irregular**. These are verbs that *do not* form the past by adding *-ed*. The past and past participle forms are irregular, and they must be memorized.

### IRREGULAR VERBS

| PRESENT | PAST | PAST PARTICIPLE |
|---------|------|-----------------|
| arise | arose | arisen |
| be (am, is, are) | was, were | been |
| beat | beat | beaten |
| become | became | become |
| begin | began | begun |
| bend | bent | bent |
| bet | bet | bet |
| bid | bid | bid |
| bind | bound | bound |
| bite | bit | bitten |
| bleed | bled | bled |
| blow | blew | blown |
| break | broke | broken |
| breed | bred | bred |
| bring | brought | brought |
| build | built | built |
| burst | burst | burst |
| buy | bought | bought |
| cast | cast | cast |
| catch | caught | caught |
| choose | chose | chosen |
| cling | clung | clung |
| come | came | come |
| cost | cost | cost |
| creep | crept | crept |
| cut | cut | cut |
| deal | dealt | dealt |
| dig | dug | dug |
| do | did | done |
| draw | drew | drawn |

| PRESENT | PAST | PAST PARTICIPLE |
|---------|------|-----------------|
| dream | dreamed/dreamt | dreamed/dreamt |
| drink | drank | drunk |
| drive | drove | driven |
| eat | ate | eaten |
| fall | fell | fallen |
| feed | fed | fed |
| feel | felt | felt |
| fight | fought | fought |
| find | found | found |
| flee | fled | fled |
| fly | flew | flown |
| forbid | forbade/forbad | forbidden |
| forget | forgot | forgotten |
| forgive | forgave | forgiven |
| freeze | froze | frozen |
| get | got | gotten/got |
| give | gave | given |
| go | went | gone |
| grind | ground | ground |
| grow | grew | grown |
| hang | hung/hanged | hung/hanged |
| have | had | had |
| hear | heard | heard |
| hide | hid | hidden/hid |
| hit | hit | hit |
| hold | held | held |
| hurt | hurt | hurt |
| keep | kept | kept |
| kneel | knelt | knelt |
| know | knew | known |
| lay | laid | laid |
| lead | led | led |
| leave | left | left |
| lend | lent | lent |
| let | let | let |
| lie | lay | lain |
| light | lighted/lit | lighted/lit |
| lose | lost | lost |
| make | made | made |
| mean | meant | meant |
| meet | met | met |
| pay | paid | paid |
| put | put | put |
| quit | quit | quit |
| read | read | read |
| ride | rode | ridden |
| ring | rang | rung |

| PRESENT | PAST | PAST PARTICIPLE |
|---|---|---|
| rise | rose | risen |
| run | ran | run |
| say | said | said |
| see | saw | seen |
| seek | sought | sought |
| sell | sold | sold |
| send | sent | sent |
| set | set | set |
| shake | shook | shaken |
| shed | shed | shed |
| shine | shone/shined | shone/shined |
| shoot | shot | shot |
| show | showed | shown/showed |
| shrink | shrank | shrunk |
| shut | shut | shut |
| sing | sang | sung |
| sink | sank | sunk |
| sit | sat | sat |
| slay | slew | slain |
| sleep | slept | slept |
| slide | slid | slid |
| slink | slunk | slunk |
| slit | slit | slit |
| speak | spoke | spoken |
| speed | sped | sped |
| spend | spent | spent |
| spin | spun | spun |
| spit | spit | spit |
| split | split | split |
| spread | spread | spread |
| spring | sprang | sprung |
| stand | stood | stood |
| steal | stole | stolen |
| stick | stuck | stuck |
| sting | stung | stung |
| stink | stank | stunk |
| string | strung | strung |
| strive | strove | striven |
| swear | swore | sworn |
| sweep | swept | swept |
| swim | swam | swum |
| swing | swung | swung |
| take | took | taken |
| teach | taught | taught |
| tear | tore | torn |
| tell | told | told |
| think | thought | thought |
| throw | threw | thrown |

| PRESENT | PAST | PAST PARTICIPLE |
|---|---|---|
| understand | understood | understood |
| wake | woke/waked | woken/waked |
| wear | wore | worn |
| weave | wove/weaved | woven |
| wed | wed | wed |
| weep | wept | wept |
| wet | wet | wet |
| win | won | won |
| wind | wound | wound |
| withdraw | withdrew | withdrawn |
| wring | wrung | wrung |
| write | wrote | written |

## 6i Past participle

The past participle is one of the four principal parts of any verb. It has three main uses:

1. To act as an adjective (see Chapter 10)
2. To form the perfect aspect (or tense)* of a verb in combination with the verb *have* as the auxiliary verb
3. To form the passive voice of a verb in combination with the verb *be* as the auxiliary verb

## 6j Present perfect

In general, using the perfect aspect indicates a time before the basic time frame.

### 1 Form

The present perfect is formed by using the verb *have* as an auxiliary followed by the past participle of the verb.

She has lived there for many years.

Maria and George have studied English since 1987.

They haven't gone there for a long time.

* A distinction may be made between verb tense and verb aspect. *Tense* refers to time, while *aspect* comments on some characteristics of the verb. The present and past participles in combination with auxiliary verbs form the aspect forms of English verbs.

Have you seen the ball?

What have you done to the garden?

## 2   Use

1. The present perfect expresses a situation that at some specified time began in the past and continues to the present. The action is not complete.

   She has lived in New York for twelve years.

   They have studied English since 1979.

   Mario has not eaten since last night.

   In sentences such as this, *for* is used to express a period of time or the length of the action, and *since* indicates the point in time when the action began (see also Chapter 8).

2. The present perfect also expresses a repeated past action that may occur again.

   I have eaten two meals so far today.

   We have had two tests up to now.

   Maria has always had problems with mathematics.

   I have read Hamlet a few times.

   The present perfect often occurs with *always* or *never*, which comes before the main verb, and with phrases such as *a few times*, *up to now*, and *from time to time*, which come at the end of the sentence.

3. The present perfect may also express the idea of a situation that arose at some unspecified time in the past and persists to this day.

   He still has not paid the bill.

   George has never lived here.

   The present perfect is often used with the words *ever*, *never*, *yet*, *still*, and *already*.

   They have never lived here.

   Have you ever lived here?

   She has left town already.

   I have never read Hamlet.

   *Yet* shows that the action has not started; it is used at the end of a negative sentence.

He hasn't left yet.

They haven't gone to sleep yet.

*Just* shows that an action was completed a very short time ago. It is used in affirmative sentences and is placed before the main verb.

He has just arrived.

Maria and George have just finished the project.

4. The present perfect may also be used in subordinate clauses of time or condition.

TIME He'll be satisfied when he has finished his project.

CONDITION If you have finished the dishes, you can have dessert.

**3** **Simple past and present perfect**

The simple past is used for actions that were finished in the past; the period of time in which the action happened is over. The present perfect is used to express an action that happened some time ago but has continued or endured until now.

PAST Last week I ate three pizzas at Louie's Restaurant.

PRESENT PERFECT I have eaten three pizzas already.

PAST They had several parties last year.

PRESENT PERFECT We have had three tests this year.

## EXERCISE 6.15

## PRESENT PERFECT

---

**A.** Fill in the blanks with the present perfect.

*Example:* She *has attended* (attend) three meetings this year.

1. They _____ (make) a lot of progress since last year.

2. Joel _____ (live) in the United States since 1983.

3. Many things _____ (change) since the beginning of the century.

4. Elmer _____ (catch) three fish already.

5. He _____ (leave, not) yet.

6. She _____ (work) here for ten years.

7. Where _____ they _____ (put) my car?

8. Maria _____ (buy, just) a new car.

9. He _____ (have) some problems with his teacher from time to time.

10. She never _____ (pay) that parking ticket.

**B.** Fill in the blanks with the present perfect or the past tense. In some sentences, either may be correct, but the meaning will be different.

*Examples:* Last week, I ___*paid*___ (pay) the telephone bill.

I ___*have paid*___ (pay) the rent every month since I moved in.

1. Jose _____ (go) to school last Tuesday.

2. Maria _____ (arrive) here three years ago.

3. He _____ (work) here for three years.

4. I _____ (see, never) that movie.

5. She _____ (know) George since 1981.

6. Up to now, Daniel _____ (try) to do his best.

7. Last May, I _____ (experience) a terrible fall.

8. Professor Khouri _____ (give) three tests so far this semester.

9. In his life, Jose _____ (feel, never) better.

10. Maria _____ (know) George for three years.

**C.** Complete the sentences with appropriate time expressions.

*Example:*   He has lived here since ____*1990*____.

1.  He came to the United States in _____.

    He has lived here for _____.

    He has lived here since _____.

2.  The school opened in _____.

    The school has been open since _____.

    The school has been open for _____.

3.  He started the project in _____.

    He has worked diligently on the project for _____.

    It has been his obsession since _____.

4.  It is _____.

    He started school in _____.

    He has been a student for _____.

    He has been a student since _____.

5.  Maria first met George in _____.

    She has known him since _____.

    She has known him for _____.

**D.** Fill in the blanks with *ever, never, already, yet,* or *just.*

*Example:*   I have ____*never*____ gone water-skiing.

1.  He has _____ bought his first new car.

2.  We haven't told her the news _____.

3. He said that he has finished the project _____.

4. Have you _____ eaten sushi?

5. I've _____ eaten sushi.

## 6k  Present perfect continuous

The present perfect continuous expresses an action that started in the past and continues in the present. The action is not complete.

### 1  Form

The present perfect continuous is formed by using *have* as an auxiliary + *been* + present participle.

I have been studying for three hours.

If the verb is compound, only the participle is required for verbs after the first.

He has been working and studying for a year.

### 2  Use

1. When used with *for, since,* and phrases such as *all morning, all day,* and *all week,* the present perfect continuous indicates the duration of an activity that began in the past and continues to the present.

   I have been teaching here since 1974.

   He has been living here for twelve years.

   It has been snowing all day.

2. When there is no specific mention of time, the present perfect continuous expresses a general activity in progress recently or lately.

   She has been thinking of getting a new job.

   All the workers have been working hard on the project.

3. With some verbs (for example, *live, work,* and *teach*), there is little difference between the present perfect and the present perfect continuous.

   I have lived here for two years.

   I have been living here for two years.

4. The present perfect continuous is often used for a finished action if the action ended very recently and hardship or long duration is being emphasized.

He has been looking for his book all day. Now he has finally found it.

Oh, there you are! I've been looking for you everywhere.

## EXERCISE 6.16

## PRESENT PERFECT CONTINUOUS

A. Change these sentences from the simple present to the present perfect continuous. Use the words in parentheses.

*Example:*   He studies and works part time. (ever since)

*He has been studying and working part time ever since he graduated from high school.*

1. She studies Spanish. (ever since)

2. Mr. Duffy works as a banker. (since)

3. The friends talk on the phone. (for)

4. George and Maria are dating each other. (since)

5. George studies art. (for)

**B.** Fill in the blanks with the present continuous or the present perfect continuous.

Example: "How ___*have*___ you ___*been*___ (be) these past few weeks?"

1. "Hello. How _____ you _____ (do)?"

   "I _____ (not, feel) too well, Dr. Thompson. My stomach _____ (ache)."

   "How long _____ your stomach _____ (hurt) you?"

   "It _____ (bother) me for a while."

   "Can you be more precise. How long _____ you _____ (experience) the pain?"

   "I _____ (have) the pain since last Tuesday."

2. "Hello, pal, what _____ you _____ (do)?"

   "I _____ (study and clean)."

   "How long _____ you _____ (do) this?"

   "I _____ (do) it since this morning. What _____ you _____ (do)?"

   "I _____ (work)."

"How long _____ you _____
(work)?"


"I _____ (sit) at this desk all day."


**C.** Write a complete sentence in the present perfect continuous, ending
with the expression given. Then write an appropriate question asking
"how long?"

*Example:*   since 1989

*I have been living here since 1989.*

*How long have you been living here?*

1. for three years



2. ever since I came to this country



3. since he was a child



4. for a long time



5. ever since he got the job

## 6l Past perfect

The past perfect is always used in conjunction with the past tense. It indicates an activity that was completed before another activity or time.

### 1 Form

To form the past perfect, the auxiliary *had* is combined with the past participle.

### 2 Use

1. The past perfect is used when there is a jump back from the past tense to an earlier action.

   He was tired because he had not slept.

   They were hungry although they had eaten earlier.

   The past perfect is often used in subordinate clauses beginning with *until*, *before*, *after*, *when*, *because*, and *although*.

2. The past perfect is often used in noun clauses to indicate reported (indirect) speech.

   "I ate the pie," he said.
   He said that he had eaten the pie.

   "Why did you leave?" she asked.
   She asked me why I had left.


## 6m Past perfect continuous

### 1 Form

The past perfect continuous is formed with the auxiliary verb *had* + *been* + present participle.

   She had been looking for an apartment for two weeks before she found one to her liking.

### 2 Use

The past perfect continuous expresses the duration of an action that was in progress before another activity in the past.

By the time the doctor saw him, the patient had been waiting for two hours.

## EXERCISE 6.17

## PAST PERFECT AND PAST PERFECT CONTINUOUS

**A.** Use the simple past or the past perfect.

Example: The film _had already begun_ (begin, already) by the time we ___got___ (get) there, so we ___took___ (take) a seat in the back.

1. In colonial times, the colonists _____ (develop) their farms, but the Native American Indians _____ (live) there before them.

2. I _____ (hear, never) of Mozart until I _____ (attend) your class.

3. Yesterday, Elke _____ (see) her old teacher at the museum; she _____ (see, not) him in three years. At first, her teacher _____ (recognize, not) her because she _____ (lose) a lot of weight.

4. He almost _____ (miss) his train. All of the passengers _____ (board, already) by the time he _____ (get) there.

5. I _____ (attend, never) a professional baseball game until my father _____ (take) me.

**B.** Change these past-tense quotes to the reported speech pattern using the past perfect.

*Example:* "They left yesterday," he said.

*He said that they had left yesterday.*

1. "You took my seat," she said.

2. "What did you eat tonight?" she asked.

3. "Jose studied English last year," Maria said.

4. "Naoko had a baby," Anne said.

5. "The teacher was absent yesterday," she said.

**C.** Use the past perfect continuous in the following sentences.

*Example:* When she finally woke up, she *had been sleeping* (sleep) for ten hours.

1. The teacher asked me a question yesterday, but I couldn't answer

   because I _____ (daydream) in class.

2. We were waiting in line with a lot of people; some of them

   _____ (wait) for three hours.

3. It was noon; I _____ (work) since 6 A.M.

4. Joe had a terrible day yesterday; he _____ (walk)
   to work when someone drenched him with water.

5. The students were getting registered last week; some of them

   _____ (stand) in a long line for most of the morning.

## 6n Future continuous

### 1 Form

The future continuous is formed of *will* + *be* + present participle or *be going to* + *be* + present participle.

I will be walking to school tomorrow.

I am going to be walking to school tomorrow.

### 2 Use

The future continuous is used to express an activity that will be in progress at some time in the future. Sometimes there is little difference between the simple future and the future continuous tense.

I will walk to school tomorrow.

I will be walking to school tomorrow.

## EXERCISE 6.18

## FUTURE CONTINUOUS

Fill in the blanks with the future continuous or the simple present.

*Example:* When I ___*see*___ (see) you tomorrow, I *will be wearing* (wear) my new topcoat.

1. I am doing my homework now; last night I was studying, and tomorrow I _____ (go) to the movies with my friends.

2. Next week, I will go on vacation. When I _____ (arrive) at the hotel, my friends _____ (wait) for me.

3. I _____ (leave) tomorrow, so I _____ (not, see) you for a while.

4. He _____ (graduate) in June; then he _____ (plan) to move to Florida.

5. When dusk _____ (come), the birds _____

(chirp) and the fish _____ (jump).

## 6o Future perfect

### 1 Form

The future perfect is formed of *will* + *have* + past participle.

By tomorrow, I will have finished all the writing.

### 2 Use

The future perfect expresses an activity that will be completed before a specific time or event in the future.

## 6p Future perfect continuous

### 1 Form

The future perfect continuous is formed of *will* + *have* + *been* + present participle.

At noon, he will have been sleeping for ten hours.

### 2 Use

The future perfect continuous emphasizes the duration of an activity that will be in progress at a specific time or event in the future.

## EXERCISE 6.19

## FUTURE PERFECT AND FUTURE PERFECT CONTINUOUS

Fill in the verb in the appropriate tense.

*Example:*   By the time we arrive, they *will have finished* (finish) the game.

1. They have been studying English for years; by next month, they

_____ (study) it for ten years.

2. By the year 2000, the world _____ (live) with nuclear energy for more than half a century.

3. At this rate, he _____ (live) in ten countries by the time he dies.

4. On our anniversary this year, we _____ (marry) two years.

5. In September, I _____ (teach) here for seventeen years.

## 6q Passive voice

A major use of the past participle is to form the passive voice.

### 1 Form

The passive voice consists of *be* + past participle.

I was hit by a car.

They were arrested three weeks ago.

In the active voice, the subject is the doer or performer of the action and the object is the receiver of the action. In the passive voice, the subject receives the action and the doer or performer is expressed or implied in the *by* phrase.

| ACTIVE | Louise made the cake. |
| PASSIVE | The cake was made by Louise. |
| ACTIVE | Columbus explored the New World. |
| PASSIVE | The New World was explored by Columbus. |

Only an active sentence with an object can be passive. If there is no object, the sentence cannot be put into the passive. Therefore, only verbs that are transitive may be made passive, and basic sentence pattern 1 (see Section 2b.3) may not be made passive. For example, the following sentences cannot be made passive.

The students live in a dormitory.

The car stopped by the fence.

If the sentence mentions the doer of the action, we use *by* + the doer. If the doer is in pronoun form, we use the objective case.

The car was driven into the tree by Elmer.

The test was given by her.

Many sentences are "agentless passives"; that is, the *by* phrase is deleted because the performer of the action is either obvious or unimportant.

The homework was handed in late. (obviously, by the student)

The test is being corrected right now. (obviously, by the teacher)

This cake was made for my birthday. (by someone unknown)

## FORMING THE PASSIVE

|  | ACTIVE | PASSIVE |
|---|---|---|
| Simple present | reads | is read |
| Present continuous | is reading | is being read |
| Simple past | read | was read |
| Past continuous | was reading | was being read |
| Future | will read | will be read |
| Present perfect | has read | has been read |
| Past perfect | had read | had been read |
| Modal | will read | will be read |
|  | can read | can be read |
|  | should read | should be read |
|  | had better read | had better be read |
|  | ought to read | ought to be read |
| Infinitive | to read | to be read |

## 2 Use

Though some people consider the passive voice a sign of weak writing (which it is if overused or used for no particular reason), the passive is actually a viable option when used for stylistic reasons or for emphasis. These are the most common reasons for using the passive:

1. When the performer or doer of the action is unknown or of secondary interest. The passive voice allows the writer to avoid using such vague sentences as:

Someone unknown stole my bicycle last month.

Thousands of weavers make fine rugs in China.

These become instead:

My bicycle was stolen last month.

Fine rugs are made in China.

2. To emphasize the receiver of the action.

   Maria was hit by the car and injured severely.

   The project was completed by two students.

3. To make general statements about people or to invoke an impersonal mood as in textbooks or reports.

   Spanish is spoken by many people in the United States.

   The Constitution was ratified in 1787.

4. In discussing discoveries and constructions, often using the verbs *build, find, invent, compose, do,* and *found*. This type of passive usually mentions the performer in the *by* phrase, since this is significant information.

   The cotton gin was invented by Eli Whitney.

   That giant mural was painted by Marc Chagall.

## EXERCISE 6.20

## PASSIVE VOICE

A. Put these active sentences into the passive.

*Example:* Columbus discovered the New World.

*The New World was discovered by Columbus.*

1. Maria has already done the homework.

2. She opened a newsstand.

3. Elmer invited George to go to the movies.

4. Atsushi prepared that report.

5. Evan has bought that car.

6. Larry will help Maria.

7. The teacher is allowing us to study together.

8. She is asking them for a refund.

9. We use a dictionary in this class.

10. He treated them badly.

**B.**  Fill in each blank with the passive voice of the verb. Use the form indicated in parentheses at the end of the sentence.

*Example:*  A grammar text *has been used* (use) in the advanced class for two years. (*present perfect*)

1. A new idea _____ (suggest) by the students. (*present continuous*)

2. Some things _____ (learn) over a long period of time. (*modal*)

3. More and more Japanese cars _____ (sell) in the United States. (*future*)

4. The homework has _____ (hand in) each day. (*infinitive*)

5. The corrections _____ (make) by the teacher. (*past*)

6. The exam _____ (take) by all the license candidates by that time. (*future perfect continuous*)

7. The orders _____ (write up) right now. (*modal*)

8. Everyone _____ (notify) within a week. (*future*)

9. The exams _____ (correct) and _____ (return) last week. (*past*)

10. Much progress _____ (report) in the area of biological research. (*present continuous*)

C. Match the agent or maker with the result or creation. Then write a passive sentence about each pair. The first one is done for you as an example.

| | | |
|---|---|---|
| _c_ | 1. Leonardo da Vinci | a. polio vaccine |
| _____ | 2. Vincent van Gogh | b. telephone |
| _____ | 3. Albert Einstein | c. *Mona Lisa* |
| _____ | 4. Ludwig von Beethoven | d. *Sunflowers* |
| _____ | 5. Herman Melville | e. Moonlight Sonata |
| _____ | 6. William Shakespeare | f. *Moby Dick* |
| _____ | 7. Eli Whitney | g. *Romeo and Juliet* |
| _____ | 8. Jonas Salk | h. theory of relativity |
| _____ | 9. Frank Lloyd Wright | i. cotton gin |
| _____ | 10. Alexander Graham Bell | j. Guggenheim Museum |

1. *The Mona Lisa was painted by Leonardo da Vinci.*

2.

3.

4.

5.

6.

7.

8.

9.

10.

**D.** Change the following sentences into "agentless passives." In doing so, the *by* phrase is deleted.

*Example:*  Teachers teach multiplication in the second grade.

*Multiplication is taught in the second grade.*

1. Teachers teach biology in the first year of high school.

2. Someone invited me to go to the movies.

3. People grow their own vegetables during the summer.

4. Someone told you to wait at the corner.

5. Students do their homework every night.

6. Doctors have been performing this type of surgery for many years.

7. The secretary is typing the letter.

8. Someone is broadcasting the game right now.

9. The police arrested the driver for drunk driving.

10. Someone has purchased that land for development.

E. Write a paragraph explaining how a special day is celebrated in your native country. Write a second paragraph describing how the Fourth of July is celebrated in the United States.

1.

2.

### 3 | Indirect objects as passive subjects

The subject of a passive sentence may be the direct or indirect object from an active sentence.

Someone gave **him** a **ticket** to the game.

(IO = him, DO = a ticket)

A ticket to the game was given to him.

He was given a ticket to the game.

When the direct object is made the subject of a passive sentence, *to* precedes the indirect object.


## EXERCISE 6.21

## INDIRECT OBJECTS AS PASSIVE SUBJECTS

In each sentence, underline the indirect object and then use it as the subject in a passive sentence. Delete the *by* phrase when possible.

*Example:*    Someone gave <u>me</u> a beautiful puppy.

*I was given a beautiful puppy.*

1. Someone gave Alfred a job in the park.


2. Harvard has offered him a scholarship.


3. Someone paid the taxi driver the twenty-dollar fare.


4. They will send you the results as soon as the lab calls.


5. The teacher awarded Louise first prize.

**4**  **Passives with *get***

A common colloquial form of the passive is formed with *get* + past participle.

Jose was hurt in an accident.
Jose got hurt in an accident.

Maria was invited to a party.
Maria got invited to a party.

## EXERCISE 6.22

## PASSIVES WITH *GET*

Complete the following passive sentences with the verbs in parentheses and *get*.

*Example:* If you play with fire, you might *get burned* (burn).

1. Jim _____ (fire) because he was late too often.

2. I always _____ (pay) on a Tuesday.

3. Marissa _____ (depress) when she first left her country.

4. He told his wife, "Don't _____ (upset). I'll fix the car."

5. She _____ (worry) when he didn't arrive on the noon train.

6. Will they _____ (marry)?

7. After the phone call, he _____ (dress) as fast as possible.

8. I forgot the address, so we _____ (lose).

9. He _____ (tire) and went home.

10. They _____ (disgust) when their car is unavailable.

# CHAPTER 7

# Determiners

## 7a Nouns and determiners

Whenever a noun is used in English, the sentence must indicate how the noun relates to objects, events, or concepts in the real world (for example, is it a count or a noncount noun, singular or plural, definite or indefinite, known or unknown?). This is usually done by using a determiner.

**Determiners** are modifying words that come before nouns and signal that a noun is coming. Functioning like adjectives, determiners tell which instance of the noun is being talked about.

### 1 Articles

The determiners most often used are *the* (the **definite article**) and *a/an* (the **indefinite article**). *The* derives from *that*, so it specifies. *A/an* derives from *one* and counts the noun.

### 2 Definite determiners

Besides *the*, the **definite determiners** include the demonstrative pronouns *this, that, these*, and *those*.

The possessive pronouns (or adjectives), which indicate ownership or possession of a noun, are also considered definite determiners.

| SUBJECTIVE | POSSESSIVE |
|------------|------------|
| I | my |
| you | your |
| he, she, it | his, her, its |
| we | our |
| they | their |

### 3 Indefinite determiners

Besides *a/an*, the **indefinite determiners** include *some, any, all, another, each, either, every, neither*, and *no*.

# EXERCISE 7.1

## ARTICLES

Read the following student fable. When you are finished reading it over, underline all the articles: *a/an* and *the.*

THE HORSE, THE BEAR, AND THE MAN FROM ANOTHER PLANET

"Hi, how are you? Nice to meet you again. How was your summer vacation?" the horse said to the bear.

"I'm fine. It was a good vacation for me. I went to Paris by myself. I tried to use my broken French, and most of the people understood my broken French. In other words, they were kind and tried to understand what I said," the bear said to the horse.

"So it was a good experience, right? But they know English, don't they? If I go there, I will use my own language, English, instead of using French. English is the most powerful language in the world," the horse said proudly.

While the horse and the bear were talking, something fell from the sky to the middle of the road. It was a very small spaceship. The horse and the bear hid behind a bush. Then someone came out from the tiny door and tried to say something in a shaky voice.

"I guess he wants help. He might have trouble with the spaceship," the bear said. The man from outer space tried to say something again. "I cannot understand what he saying," the bear stood up and said to the horse, "but let's help him!"

"I will stay here. You can go by yourself. I will have nothing to do with him," the horse said and ran away.

The moral of this fable is: You should help someone in trouble.

The moral of this fable is: You will be able to communicate without any language.

The moral of this fable is: Don't be a coward.

—Atsushi Tanaka, Japan

## 7b Functions of articles

Articles have three functions: the discourse function, the identification or definition function, and the generic function.

### 1 Discourse function of articles

In this text, *discourse* means any group of connected words, written or spoken, including phrases, clauses, sentences, and paragraphs.

A **first-time noun** is a noun mentioned for the first time in the connected words or discourse; a **second-time noun** is a noun mentioned for the second time in the discourse.

#### Singular count nouns and articles

The first time a singular count noun is used, the article *a/an* must be put before it. This marks it as something unknown and not yet identified to the listener or reader.

I have a car.

He owns a watch.

The second time the same count noun is used, the article *the* must be put before it. This marks it as something known and identified, something specific because it was previously mentioned.

The car is brown.

The watch is on his wrist.

This is the anaphoric (referential) discourse function of articles: to mark whether a noun is known or unknown.

#### Plural count nouns and articles

The first time you use a plural count noun, you do not put an article before it.

Oranges are a kind of fruit.

People wear hats.

The second time you use this noun to name the same things, you must put *the* before it. This marks it as previously known and specific.

I see books. The books are green.
<sub>1</sub> <sub>2</sub>

We wear hats. The hats are warm.
<sub>1</sub> <sub>2</sub>

We often use *some* or another determiner before first-time plural count nouns.

I'll buy some shoes.

I see some birds.

All men are created equal.

I don't have any money.

## EXERCISE 7.2

## DISCOURSE FUNCTION

---

**A.** Complete these sentences with the first and second use of singular count nouns.

*Example:* I see (book). (book) is green.

*I see a book. The book is green.*

1. I have (pencil). (pencil) is yellow.

2. She has (car). (car) is blue.

3. He owns (watch). (watch) is on his wrist.

4. Maria has (coat). (coat) is black.

5. Carlos is reading (book). (book) is a chemistry book.

6. I know (teacher). (teacher) is Mr. Jones.

7. Claire is playing with (baby). (baby's name) is Sean.

8. They see (mouse). (mouse) is gray.

9. We see (boy). (boy) is very young.

10. Bill is studying for (test). (test) will be difficult.

**B.** Change these first- and second-time nouns to the plural when possible. Be sure that the subjects and verbs agree.

*Examples:*   He had (pencil). (pencil) was yellow.

*He had some pencils! The pencils were yellow.*   I ate (food). (food) was delicious.

*I ate some food. The food was delicious!*

1. They ate (chicken). (chicken) was delicious.

2. Theo knows (girl). (girl) is in his class.

3. Alberto needs (battery). (battery) is in the drawer.

4. Yuko is mailing (letter) now. (letter) have stamp on them.

5. Marisol has (new blouse). (new blouse) is expensive.

6. We have seven (teacher). (teacher) is very supportive.

7. We looked at all the (baby), and (baby) looked back at us.

8. They have two (car). (car) are blue and white.

9. Elmer has six (class); he says (class) is very good.

10. Louise is talking to (man). (man) is from the gas company.

### Noncount nouns and articles

The first time a noncount noun is used, no article is put before it. The second time it is used to name the same thing, *the* must be put before it.

She has cheese. The cheese is round.

He drinks water. The water is cold.

The first time a noncount noun is used, the determiner *some* may be used before it.

He drinks some water.

They ate some cheese.

## EXERCISE 7.3

## NONCOUNT NOUNS AND ARTICLES

Use the first-time/second-time pattern established in the example to complete the following sentences.

*Example:*   I am drinking (juice). (juice) is very sweet.

*I am drinking juice. The juice is very sweet.*

or

*I am drinking some juice. The juice is very sweet.*

1. The car needs (gas). (gas) must be unleaded.

2. Mary wants (lumber). (lumber) is for a dog house.

3. They have (milk). (milk) is for tea and coffee.

4. Helen has (butter). (butter) is for her pancakes.

5. We have (homework). (homework) is very difficult.

6. I was caught in (traffic). (traffic) was very heavy.

7. She needed (information). (information) was hard to get.

8. They had (luggage). The porter carried (luggage) to the room.

9. I ate (cabbage). (cabbage) was very tasty.

10. Last month we have (rain). (rain) raised the water table a few inches.

### Articles in questions

It is important to be aware of the first-time/second-time noun pattern in questions.

| | |
|---|---|
| FIRST-TIME QUESTION | Do you have a car? |
| FIRST-TIME ANSWER | Yes I have a car. |
| SECOND-TIME QUESTION | Is the car new? |
| SECOND-TIME ANSWER | Yes, the car is new. |

# EXERCISE 7.4

## ARTICLES AND QUESTIONS

Write a question-and-answer dialogue using the first-time/second-time pattern of article usage in the example.

*Example:*   Joe sees (dog) (brown).

*Does Joe see a dog?*
*Yes, Joe sees a dog.*
*Is the dog brown?*
*Yes, the dog is brown.*

1. Maria is eating (bananas) (tasty).

2. You have (teacher) (interesting).

3. Flavio is reading (book) (enjoyable).

4. Anne is writing (letter) (long).

5. You are eating (apple) (delicious).

**Same noun**

For the discourse function of *the* to be relevant, the second-time noun must be exactly the same as the first-time noun. If the second-time noun introduces new information, use *a/an*.

I bought a book. The book is a history book.

He is wearing a coat. The coat is a new coat.

**Pronoun substitution**

If the first-time and second-time nouns are close together, we almost always use a pronoun instead of the second-time noun.

I bought a book. It is a history book.

She has a car. It is a new car.

## EXERCISE 7.5

## PRONOUN SUBSTITUTION

Write two sentences following the example.

*Example:* John has (new pet). (new pet) is (dog).

*John has a new pet. The new pet is a dog.*
*John has a new pet. It is a dog.*

1. John bought (new shirt). (new shirt) is (cotton shirt).

2. They bought (house). (house) is (two-family house).

3. John has (new boat). (new boat) is (sailboat).

4. I saw (bird) this morning. (bird) was (blue bird).

5. He took (bus) last night. (bus) was (suburban transport bus).

6. We are in (store). (store) is (department store).

7. Pramila entered (building). (building) was (apartment building).

8. Those people went to (restaurant). (restaurant) was (Greek restaurant).

9. He bought (coat). (coat) was (sport coat).

10. They sold (house). (house) was (old house).

**Understood nouns**

Sometimes we use *the* before a first-time noun.

PATTERN 1

I have a house.

The kitchen is in the back.

This means the same as:

PATTERN 2

I have a house.

The house has a kitchen.

The kitchen is in the back.

We can say "the kitchen" in pattern 1 because we already have some information about houses in our mind; we assume that a house has a kitchen. Pattern 1 is quite common.

I have a book.

The pages are large.

We know that all books have pages, so the second sentence of pattern 2 is not necessary. The information is understood or assumed.

## EXERCISE 7.6

## DISCOURSE FUNCTION OF ARTICLES WITH UNDERSTOOD NOUNS

**A.** Write three sentences following the example.

*Example:* John has (car). (muffler) is broken.

*John has a car.*
*A car has a muffler.*
*The muffler is broken.*

1. We went to (zoo) yesterday. (animals) were interesting.

2. They are in (restaurant). (tables) are nice and clean.

3. He went to (park) last week. (trees) were beautiful.

4. Maria is eating (sandwich). (bread) is delicious.

5. His house is near (hospital). (rooms) are usually full of patients.

**B.** Write the second sentence. Make sure that the subjects and verbs agree.

*Example:*   Mother was cooking. (stove) very hot.

*The stove was very hot.*

1. He was typing. (typewriter) electric.

2. Eduardo was swimming. (pool) very crowded.

3. Esperanza was pouring coffee. (cups) very warm.

4. Juan was driving. (car) moving quite fast.

5. John was writing. (word) all in English.

6. He had a coat. (buttons) quite large.

7. He played in a soccer game. He got hit with (ball).

8. She was playing tennis. (racket) fell out of her hand.

9. I was shaving. (razor) very sharp.

10. The party was crowded. (noise) very loud.

## 2 | Identification or definition function of articles

### Indefinite article

The indefinite article *a/an* is used to classify or define objects and people.

China is a big country.

Christmas is a holiday.

The plural is expressed without an article.

China and Russia are big countries.

Thanksgiving and Christmas are holidays.

### Specific nouns

We use *the* for specific nouns. Both the communicator (writer or speaker) and the receiver (reader or listener) know of the noun because it is unique and specific for one of the following reasons.

1. Unique by common experience

   The homework is easy.

   The teacher is late.

   The hospital* is for when you are sick.

2. Unique because there is only one in our experience

   The sun is shining today.

   The president lives in the White House.

* Phrases like *the hospital, the bank, the park,* and *the zoo* are considered common to everyone's experience, even though the specific ones being talked about may be different.

3. Unique because it is specified by a prepositional phrase

I live in the house up the hill.

He has the car with the blue stripes.

## EXERCISE 7.7

## IDENTIFICATION OR DEFINITION FUNCTION OF ARTICLES

Write a sentence to classify or define each noun.

*Example:* a pencil

*A pencil is a writing implement.*

the Earth

*The Earth is a planet.*

1. New Jersey

2. the White House

3. Africa

4. a tomato

5. Boston

6. the sun

7. a Cadillac

8. an engineer

9. a refrigerator

10. the moon

11. McDonald's

12. baseball

13. the zoo

14. gold

15. a carrot

## 3 Generic function of articles

### Indefinite article

A typical member of a group is indicated by using the indefinite article *a/an*.

A cow has four legs.

An elephant eats vegetation.

We also use no articles with a plural noun to mean all members of the group or class.

Cows have four legs.

Elephants eat vegetation.

The two sets of sentences mean almost the same thing.

### The group as a unit

We use *the* with singular, concrete count nouns to talk about a group as a single unit.

The automobile is a useful invention.

The elephant lives a long time.

No article with the plural and *a/an* with a singular count noun mean almost the same thing. Compare these sentences with the two just given:

Automobiles are useful inventions.

An elephant lives a long time.

Using *the*, however, sounds more technical or scientific.

## EXERCISE 7.8

## GENERIC USAGE

**A.** Change these statements from singular to plural, making any necessary changes.

*Example:* A bird flies when it is startled.

*Birds fly when they are startled.*

1. A cat has four legs.

2. A bear hibernates in the winter.

3. A fish swims in the water.

4. The whale is the largest animal.

5. A raccoon lives in the forest.

6. The dolphin is an intelligent animal.

7. A monkey climbs trees.

8. A horse has a driver.

9. A human has the power to reason.

10. The hippo lives in the river.

**B.** Change these sentences from plural to singular, making any necessary changes.

*Example:* Bus drivers need a lot of patience.

*A bus driver needs a lot of patience.*

1. Lawyers may give people legal advice.

2. Policemen often direct traffic.

3. Nurses help sick people.

4. Teachers need a lot of education.

5. Babies like to sleep a lot.

6. Potatoes grow under the ground.

7. Trees usually lose their leaves in winter.

8. Students must study a lot.

9. Cars have to be maintained.

10. Dogs like to run and bark.

**C.** Make a generic sentence using the words given.

*Examples:* a dog

*A dog is an animal with four legs.*

dogs

*Dogs have four legs.*

the dog

*The dog is a mammal.*

1. a piano

2. teachers

3. the tree

4. a bird

5. dictionaries

6. the lion

7. monkeys

8. people

9. a library

10. the classroom

11. a school

12. universities

13. a politician

14. the police

15. cows

## THE USE OF ARTICLES

**INDEFINITE**

The indefinite article *a/an\** comes before a singular count noun. *A/an* is used:

1. To indicate an indefinite, nonspecific item not previously mentioned (discourse function):

> Is there a phone here?
>
> I have a dog.

2. For definition/classification.

> New York is a big city.
>
> Man is a rational being.

3. To indicate a typical member of a group (generic):

> A lion has four legs.
>
> An automobile has wheels.

**DEFINITE**

The definite article *the* can come before either singular or plural nouns. *The* is used:

4. To indicate specific or common experience in three ways.

   a. Previously mentioned or known (discourse function):

   > Is there a phone here? Yes, the phone is over there.
   >
   > I have a dog. The dog is brown and gray.

   b. Common or unique:

   > The park is crowded.
   >
   > Go see the doctor.
   >
   > The president lives in the White House.
   >
   > The sun rises every day.

c. Specified nouns:

>> The houses on the beach are lovely.

>> The coffee on the shelf is fresh.

5. The group as a unit (generic):

>> The lion has four legs.

>> The elephant has a trunk.

> \* *A* is used before words beginning with a consonant; *an* is used before words beginning with a vowel.
>
>> A lion is fierce.
>
>> An elephant is huge.
>
>> He is wearing an elegant vest.

## EXERCISE 7.9

## ARTICLES

**A.** Fill in the blanks, using *a/an* or *the*.

### LATE-NIGHT FABLE

(1) _____ cow and (2) _____ elephant meet. They are standing on (3) _____ corner in (4) _____ middle of (5) _____ night.

(6) _____ cow says to (7) _____ elephant, "I knew you'd be here; I knew it!"

(8) _____ elephant says to (9) _____ cow, "How did you know?"

(10) _____ cow says, "I can read minds."

Just then (11) _____ cloud blows overhead, and (12)

_____ planet twinkles far out in (13) _____ night sky. (14) _____ planet is Mars, (15) _____ Red Planet, and (16) _____ cloud is (17) _____ gray and blue one.

Annoyed, (18) _____ elephant says, "If you're so smart, what am I thinking of right now?"

(19) _____ cow replies, "Why, about (20) _____ gray-blue cloud and (21) _____ planet twinkling in (22) _____ night."

(23) _____ moral to this fable is: There are some things you just can't explain.

**B.** Use the numbers from the box "The Use of Articles" to indicate why a particular article is used in the fable in A. Two have already been filled in for you as examples.

| ARTICLE | USE | | ARTICLE | USE |
|---------|-----|---|---------|-----|
| 1. *A* | *1* | 13. *the* | *4b* |
| 2. _____ | _____ | 14. _____ | _____ |
| 3. _____ | _____ | 15. _____ | _____ |
| 4. _____ | _____ | 16. _____ | _____ |
| 5. _____ | _____ | 17. _____ | _____ |
| 6. _____ | _____ | 18. _____ | _____ |
| 7. _____ | _____ | 19. _____ | _____ |
| 8. _____ | _____ | 20. _____ | _____ |
| 9. _____ | _____ | 21. _____ | _____ |
| 10. _____ | _____ | 22. _____ | _____ |
| 11. _____ | _____ | 23. _____ | _____ |
| 12. _____ | _____ | | |

# MISCELLANEOUS USES OF THE DEFINITE ARTICLE

| DON'T USE *the* | USE *the* |
|---|---|
| 1. Cities, states, countries, continents <br><br> Chicago, New York, England, Africa | 1. Collective and plural names <br><br> the United States, the United Kingdom |
| 2. Mountains <br><br> Mount Everest | 2. Mountain ranges <br><br> the Rocky Mountains |
| 3. Islands <br><br> Long Island | 3. Collective islands <br><br> the Galapagos Islands |
| 4. Lakes <br><br> Lake Erie | 4. Collective lakes <br><br> the Great Lakes |
| 5. Beaches <br><br> Orchard Beach | 5. Rivers, oceans, seas, canals <br><br> the Mississippi River, the Atlantic Ocean, the Red Sea, the Suez Canal |
| 6. Streets and avenues <br><br> Logan Avenue, Wall Street | 6. Well-known buildings <br><br> the World Trade Center, the Sears Tower |
| 7. Parks <br><br> Central Park | 7. Zoos <br><br> the Bronx Zoo |
| 8. Directions <br><br> north, south, east, west | 8. Sections of a country or city <br><br> the Southwest, the east side, the Sun Belt |
| 9. School subjects <br><br> sociology, mathematics | 9. Unique geographical points <br><br> the south pole, the Vatican |
| 10. Names of colleges and universities without *of* <br><br> Iona College, Harvard University | 10. Names of colleges and universities containing *of* <br><br> the University of California, the College of New Rochelle |
| 11. Magazines <br><br> *Time, Sports Illustrated* | 11. Newspapers <br><br> the *New York Times*, the *Washington Post* |
| 12. Months and days <br><br> October, Tuesday | 12. Ships <br><br> the *Titanic* |
| 13. Holidays <br><br> Christmas, New Year's Day | 13. Holiday exception <br><br> the Fourth of July |

| | |
|---|---|
| 14. Diseases<br>cancer, pneumonia | 14. Ailments<br>the flu (but a cold, a head-ache) |
| 15. Games and sports<br>poker, baseball | 15. Musical instruments<br>the piano, the guitar |
| 16. Languages<br>French, Japanese | 16. Language exception<br>the French language, the Thai language |
| 17. Locations<br>school, work, church, bed, jail, prison, class, home, downtown, college | 17. Location exception<br>the university |
| 18. Personal names<br>Jimmy Carter | 18. Families<br>the Carters |
| 19. Titles with names<br>King Joseph | 19. Titles without names<br>the king |
| 20. Cardinal numbers after nouns<br>World War One, Chapter Three | 20. Ordinal numbers before nouns<br>the First World War, the third chapter |
| 21. Heavenly bodies and constellations<br>Venus, Halley's Comet, Sirius, Orion | 21. Astronomical exceptions<br>the sun, the moon, the earth |

## EXERCISE 7.10

## USE OF ARTICLES

Fill in the blank where appropriate. Mark an X if no article is necessary.

*Example:* On our trip to ___*X*___ Japan, we crossed ___*the*___ Pacific Ocean.

1. He lives in _____ Buffalo, New York, which is on _____ Great Lakes.

2. When we drove into _____ Colorado, we saw _____ Rocky Mountains.

3. _____ prince was speaking with _____ Lady Carlotta in _____ Italian.

4. _____ United States and _____ England share many bonds.

5. _____ Greek Islands are popular with tourists.

6. _____ Roslyn Carter is _____ Jimmy Carter's wife.

7. _____ Carters live in _____ Georgia.

8. _____ Queen lives in _____ Buckingham Palace.

9. _____ *Washington Post* is an important newspaper in _____ Washington, D.C.

10. _____ People's Republic of China has _____ earth's largest population.

11. _____ Long Beach Island is located in _____ New Jersey.

12. At _____ college, there are a few students from _____ Peru and from _____ Republic of Haiti.

13. _____ California is _____ state with the largest population in _____ United States.

14. _____ Phoenix Zoo is located on _____ east side of town.

15. She said she didn't have _____ flu, just _____ cold and _____ headache.

16. Please come to my house on _____ New Year's Day.

17. Esperanza speaks _____ French language as well as her native _____ Spanish.

18. I was born in _____ October.

19. _____ Chicago is located on the shores of _____ Lake Superior.

20. He climbed _____ Mount Everest, which is in _____ Himalayas.

21. After _____ work at _____ university, she goes _____ home and goes to _____ bed.

22. In _____ history, we studied _____ fourth chapter last week; it's about _____ World War Two.

23. Her mother died of _____ cancer.

24. He studied at _____ Yale University but graduated from _____ University of Southern California.

25. He likes to read _____ *Newsweek* and _____ *Chicago Tribune*.

## 7c  Other determiners

### 1  Indefinite determiners

The **indefinite determiners** are *a/an, all, some, any, another, each, every, either, neither*, and *no*. These words do not refer to specific items or people.

> He is looking for a book.

> She is cooking some beans.

> They don't have any money.

> All people love music.

### 2  Definite determiners

The **definite determiners** are *the, this, that, these*, and *those*, plus the **possessive pronouns/adjectives** *my, your, his, her, its, our*, and *their*. In various ways, these words tell that the communicator and receiver should be able to identify exactly what the noun refers to.

> Please give me that book.

> He pointed to those books.

> She borrowed our car.

I visited their house.

He ate the bread.

### Possessive pronouns/adjectives

The possessive pronouns/adjectives are determiners used to indicate the owner of an object, feature, or quality.

My car is a Buick.

These are their books.

His feelings on the subject are well known.

## EXERCISE 7.11

## POSSESSIVE PRONOUNS/ADJECTIVES

Rewrite each sentence according to the example, using the possessive pronouns/adjectives.

*Example:*   I own this book.

or   *This book is my book.*

*This is my book.*

1. He owns this car.

2. They own these pens.

3. She owns this book.

4. You own those books.

5. We own that boat.

6. He owns the green house.

7. She owns that coat.

8. They own this car.

9. We own the pony.

10. You own that hat.

### Demonstrative pronouns

The **demonstrative pronouns** (*this, that, these,* and *those*) are determiners used to refer to things that have already been mentioned or to things that are around in the world. *This* and *these* are used to refer to a noun near the speaker. *That* and *those* refer to a noun more distant.

I saw that woman yesterday.

I'll take that hat please.

Please give me one of those cookies.

Those books are mine.

## EXERCISE 7.12

## DEMONSTRATIVE PRONOUNS

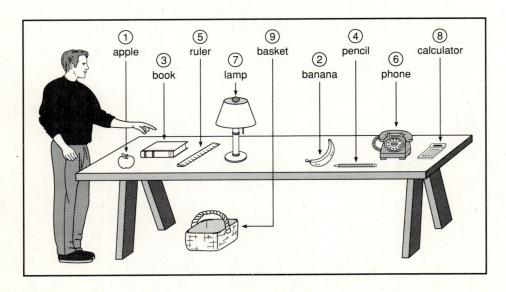

**A.** Use the illustration to write sentences about each object the man might point to.

*Examples:* 5. *Hand me that ruler.*

        8. *How much is this calculator?*

1.

2.

3.

4.

5.

6.

7.

8.

9.

10.

**B.** Complete each sentence by circling the correct word in parentheses.

*Example:* (*This,* (*These*)) books belong to Maria.

1. (*This, These*) car is his; (*that, those*) car is mine.
2. (*This, These*) hat is green. (*That, Those*) gloves are brown.

3. (*This, These*) cars are illegally parked. (*That, Those*) car is parked legally.

4. (*This, These*) shoes are mine. (*That, Those*) shoes are yours.

5. (*This, These*) seat is the teacher's. (*That, Those*) seats are for the students.

6. (*This, These*) rooms are for the team. (*That, Those*) room is the coach's.

7. (*This, These*) desks are empty, but I am sitting in (*that, those*) desk.

8. The members of the team drive (*this, these*) cars, and the manager drives (*that, those*) car.

9. (*This, These*) bananas are fresh, but (*that, those*) bananas are not.

10. I've read all of (*this, these*) books, but I still haven't read (*that, those*) books.

**3**  **Nonspecific determiners**

### *Some* and *any*

*Some* is a nonspecific determiner used to quantify count and non-count nouns but not precisely. *Any* is the negative form.

I have some money.

I don't have any money.

He has some apples.

She doesn't have any apples.

## EXERCISE 7.13

## *SOME* AND *ANY*

**A.** Fill in each blank with *some* or *any*.

*Example:*  I don't have ___*any*___ food.

1. I can't use the vending machine because I don't have

_____ change.

2. I need _____ help.

3. I don't have _____ apples today.

4. He said he needs _____ help on Saturday.

5. Marvin usually doesn't get _____ mail.

6. There aren't _____ people living in that old abandoned house.

7. We don't have _____ more food.

8. We have _____ bananas and _____ corn.

9. We gave them _____ food, but we didn't have _____ water.

10. We looked all over for _____ wood because without it there wouldn't be _____ fire.

11. He had _____ luggage, but he didn't have _____ money for the train.

12. She asked them for _____ information about Europe.

13. Amy bought _____ curry powder at the store.

14. He told me that they didn't have _____ spinach.

15. _____ people never learn.

**B.** Write sentences about each location, following the example.

*Example:* at home

*At home, I have some books. I also have some clothes, and I have some furniture.*

*At home, I don't have any snakes. I don't have any trucks, and I don't have any boats.*

1. at school



2. in the classroom



3. in my country



4. in the United States



5. in the hospital



### A note on singular determiners

Most determiners can be used with any noun, singular or plural, count or noncount. Some indefinite determiners, however—*a/an, another, each, either, every,* and *neither*—are inherently singular. These words are used with singular count nouns only.

### Another

*Another* means "one other" (*an* = *one*), or one more in addition to the number already mentioned or known.

I caught another fish.

He has another coat.

*Another* is often used with expressions of time, money, and distance, even if these expressions contain plural nouns.

He will be here for another five years.

We need another hundred dollars.

We drove another ten miles.

## EXERCISE 7.14

### *ANOTHER*

Write a paragraph about your hand, foot, face, home, and school. Differentiate the parts using *another*.

*Examples:* My hand has five fingers. One of the fingers is the thumb. Another finger is the index finger....

One part of my home is the kitchen. Another part is the garden....

1. hand

2. foot

3. face

# CHAPTER 8

# Prepositions

## 8a Use of prepositions

A **preposition** shows a modifying or descriptive relationship between its object and other words in a sentence. Among the relationships expressed by prepositions are place or position, direction, time, manner, and agent.

**PLACE OR POSITION**

He lives in San Francisco.

**DIRECTION**

The plane flew toward Rome.

**TIME**

I'll meet you at 2:15.

**MANNER**

He ate the meal with gusto.

**AGENT**

Mariko was driven there by her mother.

A **prepositional phrase** is a preposition plus a noun phrase. The noun phrase that occurs in a prepositional phrase may consist of various structures.

**NOUN**

The dog ran after the cat.

**PRONOUN**

She is standing behind me.

**GERUND**

He was arrested for stealing.

**NOUN + PREPOSITIONAL PHRASE**

They arrived in a bus with dirty windows.

They moved into the first house they saw.

The preposition may be in the form of one word (*in, at, of*) or a group of words (*in front of, by way of, because of, alongside of*).

**ONE WORD**

He lives on Long Island.

At the moment, I have no money.

**GROUP OF WORDS**

He was standing in front of me.

The train station is located alongside of the mall.

---

## COMMON PREPOSITIONS IN ENGLISH

| | | | |
|---|---|---|---|
| about | beside | in place of | outside of |
| above | between | in regard to | over |
| across | beyond | inside | round |
| after | but | in spite of | since |
| against | by | instead of | through |
| along | by means of | in the event of | till |
| along with | despite | into | to |
| alongside of | down | like | toward |
| among | down from | near | under |
| around | due to | of | underneath |
| as | during | off | unlike |
| at | except | off of | until |
| back of | from | on | unto |
| because of | in | onto | up |
| before | in addition to | on top of | up with |
| behind | in case of | opposite | with |
| below | in front of | out | within |
| beneath | | out of | without |

---

**1**  **The most common prepositions**

The prepositions most often used in writing are, in decreasing order of frequency, *of, in, to, for, at, on, from, with,* and *by.*

# EXERCISE 8.1

## THE NINE MOST COMMON PREPOSITIONS

The nine most common prepositions are among the most frequently used words in English. All ESL students are encouraged to investigate the various semantic functions (meanings) of these prepositions. A long-range goal is to look up these words in the dictionary and use each of the various definitions in an original sentence. As the class reviews these sentences, through discussion and in consultation with your instructor, a short list of four or five core definitions can be arrived at. Use this exercise as a model.

**Dictionary exercise:** Look up the word *of* in your dictionary. There will be at least ten meanings. Write five new sentences in your own words, each using a different meaning.

*Example:* Definition: *Containing or carrying*

Sentence: *I brought home two bags of groceries.*

1. Definition:

   Sentence:

2. Definition:

   Sentence:

3. Definition:

   Sentence:

4. Definition:

   Sentence:

5. Definition:

   Sentence:

After everyone has completed this, the teacher and students should come up with a list of the four most important definitions of *of*. Students may copy this list and illustrative sentences into the "Preposition" section of their notebooks.

### 2  Prepositional phrases in sentences

A prepositional phrase can come in a variety of positions in a sentence. Since prepositional phrases are also used quite frequently to expand the basic sentence pattern, sentences may contain more than one prepositional phrase. Prepositional phrases often ride "piggyback," one after another.

> In the morning after my bath, I drove to the beach with my friends from high school.

> At eight o'clock in the evening, he located his car on the dirt road by the cemetery.

## EXERCISE 8.2

## PREPOSITIONAL PHRASES

Underline the prepositional phrases in the following sentences. Then write the basic sentences.

*Example:*  He met me <u>by the station</u> <u>at three o'clock</u> <u>in the afternoon</u>.

*He met me.*

1. Marianne cooked his favorite dish as a surprise for his birthday.

2. After a short time, I found my watch by the pile of leaves in the back yard.

3. With some anger in his voice, Jose told them to leave in a hurry.

4. In the afternoon, I often see him walking on the street with his family.

5. In our class of two thousand, we have students from many countries around the world.

6. Besides sustaining an injury to his head, he also hurt his hand.

7. Unlike me, she eats spicy food from all over the world.

8. He gave them until Thursday to complete the assignments.

9. After lunch in the garden, they went into the house for a nap.

10. Despite his reluctance to make a move, he did what he was asked.

### 3    Functioning as an adjective or an adverb

A prepositional phrase usually functions as an adjective or an adverb.

**ADJECTIVE**

The news of the week was bad.

I read a book about that war.

**ADVERB**

We go to class at nine o'clock.

I ran as fast as the wind.

## EXERCISE 8.3

## PREPOSITIONAL PHRASES AS ADJECTIVES AND ADVERBS

Underline each prepositional phrase in these sentences. Then indicate if it is used as an adjective (*ADJ*) or an adverb (*ADV*).

*Examples:* Herman is the leader <u>of the group</u>.
ADJ

They live one floor <u>below us</u>, <u>on the sixth floor</u>.
ADV             ADV

1. He was the chairman of the company.

2. Iris lives in a little town in Puerto Rico.

3. We were supposed to meet them at three o'clock in the afternoon.

4. Naoko traveled by express train to Philadelphia.

5. She wrote that poem about her father.

6. Please give me three pounds of cheese and a quart of milk.

7. Clara looks like her sister.

8. Milton has a job as a cook.

9. We will be able to decide in the morning.

10. His demands were beyond reason.

11. He called me in regard to my raise.

12. Despite the heavy rain, Joe rode his bike to Alice's house.

13. I have been living in Mexico City since 1989.

14. Without knowing it, she left the lamp lit all night.

15. The house opposite us is my mother's.

16. He failed the test due to fatigue.

17. I put the books on top of the table.

18. In front of the movie theater is a large pool of water.

19. Unlike my wife, I love to swim in cold water.

20. He said that man lives within three miles of here.

## 4   Objective case

In a prepositional phrase, if a pronoun occurs as the **object of the preposition**, it must be in the **objective case** (see Chapters 2 and 9).

| INCORRECT | *I borrowed the book from she. |
| CORRECT | I borrowed the book from her. |

| INCORRECT | *Maria talked with they about the test. |
| CORRECT | Maria talked with them about the test. |

The objective pronouns are *me, you, him, her, it, us,* and *them.*

## EXERCISE 8.4

## OBJECT OF A PREPOSITION

Fill in each blank with the appropriate pronoun in the objective case.

*Example:* That poem was written by _____ *her* _____ (she).

1. I offered to send a letter for _____ (they).

2. He told me to go with _____ (he).

3. John stood by _____ (we).

4. He arrived by train without _____ (she).

5. He threw the ball at _____ (I).

6. She is the sister of _____ (he).

7. Li bought the car from _____ (we).

8. I took the bus with _____ (they).

9. The whole day was arranged by _____ (he).

10. She told me she would do it for _____ (you).

11. Miss Chen waited for _____ (he) for two hours.

12. I told Mr. Alvarez that the discussion was between _____ (we).

13. The check was paid by _____ (he).

14. The conference was attended by all of _____ (we).

15. Mary hurried to meet with _____ (they).

16. Alphonso talked with _____ (I) early in the morning.

17. Young Kim always sits by _____ (she).

18. Miss Peng speaks carefully when talking with _____ (I).

19. Living so far from _____ (we), she has been very depressed.

20. Unlike _____ (I), she loves to dance.

21. Without _____ (he), the plan is doomed.

22. He borrowed the car from _____ (she).

23. To _____ (they), money is nothing.

24. He tried to blame all his problems on _____ (we).

25. The judge ruled against _____ (he).

## 8b Prepositions of place or position

The following sentences show place or position expressed by a number of prepositions.

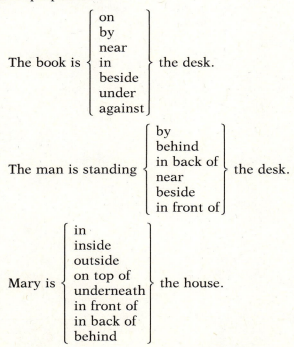

The book is $\left\{\begin{array}{l}\text{on}\\\text{by}\\\text{near}\\\text{in}\\\text{beside}\\\text{under}\\\text{against}\end{array}\right\}$ the desk.

The man is standing $\left\{\begin{array}{l}\text{by}\\\text{behind}\\\text{in back of}\\\text{near}\\\text{beside}\\\text{in front of}\end{array}\right\}$ the desk.

Mary is $\left\{\begin{array}{l}\text{in}\\\text{inside}\\\text{outside}\\\text{on top of}\\\text{underneath}\\\text{in front of}\\\text{in back of}\\\text{behind}\end{array}\right\}$ the house.

The people walked {
across the street.
around the park.
on the grass.
under the ladder.
into the house.
through the park.
down the lane.
over the hill.
up the hill.
}

The following list contains the most common prepositions of place or position.

| | |
|---|---|
| *above* | We saw the blimp flying above the stadium. |
| | On the list, his name was above mine. |
| *across* | They live across the street. |
| *after* | After dinner, we'll do the dishes. |
| *against* | He leaned the ladder against the house. |
| *among* | The paper is somewhere among the books. |
| *around* | He walked around the block. |
| *at* | Jose is at the door. |
| | Is Anna at home? |
| *at the bottom of* | His house is at the bottom of the hill. |
| *at the head of* | She is at the head of her class. |
| *at the top of* | Her house is at the top of the hill. |
| *before* | She stood before me and wept. |
| *behind* | The garden is behind the house. |
| *below* | His house is below the big hill. |
| | My marks were below the average. |
| *beneath* | The storage room is beneath the stairs. |
| *beside* | The pencil is beside the pad. |
| *between* | Last night, I sat between Maria and Juan. |
| *by* | He is standing by the desk. |
| *down* | The store is about a mile down the road. |
| *from* | His family is from Cyprus. |
| *in* | Amy is sitting in the chair in the lobby. |
| *in back of* | Jose is the man in back of Maria. |
| *in front of* | Jose stood in front of the store. |
| *inside* | He grows some plants inside the house. |
| *near* | He is standing near the car. |
| *on* | Please sit on the sofa. |
| | He put a stamp on the letter. |
| *on top of* | He lives in the house on top of the hill. |
| *outside* | Some plants can only grow outside the house. |
| *over* | His room is over the garage. |
| | The bird flew over the house. |
| *through* | We walked through the building yesterday. |
| *to* | Maria went to the store. |
| *under* | The shoes are under the bed. |
| *underneath* | He swept the dust underneath the rug. |
| *up* | Jose saw Pedro climb up the ladder. |

# EXERCISE 8.5

## PREPOSITIONS OF PLACE OR POSITION

**A.** Using the prepositions of place or position, write a paragraph describing the spatial relationships in the accompanying illustrations. When you have finished, go back and underline each prepositional phrase you have used.

1.

2.

*Examples:*   The dog is <u>underneath the bed</u>.

There are clouds <u>in the sky</u>.

1.

2.

**B.** One student can ask another student direct questions about the illustrations.

Examples: *Where is the dog in drawing 1?*
*Where are the clouds in drawing 2?*

### *In, on, at*: Expressions of place

These three prepositions have different specific functions when referring to place and location. *In* is used for large areas, *on* is used for street names, and *at* is used for specific addresses and institutions.

---

*In, on, at*: EXPRESSIONS OF PLACE

**IN IS USED FOR LARGE NAMED AREAS**

| | |
|---|---|
| **CONTINENTS** | I live in South America. |
| **COUNTRIES** | I live in Germany. |
| **STATES** | I live in California. |
| **MUNICIPALITIES** | I live in Detroit. |

**ON IS USED FOR IDENTIFIED PLACES**

| | |
|---|---|
| **STREET NAMES** | I live on Logan Avenue. |
| **ISLAND NAMES** | I live on Long Island. |
| **FLOORS** | I live on the first floor. |

**AT IS USED FOR SPECIFIC LOCATIONS**

| | |
|---|---|
| **NUMBERED ADDRESSES** | I live at 739 Logan Avenue. |
| **INSTITUTIONS** | I work at the hospital. |
| | I study at Harvard University. |
| | I live at school. |

---

## EXERCISE 8.6

## *IN, ON,* AND *AT* IN EXPRESSIONS OF PLACE

**A.** Write a short paragraph answering the following questions about your past and present places of residence. What country were you born in? On what continent? What street did you live on? What address did you live at? Then answer these same questions about your present living situation.

(*past*)

(*present*)

**B.** Fill in the correct preposition of place—*in*, *on*, or *at*. Two have been done for you as examples.

1. _*in*_ the universe
2. _____ the world
3. _____ 79 Elmer Road
4. _____ 739 Hollywood Avenue
5. _____ Asia
6. _____ Vietnam
7. _____ California
8. _____ Europe
9. _____ Australia
10. _____ University Avenue
11. _____ Thirteenth Street
12. _____ Columbus, Ohio
13. _____ the Pentagon
14. _____ Europe
15. _____ Thirty-fifth Street
16. _____ Africa
17. _____ Paradise Island
18. _____ Treasure Island
19. _____ Queens Community College
20. _____ the Soviet Union

21. _*on*_ First Avenue
22. _____ Second Avenue
23. _____ New Jersey
24. _____ New Jersey Avenue
25. _____ Mississippi Street
26. _____ 740 Mississippi Street
27. _____ Highway 101
28. _____ Fordham University
29. _____ Lehmann High School
30. _____ La Guardia Hospital
31. _____ 13 Grove Street
32. _____ Columbia University
33. _____ Fort Bragg
34. _____ Buckingham Palace
35. _____ 35 Brown Place
36. _____ Phoenix
37. _____ the Chrysler Building
38. _____ Mercy General Hospital
39. _____ Dawson County
40. _____ Union Seminary

**C.** Fill in the blanks with the correct word—*in, on,* or *at.*

*Example:*  My teacher lives ___*on*___ Fifth Avenue.

1. We vacationed _____ Andros Island _____ the Bahamas.

2. Miss Wong visited her parents _____ Asia last year.

3. Have you studied _____ Harvard for a long time?

4. John works _____ 686 East Market Street.

5. Is the building _____ Park Avenue?

6. Immigrants from many nations live _____ New York City.

7. I know some German students who will be _____ this country next year.

8. Marianne has a big family _____ the Philippines.

9. He said he lived _____ the United States, _____ Long Island, _____ 34 Maple Street _____ the town of Hempstead.

10. While he was waiting, an ambulance arrived _____ the school.

11. She doesn't live _____ 1027 Wilcox Avenue anymore.

12. The patient is still _____ the hospital, _____ the fourth floor.

13. She said she lived _____ home with her parents.

14. Jacques was born _____ Port-au-Prince _____ Haiti, which is _____ the island of Hispaniola.

15. If you are ever _____ town, visit me _____ my home.

16. I have worked _____ this hospital for fifteen years.

17. Mario was born _____ Italy, _____ the island of Sicily.

18. She lives _____ Roosevelt Island, which is located right _____ New York City.

19. Pierre lives _____ the third floor.

20. Carmencita used to work _____ the United Nations as a translator.

## 8c Prepositions of direction

Prepositions may also indicate relationships of direction. Common prepositions of direction are *(away) from, toward, by way of, through,* and *to.*

He walked toward the science lab.

You can go by way of Stewart Avenue.

To get there, you have to drive through the tunnel.

He drove his car to the hospital.

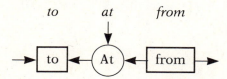

Some words, such as *up, down, over, under,* and *at,* can function as prepositions of direction as well as prepositions of place or position.

He drove down Atlantic Street.

She pointed at the stars.

**1** **Cooccurrence of prepositions of direction**

Some prepositions of direction often occur with another preposition.

He drove *from* the oceanside *to* the mainland.

She took the train *from* Denver *to* Seattle.

He came *out of* the car and *into* the airport.

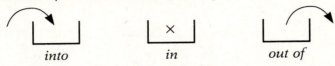

Get *off of* the bus at Thirty-fourth Street and *onto* the train there.

## EXERCISE 8.7

## PREPOSITIONS OF DIRECTION

**A.** Fill in the blanks with cooccurring prepositions of direction and any others necessary.

*Example:* John usually takes the train _____*to*_____ New

York _____*from*_____ his home in the suburbs.

Each day, John has a busy schedule. He wants to

be _____ bed and _____ the shower

by 6:15. Then, after breakfast, he heads _____ the

train. John usually takes the train _____ New York

_____ his home in the suburbs. He walks

_____ the train _____ Fourteenth

Street. When the train arrives _____ the station,

John gets _____ it and rides with the other

passengers _____ the city.

**B.** Write a brief report of two or three paragraphs describing your trip to the United States by plane, boat, train, bus, or car. Tell where you came from, what route you took, and what forms of transportation. Use any of the prepositions listed in section 8c.

## 2 *In* and *into*

*In* usually indicates a place or position.

He is in his house now.

*Into* indicates motion or action, though *in* is used interchangeably in this case.

She saw him go into (in) the chairman's office two hours ago.

We went into (in) the theater at eight o'clock.


## EXERCISE 8.8

## *IN* AND *INTO*

Fill in each blank with *in* or *into*, as appropriate.

*Example:*   Marianne walked _____*into*_____ the restaurant and sat down.

1.  He raced _____ the burning building.

2.  _____ my office I have three computers.

3.  They will be _____ class all evening.

4.  Jose sat _____ the café for an hour.

5.  The boat sailed _____ the sunset.

## 8d  Prepositions of time

Prepositions also indicate relationships of time.

We will start the meeting $\left\{\begin{array}{l} \text{at} \\ \text{by} \\ \text{before} \\ \text{after} \end{array}\right\}$ ten o'clock.

Some common prepositions of time are *about, after, around, at, before, by, for, in, on, since,* and *until.*

He arrived about three hours ago.

He left home after ten o'clock.

I'll be there around three.

The game will begin at two o'clock sharp.

The store opens at noon and closes at eight.

He was at home before midnight.

The paper must be handed in by August 1.

I have been in this country for three years.

The train will arrive in an hour.

I have to leave in a few minutes.

He celebrates his birthday on March 17.

He has been here since 1987.

He stayed until nine in the evening.

## 1 *For, during,* and *since* in expressions of time

*For* refers to a precise amount of time, usually specified in hours, days, weeks, months, or years. *For* implies continuity and may be followed by the indefinite article (*a/an*).

I lived there for two years.

He stands for eight hours a day.

John has been reading for a long time.

Snow fell for a day or so.

*During* refers to a period of time stated as a block. It is often followed by the definite article (*the*) or another specific determiner.

During the summer, I worked as a farm hand.

I was busy during April.

It snowed during the winter.

*Since* refers to time elapsed. It refers to a period of time that extends from a point in the past to the present or to another point in time in the past. *Since* usually calls for the perfective aspect of the verb (see Section 6j).

I have been living here since October.

He has lived in New Orleans since he came from Cuba in 1959.

*Ever since* is used to convey continuity from a stated event to the present.

He has worked here ever since graduating from high school.

Ever since his accident, he has had trouble sleeping.

## EXERCISE 8.9

### FOR, DURING, SINCE, AND EVER SINCE

**A.** Fill in each blank with *for*, *during*, *since*, or *ever since*, as appropriate.

*Example:* I worked full time ___ *during* ___ the vacation.

1. Herbert has lived here _____ three years.

2. This school has been a university _____ 1959.

3. Donna has been ill _____ three years ago.

4. Ms. Nguyen has been a student _____ last year.

5. Mr. Chang worked in Hong Kong _____ ten years before coming to the United States.

6. _____ the spring, I will do some gardening.

7. _____ twelve years now, he has been principal of the school.

8. I have loved her _____ 1976.

9. He worked _____ six hours last night.

10. I've been waiting for you _____ ten o'clock.

11. He has been depressed _____ his father died.

12. They were on vacation _____ a week.

13. _____ I graduated, I have lived on my own.

14. _____ the winter, it snows a lot.

15. It has been snowing _____ three days now.

16. It hasn't snowed here _____ 1959.

17. He has owned this business _____ his parents re-tired.

18. She has been a mother _____ 1989, when her daughter was born.

19. They have been married _____ fifteen years, _____ 1975.

20. My parents have been together _____ thirty-five years.

**B.** Fill in each blank with an appropriate answer about your educational history.

My name is _____. I have been in the United States for _____ years, since _____, and during this time I have been living _____.

I attended grammar school for _____ years and high school for _____ years. I have been a high school graduate since _____. During this time, I _____.

I have been studying English for _____ years,

since _____ . During this time, I have _____

_____ .

**2** ***In*, *on*, and *at* in expressions of time**

*In* is used for specific stated periods of time.

I went to work in the summer.

I went to school in the past.

I went to Haiti in 1983.

I went to work in May.

I went to work in the morning.

*On* is used for specific days or parts of a day.

I went to work on March 26.

I went to school on Monday.

I went to school on Monday morning.

I went to work on the morning of March 26.

*At* is used for times of day.

I went to work at eight o'clock.

I went to school at noon.

I went to her house at three o'clock Monday.

I got home at midnight yesterday.

## EXERCISE 8.10

## *IN, ON,* AND *AT* IN EXPRESSIONS OF TIME

**A.** Fill in each blank with *in*, *on*, or *at*, as appropriate.

*Example:* His workday usually begins _____ *at* _____ eleven o'clock.

1. She will see her mother _____ the morning.

2. A few children visited the playground _____ Tuesday.

3. The days are shorter _____ the winter than

    _____ the summer.

4. The band stopped playing _____ midnight.

5. My high-school years began _____ 1964.

6. The physical examination is _____ January 8.

7. Liz and Rudolpho will leave _____ the morning.

8. The temperature is usually above eighty degrees _____ August.

9. He mailed the cards _____ Saturday.

10. The weather is warmer _____ May than

    _____ October.

11. I am to meet their train _____ Tuesday

    _____ ten _____ the evening.

12. The baby woke us _____ three o'clock

    _____ the morning.

13. They arrived _____ our house _____

    the thirteenth _____ 9:00 P.M.

14. Your appointment is _____ two-thirty _____ Friday, June 11.

15. It started to rain _____ dawn _____ Tuesday morning.

16. After our vacation, classes begin again _____ January 2 _____ 8 A.M.

17. He said he would see us sometime _____ the future.

18. He meditates _____ dawn and again _____ dusk each day.

19. Can you come to the dance _____ Saturday night?

20. _____ the future, we will hold classes _____ Mondays _____ the evening _____ 6:00 P.M.

**B.** Fill in each blank with *in*, *on*, or *at*, as appropriate.

Anne's labor began _____ the evening _____ October 25, 1990. The baby was born _____ eight _____ the morning _____ October 26. Now Anne's life has many new routines. Each day, _____ the morning, she feeds the baby _____ six and again

_____ eight. She eats her own breakfast and takes her shower later _____ the morning, _____ nine, while her mother cares for the baby. _____ Tuesdays and Thursdays, she leaves _____ noon to teach her class. _____ the past, this was no problem; she would leave _____ noon and arrive _____ half an hour. Now, however, she has to wait for the baby sitter, who is supposed to arrive _____ noon but is often late. _____ Thursday last week, the sitter did not arrive _____ twelve but instead _____ one _____ the afternoon. When Anne arrived _____ school, it was _____ one-thirty. She apologized to the class and promised to make up the lost time sometime _____ the near future.

## 3 Other expressions of time

### From . . . to and from . . . until

These prepositions cooccur and mean the same thing when expressing time.

I worked from nine to three.

She studied from ten until noon.

### On time and in time

*On time* means "on schedule." *In time* means before an appointed time, with time left over.

The bus arrived on time today.

I reached work in time to have a cup of tea.

*Around* and *about*

These prepositions are interchangeable and indicate approximate time. They are sometimes preceded by *at*.

He will arrive in New York (at) about 7:00 P.M.

My train leaves (at) around 8:00 A.M.

## EXERCISE 8.11

## EXPRESSIONS OF TIME

Fill in the blanks with the appropriate prepositions of time.

*Example:* I slept ___*from*___ 11:00 P.M.

___*until*___ 5:30 A.M.

1. He arrived just _____ time to eat his breakfast.

2. Every day, the post office is open _____ nine

_____ five.

3. I have been living here _____ nine or ten years.

4. The boat from Europe was right _____ time.

5. _____ six years ago, I bought a new car.

6. On Tuesday at _____ six o'clock, we will leave for Buffalo.

7. He was _____ time for dinner.

8. We waited _____ the beginning of the game

   _____ the end.

9. The train arrives _____ time most of the time.

10. _____ four or five years ago, I left my native country.

11. The fever should break _____ twenty-four hours from now, if you take the medicine.

12. He works _____ dawn _____ dusk, six days a week.

13. He said he would meet us at _____ 2:00 P.M. at the library.

14. My check arrived _____ time to pay the rent.

15. That airline's flights rarely leave _____ time.

## 8e  Prepositions of manner

Prepositions of manner introduce answers to the question *How?* Some common prepositions of manner are *by, on, in, with,* and *like.*

You can get there by car, bus, plane, train, or ship.

She traveled on foot, but I went on horseback.

I like to travel on a plane, a train, or a ship.

We came in a car; they came in a taxi.

He writes in black ink, but she writes in pencil.

He always sings in a low voice.

Because of the rain, we all left in a hurry.

He accepted the tickets with pleasure.

He signaled with a gesture.

He fell with a thud.

The baby walks like a clown.

She always acts like an authority on everything.

## EXERCISE 8.12

## MANNER AND DIRECTION

Pretend that you are traveling with a group around North America as depicted on the accompanying map. Write a few paragraphs about the journey; imagine that you are using various forms of transportation (plane, car, train). Use the prepositions of manner and direction, plus any others that are appropriate.

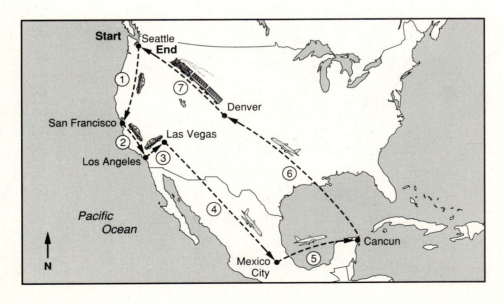

*Example:*

We left Seattle at eight o'clock in a car....

## 8f  Prepositions of measure

*Of* and *by* are the most common prepositions of measure.

He ordered three gallons of ice cream and a quart of milk.

Most of the students are from Haiti.

Gasoline is sold by the gallon and vegetables by the pound.


## EXERCISE 8.13

## PREPOSITONS OF MEASURE

Fill in each blank with the correct preposition.

*Example:*  I bought three cans _____*of*_____ soda.

Before we left town, we stopped at the supermarket. In the dairy department, we bought three quarts _____ milk and a pound _____ cheese. Then we selected three bottles _____ cider. At the bakery, they sell cookies _____ the pound and bread _____ the loaf. We bought two pounds _____ cookies and five loaves _____ bread. We also purchased two jars _____ mustard and a bottle _____ ketchup.

After that, we went to the gas station. We filled the car up with twelve gallons _____ regular gas. We also needed some oil, which they sell _____ the quart. The car took three quarts _____ oil.

Finally, we left on our camping trip.

## 8g Prepositions of purpose

To express a purpose or a reason why something is so, we use the preposition *for*.

That hose is for emergency use only.

He stopped at the market for some vegetables.

### EXERCISE 8.14

### PREPOSITONS OF PURPOSE

Why do you go shopping? Describe two different places that you shop in, and tell what you go there for. After you have finished, underline all the prepositional phrases.

*Example:* I shop at the pharmacy *for shampoo and soap*.

## 8h Prepositions of association

The preposition *of* is used to express association.

The new part of the campus is almost completed.

I heard of your baby's birth from Ruth.

## 8i Prepositions of similarity and capacity

Similarity is expressed with *like*.

You look like your brother.

She feels just like him.

*As* expresses "in the capacity of."

He got a job as a teacher.

Edward will serve as president this year.

## EXERCISE 8.15

## *LIKE* AND *AS*

Fill in each blank with the correct preposition, *like* or *as*.

*Example:* _____*as*_____ head of the committee, he will call the meetings.

1. The baby looks _____ his mother.

2. He appeared _____ Hamlet in the play.

3. Lana works _____ an elevator operator.

4. Elmer has a coat that is _____ silk.

5. Those gray clouds look _____ snow is coming.

## 8j Omission of prepositions

In some cases, prepositions may be optional. In others, the preposition must be omitted.

**OPTIONAL OMISSION**

1. When the preposition *for* expresses a span of time

   That family has lived here (for) two years.

   (For) how many years have you been married?

2. When the preposition *on* is used before days of the week

   I'll see you (on) Sunday.

   I bought the car (on) Tuesday.

3. In responses to questions that call for *in, at, on,* or *for* as prepositions of time

   How long have you been here? I have been here (for) two hours.

   When will you meet her? We will meet her (at) three o'clock.

**MANDATORY OMISSION**

4. When the noun in the time phrase contains an ordinal number or a demonstrative determiner such as *last, next, this,* or *that* or the head noun in the phrase contains *before, after, next, last,* or *this* as part of its meaning (for example, *yesterday, tomorrow, today*)

   He was working (on) that day.

   We saw him (during) last week.

   We spoke to him (on) yesterday.

   Does she leave for California (on) this Friday or (on) next Sunday?

   He is going there (on) the third.

   He will be there (for) next week.

5. When the time phrase contains a quantifier such as *every* or *all*

   She drives to church (on) every Sunday.

   They live in Florida (for) all year.

6. When a locative noun such as *home, downtown,* or *uptown* is used with a verb of motion or direction

   Henry went (to) home.

   Because of the rain, I hurried (to) inside.

7. When the adverbs *here* and *there* are used after the verb.

She goes (to) there quite frequently.

Mr. Chang comes (to) here every day.

## EXERCISE 8.16

## OMISSION OF PREPOSITONS

Read the following sentences. If the preposition in italics may be omitted, indicate in the blank whether the omission is mandatory (*M*) or optional (*O*), and give the number (1–7) of the rule you are applying.

*Examples:*   *M, 7*  I go *to* there each day.

   *O, 1*  We talked *for* two hours.

_____   1. I have lived here *for* two years.

_____   2. He said he would meet us here *on* Sunday.

_____   3. She will return *on* that Sunday.

_____   4. Mr. Smith returns *to* here on Saturday.

_____   5. They attend a lesson *on* every Monday.

_____   6. He met with Ralph *on* Monday.

_____   7. Naoko went *to* home.

_____   8. He works outside *during* all year.

_____   9. We will attend the meeting *on* Saturday.

_____   10. I was working *on* yesterday.

_____   11. They all went *to* home after the meeting.

———— 12. The children have attended that school *for* four years.

———— 13. He has come *to* here occasionally.

———— 14. He says he has been at home *for* two hours.

———— 15. I will graduate *on* next Tuesday.

## 8k  Case function

A few of the most frequently used prepositions have **case functions:** they signal relationships among people or objects rather than relationships of position, direction, time, or manner.

In case grammar, subject and object are surface slots or positions, and any noun that is not functioning as the surface subject or object of the verb must be preceded by a preposition. The preposition in turn gives clues to the semantic function of the noun it precedes.

### PREPOSITIONS AND THEIR CASE

| PREPOSITON | CASE | EXAMPLE |
|---|---|---|
| *by* | agentive | It was done by Mom. |
| *by* | means | We went home by taxi. |
| *for* | benefactive | He did some work for me. |
| *for* | proxy | She substituted for me. |
| *from* | ablative, source | Mary purchased that book from Joe. |
| *of* | eliciting | I asked a favor of him. |
| *of* | separation | They robbed us of our money. |
| *to* | dative | Iris gave the money to Dominick. |
| *with* | instrument | Jose destroyed the tree with his car. |
| *with* | comitative | She went to the movies with Carlos. |
| *with* | joining | They presented me with an award. |

The dative, benefactive, and eliciting cases may take indirect object movement. (See also Section 2c.)

I gave the pen to Mary. / I gave Mary the pen.

She bought the food for us. / She bought us the food.

He asked a favor of me. / He asked me a favor.

# EXERCISE 8.17

## CASE FUNCTION OF PREPOSITIONS

Using the box in 8k, complete these sentences according to the case indicated in parentheses.

*Examples:*  The ball was hit _____*by*_____ (agentive) Carlos.

Esperanza gave it _____*to*_____ (dative) him.

1. Tom was sent home _____ (means) taxi.

2. Marianne did some gardening _____ (benefactive) her mother.

3. Louisa attended that meeting _____ (proxy) me.

4. I danced _____ (comitative) Liz all night.

5. She requested an invitation _____ (source) the club.

6. He broke the window _____ (instrument) a ball that he threw.

7. They robbed me _____ (separation) my wallet.

8. He went to Europe _____ (means) boat.

9. Carlos ran all the way home _____ (comitative) his dog.

10. He paid _____ (proxy) his children.

## 81 Prepositions with verbs of transfer

Verbs of transfer take either *to* or *from*.

| | |
|---|---|
| sell to, buy from | give to, take from |
| lend to, borrow from | rent to, rent from |
| lease to, lease from | |

These verbs of transfer are all of a class called *phrasal verbs* (see Chapter 11). These combinations are all separable; that is, any direct object or complement is placed between the verb and the accompanying preposition.

He sold the car to his friend.

She bought a car from her brother.

We rent a house from him.

He rents a house to us.

## EXERCISE 8.18

## PREPOSITIONS WITH VERBS OF TRANSFER

Use the verbs of transfer in 81 to write pairs of sentences. One pair of sentences should be in the present tense, the other pair in the past tense.

*Example:* lease to, lease from

(*present*)

*He leases a house from his landlord.*
*They lease an apartment to their friends.*

(*past*)

*We leased the car from an agency.*
*Sally leased her apartment to a college friend.*

1. sell to, buy from
   (*present*)


   (*past*)


2. give to, take from
   (*present*)


   (*past*)


3. lend to, borrow from
   (*present*)


   (*past*)


4. rent to, rent from
   (*present*)


   (*past*)


5. lease to, lease from
   (*present*)


   (*past*)

## EXERCISE 8.19

## USING PREPOSITIONS

---

Write a fictional account of a journey you and some friends take. Using the prepositions of time, manner, and direction, as well as any other appropriate prepositions, tell the dates and times of arrival and departure, the manner of travel between points, how long each segment of the trip took, and so on. Be creative. Add any details you want, and have a good vacation!

## EXERCISE 8.20

## "SPRING AND ALL"

Read this poem by William Carlos Williams. Underline the prepositions, and list them to the right of the poem. Then tell what kind of relationship each indicates: place/position, direction, time, manner, measure, association, or agent.

*Example:*   *By* the road *to* the contagious hospital
              by—position
              to—direction

### SPRING AND ALL

By the road to the contagious hospital
under the surge of the blue
mottled clouds driven from the
northeast—a cold wind. Beyond, the
waste of broad, muddy fields
brown with dried weeds, standing and fallen

patches of standing water
the scattering of tall trees

All along the road the reddish
purplish, forked, upstanding, twiggy
stuff of bushes and small trees
with dead, brown leaves under them
leafless vines—

Lifeless in appearance, sluggish
dazed spring approaches—

They enter the new world naked,
cold, uncertain of all
save that they enter. All about them
the cold, familiar wind—

Now the grass, tomorrow
the stiff curl of wildcarrot leaf
One by one objects are defined—
It quickens: clarity, outline of leaf

But now the stark dignity of
entrance—Still, the profound change
has come upon them: rooted, they
grip down and begin to awaken

# CHAPTER 9
# Pronouns and Existentials

**Pronouns** usually replace noun phrases that have been specified previously or are assumed to be common knowledge. Whenever a noun phrase is repeated in a sentence, the second noun phrase may be replaced by a pronoun.

Yoshio said that *he* would be there.

Those people always go where *they* want.

Indefinite pronouns do not have specific referents.

*Someone* left the door open.

*Anyone* can be a fool.

The personal pronouns *we*, *you*, and *it* may also indicate indefinite reference.

*We* are all victims of pollution.

*You* must try if you are to succeed.

*It* is not my problem.

Pronoun agreement is one of the subtle ways in which writing is made coherent. The pronouns that occur create a bond between and within sentences. And pronoun selection helps the reader by identifying the voice of the speaker.

## 9a Personal pronouns

**Personal pronouns** are generally definite. They refer to a specific individual or object. The forms of the personal pronouns are irregular and must be memorized.

We select a pronoun through a grammatical process that takes person, number, gender, and case into consideration.

### 1 Pronoun agreement: person, number, and gender

A pronoun should agree with its antecedent (the noun phrase being replaced). The person, number, and gender of a pronoun are thus determined by the nature of its antecedent.

### Person

When the pronoun refers to the speaker or a group including the speaker, the **first person** is used.

*I* like to eat spinach.

*We* joined the parade at Fifth Avenue.

The **second person** is used when the speaker addresses one or more persons directly but excludes himself or herself.

Will *you* please send the information to my home?

When reference is made to someone or something other than the speaker or the person spoken to, the **third person** is used.

*He* is the culprit.

*They* live in Boston.

### Number

Number refers to whether the antecedent is singular or plural.

*Jose* is a student. *He* is from El Savador.

When the *scouts* go on a trip, *they* always have a good time.

A plural pronoun is used to refer to two or more antecedents joined by *and*, and a singular pronoun is used to refer to two or more antecedents joined by *or* or *nor*.

*Jose and Esperanza* are students. *They* are from El Salvador.

*Milk or tea* is served with lunch. *It* is your choice.

### Gender

Gender refers to whether the antecedent is masculine, feminine, or nonhuman.

*Maria* took your books. *She* is in the library.

The *dog* ate the food; then *it* ran away.

The neuter *it* is restricted in terms of verbs. This pronoun cannot occur with verbs requiring a human subject. Thus this sentence is permissible:

He recalled the past.

But this one is not:

*It recalled the past.

## 2 Pronoun agreement: case

The selection of a personal pronoun is also based on its grammatical function in the sentence. There are three categories or case functions for pronouns: nominative (subject position), accusative (object position), and genitive (possessive). The case of a pronoun depends on its use in its own clause. The **nominative case** is used when the pronoun is the subject of the sentence.

*You* are the person to contact.

*We* felt the earthquake.

The **accusative case** is used when the pronoun is a direct object, an indirect object, or the object of a preposition.

Jose saw *her* at the corner.

Jose gave *us* a photo.

Jose was looking for *her*.

The **genitive (possessive) case** is used when the pronoun shows ownership.

That hat is *his*.

That car is *mine*.

The pronoun forms that function as modifiers are the **possessive pronouns/adjectives** (*my, your, his, her, its, our, their*). These forms are considered determiners. They come before the noun, signaling that a noun is to come, and do not serve the pronoun function of replacing the noun phrase (see Section 7c).

She is *his* wife.

He is *her* husband.

## 3 Usage: case of pronouns

There are a few things to be aware of in pronoun use.

1. When a pronoun follows *and* or *or* as part of a compound unit, the pronoun is in the same case as the noun.

   The man gave Jose and *me* a ride. (*Jose* and *me* are indirect objects.)

   Just between you and me, I don't want to go. (*You* and *me* are objects of the preposition.)

   Will my brother and I be invited? (*Brother* and *I* are subjects.)

2. In comparisons after *as* and *than*, when the pronoun is the subject of an understood verb, use the nominative form.

She is taller than *he* [is].

Can you run as fast as *he* [can]?

3. Use the nominative case for subject complements (see Section 2c).

It was *he*.

It could have been *they*.

## PRONOUN FORM BY CASE FUNCTION

**PERSONAL PRONOUNS**

| *Singular* | SUBJECTIVE | OBJECTIVE | POSSESSIVE PRONOUN | POSSESSIVE ADJECTIVE |
|---|---|---|---|---|
| First person | I | me | mine | my |
| Second person | you | you | yours | your |
| Third person | he | him | his | his |
| | she | her | hers | her |
| | it | it | | its |

| *Plural* | | | | |
|---|---|---|---|---|
| First person | we | us | ours | our |
| Second person | you | you | yours | your |
| Third person | they | them | theirs | their |

**RELATIVE AND INTERROGATIVE PRONOUNS**

| | | | | |
|---|---|---|---|---|
| | which | which | — | |
| | who | whom | whose | |
| | whoever | whomever | whomever | |

**INDEFINITE PRONOUNS**

| | | | | |
|---|---|---|---|---|
| | everybody | everybody | everybody's | |

## EXERCISE 9.1

## PRONOUN USAGE

Correct the errors in pronoun use in the following paragraphs. The first two corrections have been done for you as examples.

The president of the United States and ~~he~~ *his* wife live in Washington, D.C. ~~Her~~ *She* is called the First Lady by some people. Them live in the White House. They is the official residence of the president and him family. His has an office there and him wife does too. When the president and her wife entertain official guests, them have the visitors stay in the spacious guest quarters available in the White House.

The White House was originally built of gray stone. But the British burned us to the ground during the War of 1812. He was rebuilt after the war. In 1818, President James Monroe and its wife, Elizabeth, were the first people to live in the new White House with his new white paint job. Us lived there until 1825. Since then, there have been many other residents. All of him shared the same address, 1600 Pennsylvania Avenue, and all of we are forever in American history.

## EXERCISE 9.2

## PRONOUN FORM

Look over the errors you corrected in Exercise 9.1, and list all the correct pronouns here. Write the person, number, gender, and case or possessive adjective for each. The first two have been done for you as examples.

1. *his — possessive adjective*
2. *she — third person singular feminine*
3.
4.
5.
6.
7.
8.
9.
10.
11.
12.
13.
14.
15.
16.

## EXERCISE 9.3

## PRONOUNS AND VERBS

Circle the correct choice of pronouns and verbs in parentheses. Then underline the antecedent of each pronoun.

*Example:* If the women's basketball team goes to the tournament, <u>each player</u> will pay (*her,* *their*) expenses.

1. After Joshua has run for thirteen miles, (*you feel, he feels, they feel*) tired and thirsty.

2. People who have any sense about (*his, her, their*) weight won't eat fattening foods.

3. A boy can join the group only if (*he, they, you*) can swim.

4. The couple's trip to the mountains allowed (*him, it, them*) to see a lot of the countryside.

5. It takes a great deal of character for a boy to admit that (*its, he, they*) made a mistake.

6. Marilyn finally admitted that it was (*her, she, them*) who took the book.

7. No one knew more about her country than (*her, she, we*).

8. Can her brother and (*she, it, them*) go with us?

9. The people of the army were ordered to stop what (*we were, they were, he was*) doing.

10. If you were (*me, I, them*), what would you do?

## EXERCISE 9.4

## CORRECT FORM OF PRONOUNS

---

Circle the correct form of the pronouns in parentheses.

*Example:* Jose and (*I*, *me*) invited our teacher to visit our home town.

1. (*She*, *Her*) and (*I*, *me*) shared the cost of the present.

2. Before (*we*, *us*) went to the movies, (*we*, *us*) ate dinner.

3. Evelyn said that the others would ride with (*I*, *me*).

4. (*She*, *Her*) said the children would rather ride with (*they*, *them*).

5. Edward wants to visit (*their*, *them*).

6. That green bicycle is (*her*, *hers*).

7. (*We*, *Us*) went to the concert with (*us*, *our*) friends.

8. (*He*, *Him*) gave the prize to (*us*, *ours*).

9. Elmer told (*we*, *us*) to visit after dinner.

10. The teacher told (*me*, *I*) that this book is (*your*, *yours*).

11. (*You*, *Yours*) are the hope of the next generation.

12. (*She*, *Her*) is president of the student council.

13. The principal told (*she*, *her*) to be on time tomorrow.

14. Naoko was working for (*I*, *me*) last week.

15. Jim likes work; (*he*, *him*) enjoys the people.

16. The losers were (*we*, *us*) and (*they*, *them*).

17. Mariko admitted that it was (*she*, *her*) who broke the glass.

18. The cost was more than (*we*, *us*) students could pay.

19. (*He, Him*) and Carlos caught the last bus home.

20. Amy is taller than (*I, me*).

## EXERCISE 9.5

## POSSESSIVE CASE PRONOUNS

---

In sentences 1–5, change the possessive case pronouns into possessive adjectives. In sentences 6–10, change the possessive adjectives into possessive case pronouns.

*Examples:*   That book is mine.
*That is my book.*
This is their house.
*This house is theirs.*

1. That car is ours.

2. Yours is the big piece.

3. The leftover food is theirs.

4. The blue car is his.

5. The small house on the corner is hers.

6. The book with the green cover is my book.

7. Their house is the last one.

8. He wants his book.

9. I think this is your pen.

10. She said that was their house.

## EXERCISE 9.6

## CORRECT PRONOUN FORM

Fill in each blank with the correct form of the pronoun. The first has been done for you as an example.

### MY NEIGHBOR GEORGE

This is the story of George. _____*He*_____ is a neighbor

of _____; _____ lives right next door.

_____ works in a factory all day.

George gets up early every workday. _____ once

told _____, "_____ clock wakes

_____ wife and _____ at 5:00 A.M.

_____ gets up just to cook _____

breakfast. That's why _____ really appreciate

_____."

Every day, when George starts _____ car,

_____ wakes _____. _____

car has a loud engine, and _____ always warms

_____ up for a long time. When _____

leaves, it is about 6:30 A.M. _____ like this time

because after _____ leaves, _____

can go back to sleep.

## EXERCISE 9.7

## PRONOUNS AND POSSESSIVE ADJECTIVES

**A.** Underline all the pronouns and possessive adjectives in the paragraph.

MY MORNING

This morning, I woke up at 6:00 A.M. I took a shower, brushed my teeth, and went down to breakfast. My parents were already there. Dad was reading his paper, and Mom was drinking coffee from her favorite mug. I said "good morning" to them and sat down to eat my breakfast.

**B.** Rewrite the paragraph in the third person. Start with this sentence: "This morning, he woke up at 6:00 A.M."

**C.** Rewrite the paragraph in the second person. Start with this sentence: "This morning, you woke up at 6:00 A.M."

## EXERCISE 9.8

## PRONOUNS IN USE

**A.** Write a paragraph about your week. Begin with these words: "Every week, I . . ." When you have finished, underline all the pronouns.

*Example:* Every week, <u>I</u> go to school and work at <u>my</u> job. <u>I</u> also wash <u>my</u> car at least once. . . .

**B.** Now rewrite the paragraph as if it were written about a male friend. Start with "Every week, he . . ."

**C.** Rewrite the paragraph as if it were written about a female friend. Start with "Every week, she . . ."

**D.** Finally, rewrite the paragraph as if it were written about people in general. Start with "Every week, they . . ."

**Reflexive pronouns** are used within a sentence when the subject and object have identical referents and refer to the same person.

I drove *myself*.

They showed *themselves*.

Grammatically, a reflexive pronoun is in an object position, as direct object, indirect object, or object of a preposition. Like other pronouns, reflexives must agree with their antecedents in gender, number, and person.

You rewarded yourself.

Jeanine hurt herself.

We saw ourselves in the video.

They have a strong belief in themselves.

The turtle found itself crossing the finishing line.

Sentences like the following are therefore incorrect.

*He hurt myself.

*I showed ourselves.

Reflexive pronouns are often used as intensifiers.

I'll do it myself.

Expressions of the form (*all*) *by oneself* or *for oneself* mean alone or without help.

You did your homework by yourself.

We cooked dinner for ourselves.

Some common idiomatic expressions use the reflexive.

"Help yourself" means serve your own food.

"Make yourself at home" means feel at ease, as if you were in your own home.

---

### REFLEXIVE PRONOUN FORMS

|  | SINGULAR | PLURAL |
|---|---|---|
| First person | I/myself | we, ourselves |
| Second person | you/yourself | you, yourselves |
| Third person | he/himself | they, themselves |
|  | she/herself |  |
|  | it/itself |  |

---

## EXERCISE 9.9

## REFLEXIVE PRONOUNS

Fill in each blank with the correct reflexive pronoun.

*Example:*  He's shy. He never talks about __*himself*__.

1. He's friendly. He talks about _____ to others.

2. She is vain. She is always looking at _____ in the mirror.

3. I want to welcome you. Please come in and make _____ at home.

4. Help _____ to some food.

5. We are responsible students; we can take care of _____.

6. He said, "You are conceited. You think only of _____."

7. If you live alone, you often cook for _____.

8. There are many single parents who support _____ and their children.

9. Does he live by _____?

10. As an adult, I have to support _____ economically.

11. Little children must be supervised because they may hurt _____.

12. Jose taught _____ to read basic English.

13. "The best way to succeed is for all of you students to help _____."

14. When I saw _____ in the mirror, I was surprised.

15. Alex and Micki helped _____ by studying together for long hours.

## EXERCISE 9.10

## REFLEXIVE PRONOUNS IN QUESTIONS

Form a question with the words given, and then write an answer. Ask if someone does these things for you or if you do them yourself.

*Example:* cook your meals *Do you cook for yourself? No, I don't cook for myself.*

1. cut your hair


2. pay your tuition


3. buy your clothes


4. drive a car


5. mow your lawn


6. fix your car


7. wash your clothes


8. clean your room

9. brush your teeth

10. do your homework.

## 9c Indefinite pronouns

**Indefinite pronouns** such as *anybody*, *someone*, and *everything* do not have direct referents. They are derived from combining the determiners *no*, *some*, *any*, and *every* with the nouns *body*, *one*, and *thing*.

|  | INDEFINITE PRONOUNS | | |
|---|---|---|---|
| nobody | anybody | somebody | everybody |
| no one | anyone | someone | everyone |
| nothing | anything | something | everything |

The indefinite pronouns may occupy any noun position: subject, direct or indirect object, and object of the preposition.

Everybody is here.

They found nothing in the yard.

She bought something for everyone.

In terms of subject-verb agreement, indefinite pronouns are always singular.

Nothing is wrong.

Everyone is here.

## EXERCISE 9.11

## INDEFINITE PRONOUNS

Complete this dialogue by filling in the blanks. The first one has been done for you as an example.

Joe comes up to a police officer and says, "Excuse me, sir."

The police officer says, "Is there _*something*_ I can do for you?"

"Yes, _____ took my bike from over there."

"Do you think _____ stole it?"

"It's possible. I didn't give _____ permission to ride it. I had it locked up, and I'm worried."

"Don't worry; _____ will be all right! We'll ask _____ in the area if they've seen it, and we'll find it."

A little later, Joe reports, "The first person I asked said he saw _____. Another said I should stop bothering _____."

"Well, you have _____ to worry about. _____ saw what happened and explained _____. He said your brother came and took your bike. He left this note for you."

## 9d Interrogative and relative pronouns

## 1 Interrogative pronouns

*Who*, *whom*, and *what* are sometimes referred to as **interrogative pronouns**. They take the place of a noun phrase in *wh-* questions. We use *who* if the question is about a subject or *whom* if it is about an object (see Section 5b).

> Who called last night?

> Whom did you write the letter to?

> What was the name of the street?

## EXERCISE 9.12

## INTERROGATIVE PRONOUNS

Rewrite each sentence in the form of a question about the word in italics.

*Example:*   He ate the *pizza*.

*Who ate the pizza?*

1. She drove the *car*.

2. He wrote a letter to *Luis*.

3. He wrote a *letter* to Luis.

4. Maria appointed *Carlos* chairman of the dance.

5. The committee elected *Esperanza*.

**2**  **Relative pronouns**

The **relative pronouns** are used to identify and replace a noun phrase in an embedded sentence (see Section 4d).

> The people who called on Monday got the applications first.

> The book that is on the table was written by Camus.

See Section 5c for more on relative pronouns.

## 9e Demonstrative pronouns

When not functioning as determiners, the **demonstrative pronouns** refer to concrete objects or events that are known to both the speaker and the listener.

*This* is your pen. (A definite pen is pointed out.)

*This* was a good class. (A definite class is pointed out.)

*These* are my books. (Definite books are pointed out.)

*Those* were the best years of my life. (Definite years are pointed out.)

When functioning as pronouns, the demonstratives can occupy the subject or object position.

These are delicious.

That is hers.

I want this.

He would prefer those.

### 1 Discourse function of demonstratives

Demonstratives have a common discourse function. In this capacity, their purpose is to refer to statements in a previous conversation that are known to both the speaker and the listener.

That was a bad idea.

Those were fine sentiments.

### 2 Prearticles and postdeterminers

The following list contains words considered prearticles and postdeterminers. They can also function in the place of nouns like the demonstratives and the indefinite pronouns.

| | | |
|---|---|---|
| some | both | few |
| none | all | most |
| either | many | more |
| neither | much | several |

Some will make fun of this.

All may attend if they choose.

Many have left the building.

Much has happened.

I caught several.

We didn't play much.

## 9f  Existentials: *It* and *there* in nonreferential sentences

Every sentence in English must have a surface subject, and *it* and *there* are frequently used to fill this purpose. For example, in English a sentence about the weather may read "It is raining," whereas the same sentence in Spanish would be "Is raining."

*It* and *there* are like the indefinite pronouns when they are used in sentences in which they have no antecedent. Sentences like this are called **existentials**, and they are variations on the basic sentence pattern (see Section 2c).

It's a beautiful day.

There's a book on the table.

In other contexts, these two words have a referential function.

Where is the car? It is parked in front of the house. (*it* = the car)

Let's go to the beach. It's cooler there. (*there* = the beach)

### 1  Nonreferential *it*

Nonreferential *it* is often used in simple statements and questions dealing with environmental features such as weather, temperature, time, and distance. The contracted form *it's* is often used.

**WEATHER**

What is it like outside?

It's raining.

**TIME**

What time is it?

It's eleven o'clock.

**DISTANCE**

How far is it from here?

It's one hundred miles.

**ENVIRONMENT**

What is it like here on weekends?

It's never very crowded here.

In these sentences, the use of *it* as a filler allows for shorter responses with less redundancy. In this way, it acts like a pronoun.

## EXERCISE 9.13

### NONREFERENTIAL *IT*

Using nonreferential *it* wherever possible, write a series of questions and answers about the topics indicated.

*Example:*   time (hour and minute)

*What time is it?*

*It's two o'clock.*

1. weather (today)

2. weather (yesterday)

3. weather (tomorrow)

4. weather (in July)

5. time (day of the month)

6. time (the year)


7. location


8. distance


9. atmosphere


10. environment


## EXERCISE 9.14

## NONREFERENTIAL *IT*

**A.** Answer each question accurately.

1. What time is it?

2. What day of the week is it?

3. What month is it?

4. What year is it?

5. What day of the month is it?

**B.** Match each question in the left column with its answer in the right column. Write the letter of the answer in the blank preceding the question.

_____ 1. What is this neighborhood like?  a. It's not healthy around here.

_____ 2. How far is it from here?  b. It's been raining all day.

_____ 3. What's it like there today?  c. It's the Fourth of July.

_____ 4. What day is it?  d. It's two hundred miles from here.

_____ 5. What is that street like at noon?  e. It's always too crowded.

## 2 Nonreferential *there*

Nonreferential *there*, like the demonstratives, has a discourse function. *There* signals that the sentence will state the location or existence of something. The use of nonreferential *there* also postpones the introduction of new information until later in the sentence.

There's a big park in the city.

There are many beautiful lakes in the state.

There's a class at one o'clock.

There are many activities on this field.

### Quantity with nonreferential *there*

A plural sentence with *there* may express a definite or an indefinite quantity.

There are three students from Haiti in the class.

There are a few people from Asia.

There are a lot of students from Asia.

Nonreferential *there* is used in questions and answers expressing quantity with *how much* or *how many*.

How much water is there?
There is a gallon.

How many teachers are there in your school?
There are forty teachers in my school.

**3**  **Verb agreement with *it* and *there***

With *it*, the verb tense is always singular.

It is raining a lot.

It is about ten miles from here.

Since *there* is a substitute for a postponed subject, it depends on the noun phrase following the verb, which is the logical subject. If the noun phrase is plural, the sentence uses *there are*; if the noun is singular, the sentence uses *there is*.

## EXERCISE 9.15

## THERE IS / THERE ARE

Circle *is* or *are*, as appropriate.

*Examples:*  There (*is*, *are*) a big house behind the barn.

There (*is*, *are*) many kinds of cats.

1. There (*is*, *are*) special fruits in that salad.

2. There (*is*, *are*) a post office just around the corner.

3. There (*is*, *are*) a new minister of education in my country.

4. There (*is*, *are*) many volunteers for the play.

5. There (*is*, *are*) a sign at the corner.

6. There (*is*, *are*) no children allowed.

7. There (*is*, *are*) twenty-four hours in each day.

**9f/Existentials: *It* and *There* in Nonreferential Sentences**  279

8. There (*is, are*) nine players on each team.

9. There (*is, are*) only one teacher for that course.

10. There (*is, are*) thirteen different species of flowers in the garden.

## EXERCISE 9.16

## DESCRIBING WITH *THERE IS / THERE ARE*

Write a series of sentences describing a classroom, a supermarket, and a bedroom. Use as much detail as possible.

*Example:* There are eight people in my history classroom. There is one window in the room. There are ten desks in the room. There are two pictures on the wall....

1. Classroom

2. Supermarket

3. Bedroom

## EXERCISE 9.17

## DESCRIBING WITH *THERE IS / THERE ARE*

___

Look around the room you are in. Reply to each question accurately. If an object is present, tell the location using *it's*.

*Examples:*   Is there a map in the room?

*Yes, there is a map in this room. It's on the wall.*

Is there a teacher's desk?

*There is no teacher's desk in this room.*

1. Is there a pencil sharpener?

2. Is there a wastebasket?

3. Is there a telephone?

4. Is there a clock?

5. Is there a coat rack?

6. Is there a horse?

7. Is there a fire extinguisher?

8. Is there a chalkboard?

9. Is there a basketball?

10. Is there a file cabinet?

### 4   The difference between *there* and *it*

Be aware of the difference between *there is* (*there's*) and *it is* (*it's*). *There is* is used to express the existence of things in a nonreferential way.

There are many birds in this area.

*It is* is used in a referential way for classification, description, location, and origins. This *it* has an antecedent.

What is a banana? It's a fruit. It's yellow. It's in the bowl. It's from Costa Rica.

CHAPTER 10

# Adjectives and Adverbs

Adjectives and adverbs are used to expand the basic sentence pattern by modifying or qualifying other words. They describe, limit, or restrict the words they modify.

**Adjectives** modify nouns or pronouns. They usually precede the word they modify, but not always.

PRECEDING      The round table is over there.

She had a beautiful dress.

FOLLOWING      She bought the books necessary for the course.

Adjectives may also be used as complements after the verb *be* and other linking verbs like *appear, become, feel, look, seem, smell,* and *taste*. These adjective complements refer to the subjects of their clauses.

That car is beautiful.

The weather feels wonderful.

**Adverbs** primarily modify verbs, as well as adjectives, and other adverbs.

MODIFYING VERB       She greeted the fans warmly.

MODIFYING ADJECTIVE  There were only two parking spots.

MODIFYING ADVERB     She took her responsibilities quite seriously.

An adverb indicates intensity (*very*) or explains how, why, where, or when. When adverbs modify verbs, they are usually movable; otherwise, they generally precede the words they modify.

## EXERCISE 10.1

## FORMS OF ADJECTIVES AND ADVERBS

In the following sentences, first circle the appropriate form of the word from the choices in parentheses. Then underline the word or words it modifies. Finally, identify the modifier as an adjective (*adj*) or adverb (*adv*) in the blank.

Examples: _*adj*_ The cake <u>tasted</u> too (*sweetly,* (*sweet).*)

_*adv*_ He <u>ran</u> the race ((*quickly*) *quick*).

_____ 1. David felt (*bad, badly*) when he failed the exam.

_____ 2. Harumi always takes herself (*serious, seriously*).

_____ 3. The team played (*well, good*), but it didn't win.

_____ 4. The truck sounded (*loud, loudly*).

_____ 5. She did her homework (*perfect, perfectly*).

_____ 6. Now I think (*different, differently*) about life.

_____ 7. We arrived too (*late, lately*) to meet the plane.

_____ 8. The gold watch is very (*expensive, expensively*).

_____ 9. My arm hurts so (*bad, badly*) that I can't throw.

_____ 10. The lake seems (*deep, deeply*).

_____ 11. The child pounded the door (*hard, hardly*).

_____ 12. A (*special, specially*) designed car allowed him to drive.

_____ 13. The teacher feels (*strong, strongly*) about his students.

_____ 14. They have treated the others (*cruel, cruelly*).

_____ 15. He always drives (*safe, safely*).

_____ 16. That (*unique, uniquely*) system was installed recently.

_____ 17. A (*normal, normally*) development takes six months.

_____ 18. Elmer seems (*weak, weakly*) after his illness.

_____ 19. Some animals are bred (*specific, specifically*) for strength.

_____ 20. His upper body strength is (*considerable, considerably*).

## 10a Adjectives

In sentences, adjectives function as noun modifiers, as subject complements after linking verbs, and as object complements.

>She is a beautiful child. (noun modifier)

>She is beautiful. (subject complement)

>He declared her work beautiful. (object complement)

Adjectives are used to describe, as in all three of these sentences. They may also be used to specify which of a number of alternatives is being referred to.

>The tall boy threw the rock.

Adjectives may also subclassify within a large class of objects.

>She has an electric guitar.

A variety of word forms may function as adjectives.

| | |
|---|---|
| PRESENT PARTICIPLES | laughing cow |
| PAST PARTICIPLES | broken promises |
| TWO-WORD VERBS | warmed-over food |
| NOUNS | summer clothes |
| PHRASES | state-of-the-art technology |

### 1 Participles as adjectives

Participles, the *-ing* and the *-ed* forms of verbs, serve admirably as adjectives.

The present participle (*-ing* form) is used when the noun in the phrase gives a feeling or performs the action.

>It was a boring movie.

>She is an interesting person.

When the noun feels something or is the receiver of the action, we use the past participle.

>The bored audience continued to watch the movie.

>She was interested in the movie.

A present participle may indicate that an action is still in progress.

>Growing plants need plenty of water.

A past participle shows that an action is finished.

Grown children can take care of themselves.

Participles as adjectives can come after *be* or before nouns, just like other adjectives.

## EXERCISE 10.2

## PARTICIPLES

Fill in each blank with the correct adjective derived from the verb in the model sentence.

*Examples:*   The novel excited the students.

The students read the ___*exciting*___ novel last week.

The ___*excited*___ students read the novel last week.

1. The politician charms us.

   That _____ man is a politician.

   The _____ people listen to every word he says.

2. The storm terrified me.

   That was the most _____ storm I've ever experienced.

   I was _____.

3. His story fascinated the group of friends.

   The _____ group of friends listened to every word in the story.

   His story was _____.

4. The monkey amused us.

   The _____ monkey played in its cage all morning.

   We were _____ by the monkey.

5. The full meal satisfies the woman.

   The _____ meal lasted three hours.

   She left the restaurant a _____ woman.

6. The customer annoys the waiter.

   The _____ customer left the restaurant.

   The _____ waiter complained to his boss.

7. His decision surprised his parents.

   His parents said, "What a _____ decision!"

   His parents said, "We are so _____ by your decision!"

8. The story pleased me.

   To me, it's a _____ story.

   I am _____ by the story.

9. Maria will tease Jose.

   Jose will be _____.

   Maria will be _____.

10. A difficult test can frustrate even the best students.

    Even the best students felt it was a _____ test.

    The test left even the best students _____.


## EXERCISE 10.3

## PRESENT AND PAST PARTICIPLES

Use the verb in each sentence to make two new sentences, one using the present participle and the other using the past participle.

*Example:* The news disturbed the family.

*The news was disturbing to the family.*
*The family was disturbed by the news.*

1. Action films entertain people.

2. A nap relaxes people.

3. Physical labor exhausts workers.

4. Loud noises frighten infants.

5. Sports interest children.

6. The movie amused the audience.

7. That teacher motivates the students.

8. That subject bores the students.

9. Language study frustrates some students.

10. That grammar rule confuses some students.

## EXERCISE 10.4

## PARTICIPLES AS ADJECTIVES

Circle the appropriate form of the participle in each sentence.

*Example:*   Some students are ((bored,) boring) in class.

1. Some classes are (*bored, boring*).

2. A vacation trip is always (*excited, exciting*).

3. Failing a test is a (*depressed, depressing*) experience.

4. What do you do when you are (*depressed, depressing*)?

5. Many people are (*disappointed, disappointing*) when they find out how difficult life is.

6. A business aims to have (*satisfied, satisfying*) customers.

7. We felt good after that (*satisfied, satisfying*) meal.

8. Watching baseball is sometimes (*interested, interesting*) and sometimes (*bored, boring*).

9. A long car trip can make you (*tired, tiring*).

10. A long car trip can be (*tired, tiring*).

11. Police and fire protection are (*needed, needing*) services.

12. Attaining a degree is a (*rewarded, rewarding*) experience.

13. The people are (*concerned, concerning*) about crime in their neighborhood.

14. He was blessed with a (*loved, loving*) family.

15. A (*worked, working*) mother does not have much free time.

## EXERCISE 10.5

## MORE PARTICIPLES AS ADJECTIVES

Circle the appropriate participle of each pair in parentheses.

### VISITING A GHOST TOWN

I visited a ghost town once. It was an (*interested, interesting*) experience, though I must admit it was a little (*frightened, frightening*), too.

The town was full of (*abandoned, abandoning*) and (*run-down, running-down*) buildings. Most of them had (*broken, breaking*) windows. Inside, the (*decayed, decaying*) rooms held nothing but dust and a few (*disgusted, disgusting*) smells. But I was (*surprised, surprising*) to see how much of the past was (*preserved, preserving*). For example, some of the kitchens were quite (*fascinated, fascinating*). They still had (*run, running*) water and (*worked, working*) stoves. There were also some old books in some of the houses, and we could tell that the inhabitants were (*educated, educating*) people.

I was (*amazed, amazing*) by the whole experience. It certainly

was (*enlightened, enlightening*).

## 2 | The order of adjectives

There are four categories of adjectives: size, shape, color, and other descriptives. If two or more adjectives precede the noun, they are always in a precise order.

Size, shape, and color always occur in that order: *the big round table, the large blue table, the round blue table*. Other descriptive adjectives come before color but after size and shape: *beautiful blue dress, large cardboard box, round glass table*. Nouns as descriptive adjectives directly precede the head noun: *winter hat, table lamp*.

## EXERCISE 10.6

## ORDER OF ADJECTIVES

Fill in the blanks with adjectives of description (including nouns), size, shape, and color as indicated in parentheses.

*Examples:* She wore a ___*big*___ ___*red*___ (size, color) hat.

He wore a ___*black*___ ___*wool*___ (color, descriptive noun) coat.

1. He carried a _____ _____ (shape, color) envelope.

2. The _____ _____ (size, color) cat lay on the bed.

3. The _____ _____ _____ (size, shape, color) boat left port this morning.

4. She wore a _____ _____ (color, descriptive noun) dress to the movie.

5. In the yard is a _____ _____ (descriptive adjective, color) bike.

6. He has a _____ _____ (shape, color) coat on today.

7. We strolled around the _____ _____ (shape, color) garden.

8. I always wear my _____ _____ (color, descriptive noun) when I ski.

9. He complained about the _____ _____ (size, color) building materials in the driveway.

10. I bought a _____ _____ (size, color) car.

## 10b Adverbs

Adverbs qualify verbs, adjectives, and other adverbs.

## 1 Five categories of adverbs

1. Adverbs of manner (how): *carefully, loudly, quickly, fast, nearly, well, hard, together, quietly*
2. Adverbs of place (where): *above, apart, around, away, behind, close, down, downstairs, everywhere, here, in, inside, near, out, outside, over, right, sideways, there*
3. Adverbs of frequency (how often): *scarcely, hardly, rarely, never, seldom, occasionally, sometimes, frequently, again, always*
4. Adverbs of time (when): *after, already, before, early, first, last, later, now, soon, still, today, tomorrow, yesterday, yet*
5. Adverbs of degree (to what degree): *quite, very*

Adjectives and adverbs of degree are called **qualifiers** and may precede adjectives or other adverbs. *Very* is the most common.

He ran very quickly.

Here are some other qualifiers:

| | | |
|---|---|---|
| a bit | mighty | so |
| a little | quite | somewhat |
| indeed | pretty | rather |
| too | enough | exceedingly |
| enormously | extremely | moderately |
| entirely | really | wholly |

She was wearing a really pretty dress.

He wrote an enormously popular book.

## 2 Adverb formation

Many common adverbs are formed by adding the suffix *-ly* to nouns or adjectives.

quickly    weakly
loudly     hourly

Less frequent but common additions are *-wise* and *-ward*.

lengthwise

clockwise

backward

## EXERCISE 10.7

## USING ADVERBS

Complete each sentence using an adverb from the category indicated.

*Example:*  She traveled to King's Island ___*weekly*___ (time).

1. When he saw the rain, he _____ (manner) closed the door.

2. He _____ (frequency) does that.

3. He said that old book was _____ (qualifier, degree) rare.

4. He said he would meet us _____ (place).

5. The bride and groom slipped _____ (manner) away from the reception.

6. The students reminded the teacher that they had done that lesson _____ (time).

7. He _____ (frequency) touched his dinner.

8. The people protested the _____ (degree) harsh new penalties.

9. It was late when I got home, so I closed the door _____ (manner) and _____ (manner) got into bed.

10. He said he would finish the job _____ (time).

11. The jokes were _____ (degree) funny.

12. Jose and Maria _____ (frequency) visit their homeland.

13. He is _____ (frequency) late.

14. When we arrived at the hotel, we were _____ (degree) tired.

15. We slept _____ (place) in the basement.

## EXERCISE 10.8

## ADVERBS OF DEGREE

Write ten complete sentences that use adverbs of degree. Underline the word modified.

*Examples:*

*She was very <u>well</u> prepared.*
*The team was extremely <u>tired</u>.*

1.

2.

3.

4.

5.

6.

7.

8.

9.

10.

## 10c Comparative and superlative

An important feature of adjectives and adverbs is to compare and contrast two or more items that are alike in basic features. For example, this sentence is permissible.

My cat is prettier than your dog.

But the following is incorrect.

*My cat is prettier than your house.

The **comparative form** of the adjective or adverb is used in the comparison of two items. The **superlative form** is typically used when comparing more than two items and one is ranked at either extreme of the particular dimension being discussed.

### 1 Basic patterns for the comparative

For adjectives and adverbs of one syllable and two-syllable adjectives ending in -y, the basic pattern is this:

$$\mathbf{A} + \left\{ \begin{array}{l} \text{is} \\ \text{looks} \\ \text{seems} \\ \text{works} \end{array} \right\} \underline{\hspace{2cm}} + \textit{-er than } \mathbf{B}.$$

For -ly adverbs and long adjectives, we use this pattern:

**A** (verb) more _____ than **B**.

### Better/worse, more/less/fewer

We can also use *better/worse* or *more/less/fewer* before nouns to make a comparison.

A small town has fewer people than a big city.

*Than* is used with all comparisons.

## EXERCISE 10.9

## Comparatives

Fill in the blank with the correct comparative form of the adjective in parentheses.

*Example:* That cow is ___*fatter*___ (fat) than this cow.

1. She thinks reading a book is _____ (interesting) than watching sports.

2. My brother is _____ (young) than I.

3. The scenery is even _____ (beautiful) than I remembered.

4. The exam was _____ (difficult) than I expected it to be.

5. The Empire State Building is _____ (tall) than the CitiCorp Building.

6. This painting is _____ (colorful) than that one.

7. The flight was _____ (long) than usual due to inclement weather.

8. Our new home is much _____ (spacious) than our old one.

9. This city is _____ (crowded) than the village where I come from.

10. That singer is _____ (popular) than she used to be.

## EXERCISE 10.10

## COMPARING PLACES

**A.** Write a paragraph comparing where you live now and your native country.

*Example:* Once I lived in Haiti; now I am in New York. Haiti is hotter than New York. New York has more people than Haiti....

**B.** Write a paragraph comparing where you live now to where your grandfather lived. Use the adjectives *crowded, modern, beautiful, big, noisy, interesting,* and *cold.*

*Example:* Our house in Saint Louis is bigger and more modern than Grandfather's hut in Phnom Penh.

**C.** Write another paragraph, comparing where you live now to where your grandfather lived. Use *worse/better* and *more/less/fewer* with the words *traffic, people, job opportunities, tall buildings, climate, rain, crime,* and *pollution.*

*Example:* My grandfather's town had less crime than Detroit but more pollution from heavy industry.

## 2 No comparison

There are a number of adjectives that should not be compared because they represent an absolute state.

| | | |
|---|---|---|
| perfect | unique | universal |
| single | supreme | empty |
| vertical | full | dead |
| final | mortal | wrong |
| straight | blind | fatal |
| instantaneous | impossible | infinite |

Adjectives of shape, such as *round* and *square*, should not be compared either.

## 3 Basic patterns for the superlative

When three or more items are compared, we use the superlative form.

For one-syllable adjectives and adverbs and for two-syllable adjectives ending in *-y*, we use this pattern:

**A** (verb) + *the* _____ *-est.*

For *-ly* adverbs and for long adjectives, use this pattern:

**A** (verb) *the most* _____ .

The definite article *the* must be used before a superlative form.
A prepositional phrase often occurs after a superlative form.

She is the smartest girl in the class.

He read the most interesting story in the book.

## 4   Irregular forms of comparatives and superlatives

Some adjectives have irregular comparative and superlative forms.

| BASE | COMPARATIVE | SUPERLATIVE |
|------|-------------|-------------|
| bad/badly | worse | worst |
| well/good | better | best |
| less | lesser | least |
| little | less/littler | least/littlest |
| far | farther/further | farthest/furthest |
| much | more | most |

## EXERCISE 10.11

## FORMING SUPERLATIVES

Complete each sentence with the proper form of the superlative followed by an appropriate prepositional phrase.

*Example:* He is the _____*tallest*_____ (tall) in _____*the class*_____.

1. That dog is the _____ (large) animal of _____.

2. He has done the _____ (much) work of _____.

3. She is the _____ (intelligent) woman in _____.

4. My brother is the _____ (fast) swimmer on _____.

5. Pollution is one of the _____ (bad) problems in _____.

6. Those roses are the _____ (beautiful) flowers in _____.

7. The job of police officer is one of the _____ (dangerous) in _____.

8. This is the _____ (busy) airport in _____.

9. He thinks *The Simpsons* is the _____ (funny) show on _____.

10. Some people feel that Chinese is the _____ (difficult) language of _____.

# EXERCISE 10.12

## USING THE SUPERLATIVE

Use the superlative to write about the United States on each topic.

*Example:* popular food

*Hamburgers are the most popular food.*

1. popular sport

2. high mountain

3. tall building

4. crowded city

5. popular car

6. common man's name

7. common woman's name

8. hot month

9. cold month

10. big lake

# EXERCISE 10.13

## CHOOSING THE CORRECT SUPERLATIVE

From each group of three, choose the superlative item, and write an appropriate sentence using the adjective in parentheses.

*Example:* (cold) January, March, April

*January is the coldest month.*

1. (big) a cat, a dog, a tiger

2. (slow) a dog, a cat, a turtle

3. (fattening) cream, milk, water

4. (juicy) an orange, a banana, a potato

5. (spicy) bread, a pickle, milk

6. (difficult) physics, chemistry, biology

7. (delicious) chocolate, vanilla, strawberry

8. (strenuous) swimming, running, bicycling

9. (quick) driving, flying, train

10. (relaxing) listening to music, watching television, reading a book

11. (crowded) Chicago, Denver, New York City

12. (sweet) mangoes, oranges, cherries

13. (easy) skipping rope, bouncing a ball, riding a bicycle

14. (beautiful) the sunrise, the sunset, the full moon

15. (hard) a diamond, a pearl, gold

## EXERCISE 10.14

## COMPARISONS WITH *MORE*, *LESS,* AND *FEWER*

For each group of words, write two sentences making comparisons using *more*, *less*, and *fewer*.

*Example:*   cholesterol, an egg, a piece of bread

*An egg has more cholesterol than a piece of bread.*

*A piece of bread has less cholesterol than an egg.*

1. artificial additives, processed foods, organic foods

2. fat, fish, pork

3. vitamins, an orange, a piece of candy

4. calories, an egg, a glass of water


5. sugar, candy, a piece of bread


## EXERCISE 10.15

## WRITING WITH SUPERLATIVES

Write three complete sentences that answer each question.

1. What are the three best things about this school?


2. What are the three worst things about this school?


3. What are the three best things about this country?


4. What are the three worst things about this country?


5. What are the three best things about this city?

6. What are the three worst things about this city?

7. What are the three best things about your native country?

8. What are the three worst things about your country?

9. What are the three best things about yourself?

10. What are the three worst things about yourself?

## EXERCISE 10.16

## USING COMPARATIVES AND SUPERLATIVES

Circle the correct form of the word in parentheses.

Yesterday was a (*perfect, perfecter*) day. It was the (*good, best*) day of our vacation so far. The (*worse, worst*) day was Tuesday. That was the day it rained, and things went from (*bad, worse*) to (*bad, worse*) all day. First we had a flat; that tire was the (*flatter, flattest*) tire I ever saw! Then we got a ticket for an expired registration, but (*worse, worst*) of all, we were late for dinner.

Tomorrow we'll drive a little (*far, farther*) to the lake and stay there for a few days.

## 5  Comparative questions

We frequently use three different types of questions to make comparisons.

1.  We can use information questions with *who*, *which*, and *whose*.

> Who is better at math, this boy or that girl?
>
> Which exercise is more strenuous, yoga or running?
>
> Whose book is this, yours or mine?

2.  We may use the yes/no question form.

> Do professors rank higher than instructors?
>
> Is physics harder than calculus?

3.  We can use the yes/no question form with *as . . . as*.

> Is New York as large as Tennessee?
>
> Does the heat affect you as much as it affects me?

## EXERCISE 10.17

## COMPARATIVES IN QUESTIONS

Use the adjective in parentheses to write three questions, each of a different form, comparing the items given.

*Example:*  (busy) Broadway, Main Street

*Which is busier, Broadway or Main Street?*
*Is Broadway busier than Main Street?*
*Is Broadway as busy as Main Street?*

1.  (neat) Mr. Smith, Mrs. Smith

2. (interesting) algebra, biology

3. (athletic) Jose, George

4. (sociable) a cat, a dog

5. (heavy) an elephant, a zebra

<h2>6    Comparison of nouns</h2>

It is possible to compare the number or amount of two nouns. To express the idea of more, we use this pattern

*more* + plural noun + *than* + noncount noun

Texas has more oil wells than Ohio.

A cafeteria has more food than a refreshment stand.

To express the idea of less there are two patterns:

1. *not* + *as many/as much* + plural or noncount noun + *as*

   There aren't as many people in a small town as in a large city.

   There isn't as much water in a lake as in an ocean.

2. *fewer* + plural noun + *than*
   *less* + noncount noun + *than*

   A small town has fewer people than a large city.

   A lake has less water than an ocean.

## EXERCISE 10.18

## COMPARING NOUNS

Using the patterns for comparing nouns, compare two places you know. Use the words given.

*Example:* big buildings

*Los Angeles has more big buildings than San Jose.*
*San Jose does not have as many big buildings as Los Angeles.*

1. pollution

2. cultural life

3. noise

4. traffic

5. crime

6. hospitals

7. people


8. public transportation


9. nightlife


10. music


## EXERCISE 10.19

## USING ADVERBS AND COMPARATIVES

Fill in each blank with the correct form of the adverb or the comparative form of the adverb, adjective, or noun. The first one has been done for you as an example.

People throughout the world are now becoming _more_ _concerned than_ (concerned) in the past about environmental issues. One of _____ (serious) problems today is the greenhouse effect. Every day, power plants, cars, and factories are releasing _____ (great) amounts of gases into the air. These gases become trapped in the atmosphere above, creating a layer of heat like a giant greenhouse. As a result, our planet is now heating up _____ (fast) in the past.

Countries with warm climates are feeling the effects of rising temperatures _____ (seriously) those with cold climates. This global warming trend is also creating _____ (floods, droughts, and storms) before.

Temperatures are becoming _____ (warm) before, and the ultraviolet rays of the sun are becoming _____ (strong). The rate of skin cancer from exposure to the sun is increasing _____ (rapid).

The more gases we release into the air, the _____ (bad) the greenhouse effect becomes. The only way to curtail this effect is to _____ (immediate) make some adjustments in our lifestyle. Car exhaust fumes create _____ (pollution) any other single source, so by taking _____ (few) car trips, we gain _____ (clean) air. Carpooling and public transportation are the _____ (good) ways to reduce the number of automobiles on the road.

We must become _____ (conscious) of our environment and learn to make choices in the energy we use. Air conditioners use much _____ (energy) electric fans. Disposable diapers create _____ (significant) _____ (waste and pollution) cloth diapers.

The _____ (efficient) we use any source of power, the _____ (good) it will be for the environment. If everyone is _____ (careful) about using electricity, the amount of harmful gases going into the air will decrease.

Some countries have _____ (environmental laws) others. The industrialized nations of Western Europe have _____ (extensive) environmental programs in the world.

## 10d Equality, similarity, difference

### 1 Equality of adjectives and adverbs

By using the following pattern with adjectives and adverbs, we can say that two items are equal or not equal.

**A** (verb) as _____ as **B**.

Jose is as old as I.

Jose does not run as fast as I.

## EXERCISE 10.20

## EQUALITY OF ADJECTIVES AND ADVERBS

Using the words in parentheses, compare two people. Add a comparative statement if there is inequality.

*Examples:*  (fast), equality

*Jose runs as fast as Elmer.*

(old), inequality

*Maria is not as old as Esperanza.*
*Esperanza is older.*

1. (quiet), inequality

2. (lazy), equality

3. (strong), inequality

4. (big), equality

5. (educated), inequality

6. (friendly), inequality

7. (responsible), equality

8. (honest), equality

9. (patient), inequality

10. (talkative), inequality

**2** **Equality of nouns**

By using the following patterns with nouns, we can say that two items are equal or not equal.

$$\textbf{A} \left\{ \begin{array}{l} \text{is/is not} \\ \text{has/does not have} \end{array} \right\} \text{ the same } \underline{\hspace{2cm}} \text{ as } \textbf{B.}$$

$$\textbf{A and B} \left\{ \begin{array}{l} \text{are/are not} \\ \text{have/do not have} \end{array} \right\} \text{ the same } \underline{\hspace{2cm}}.$$

A lemon has the same shape as a lime.

A lemon and a lime do not have the same shape.

### EXERCISE 10.21

### EQUALITY OF NOUNS

Considering the topics given, compare yourself to another student in the class, following the appropriate pattern in the example. If inequality is expressed, add a qualifying statement.

*Examples:* (age)

*Jose and I are the same age.*

*Jose and I are not the same age. He is older than I.*

1. nationality

2. height

3. religion

4. age

5. weight

## EXERCISE 10.22

## NEGATIVES AND AFFIRMATIVES

Make a negative or an affirmative statement with the words given; use the appropriate pattern in the example.

*Examples:*    an apple and a peach

(*size/be*)

*An apple and a peach are the same size.*

beer and soda

(*ingredients/have*)

*Beer and soda do not have the same ingredients.*

1. an orange and an apple

   (*color/by*)

   (*size/be*)

   (*shape/be*)

2. bread and cheese

   (*price/be*)

   (*ingredients/have*)

   (*package/have*)


3. a nickel and a quarter

   (*size/be*)

   (*shape/be*)

   (*value/have*)


4. my instructor and I

   (*nationality/be*)

   (*age/be*)

   (*height/be*)


5. a banana and a peach

   (*shape/be*)

   (*color/be*)

   (*price/have*)

## 3 Similarity and difference

To indicate that two items are the same or different, we use these patterns:

**A** is the same as **B**.
**A** and **B** are the same.

A sentence is the same as an independent clause.
A sentence and an independent clause are the same.

**A** is different from **B**.
**A** and **B** are different.

A sentence is different from a fragment.
A sentence and a fragment are different.

## EXERCISE 10.23

## SIMILARITY AND DIFFERENCE

Tell if the two words are the same or different. Use both patterns for each pair.

*Example:*   big, large

*Big is the same as large.*
*Big and large are the same.*

1. winter, summer

2. little, small

3. sell, buy

4. stupid, ignorant

5. my name, my instructor's name

**4**  **Similarity of appearance**

To indicate that two items are the same in appearance, we use these patterns:

**A** looks like **B**.
**A** and **B** look alike.

A horse looks like a donkey.
A horse and a donkey look alike.

## EXERCISE 10.24

## SIMILARITY OF APPEARANCE

Answer each question accurately.

*Examples:*  Do horses look like donkeys?

*Yes, horses look like donkeys.*

Do cows look like horses?

*No, cows do not look like horses.*

OR

*No, cows and horses do not look alike.*

1. Do you look like your instructor?

2. Do you look like your mother?

3. Does a cat look like a dog?

4. Does water look like cola?

5. Do people from your country look like people from the United States?

**5** **Other similar aspects**

To indicate that two items are similar in ways other than appearance, we use the relevant sense perception words.

**A** smells like **B**.
**A** and **B** smell alike.

**A** tastes like **B**.
**A** and **B** taste alike.

**A** sounds like **B**.
**A** and **B** sound alike.

Coca-Cola tastes like Pepsi-Cola.
Coke and Pepsi taste alike.

We can also use the following pattern to indicate that two items are similar in some way:

**A** is like **B**. They are both _____.

Jose is like Maria. They are both hard workers.

## EXERCISE 10.25

## SIMILARITY PERCEIVED THROUGH THE SENSES

First, form a question using the words given. Then write an answer to it.

*Example:* taste, water, soda

*Does water taste like soda?*
*No, water does not taste like soda.*

OR

*No, water and soda do not taste alike.*

1. taste, Pepsi-Cola, Coca-Cola


2. look, salt, sugar


3. sound, the radio, a live voice


4. smell, coffee, tea


5. feel, cotton, leather

# CHAPTER 11
# Phrasal Verbs and Other Idioms

## 11a Idioms

**Idioms** and **idiomatic expressions**, including phrasal verbs, are an important part of normal English. An idiom is a phrase that has a meaning that cannot be understood from the individual meanings of its components.

An idiom is peculiar to itself and cannot be translated literally from one language to another without some change in the meaning or connotation. Since each idiom has such a peculiar meaning, it must be studied as a separate vocabulary item.

## 11b Phrasal verbs

Two- and three-word verbs, called **phrasal verbs**, are the most common idioms. These verbs are altered in meaning by the addition of one or two prepositionlike words known as **particles** that do not function as prepositions. Here are some phrasals using the verb *break*:

*break down*, to stop working

*break in*, to adapt something new through use; to train a new employee

*break into*, to enter by force

*break loose*, to become free, escape

*break off*, to terminate; to remove a piece

*break out*, to occur suddenly

*break up*, to divide completely into small pieces

A phrasal verb may be either *separable* or *nonseparable*. If the particle is nonseparable, the two parts always occur together.

I came across that book yesterday.

We cannot say:

*I came that book across yesterday.

If the particle is separable, a direct object or complement may come between the verb and the particle. The separation is obligatory when the direct object is a pronoun. In general, the shorter and simpler the direct object is, the more likely it is for the verb and particle to be split.

OPTIONAL    He backed the car up. / He backed up the car.

MANDATORY   He backed it up.


## 1  Nonseparable phrasal verbs

### Verb + particle + object

1. Some verbs take a particle only if an object follows.

*decide on*, to choose
Have you decided on your schedule yet?

*hear about*, to hear the news
I heard about the accident.

*hear of*, to recognize the name
She had never heard of Frederick Douglass.

*insist on*, to require
The teacher insists on neat papers.

*listen to*, to hear a sound; obey
I listened to the music.
Children should always listen to their parents.

*look at*, to use the eyes to see
He looked at the pictures.

*look for*, to search for
I looked for you all over.

*wait for*, to stay and wait
He waited for the bus in front of the building.

2. If an object does not follow these verbs, the particle is not used.

What happened last night?

I haven't heard.

What did she say?

I wasn't listening

3. In informal information questions, we leave the particle after the verb:

What does she insist on?

In formal written information questions, the particle precedes the *wh* word.

On what does she insist?

## EXERCISE 11.1

## NONSEPARABLE PHRASAL VERBS

Fill in each blank with the correct particle.

*Example:*  He was looking _____ *at* _____ his watch.

1. I always listen _____ my older brother's advice.

2. Did you decide _____ a career yet?

3. If you can't wait _____ the final report, insist _____ a preliminary one.

4. If you are looking _____ a job, go to the counseling office.

5. He said he never heard _____ Mayor Young.

6. Esperanza heard _____ the earthquake.

7. I was listening _____ Mozart when you called.

8. The teacher insists _____ typed reports.

9. She asked us to wait _____ her right here.

10. Maria has decided _____ nursing as her major.

**No object**

Some phrasal verbs are not followed by an object.

*come back*, to return to a place
I always come back at eight o'clock.

*come over*, to visit someone's home
I asked them to come over.

*get up*, to arise
She finds it hard to get up in the morning.

*go back*, to return to a place
He always goes back to his own country.

*go on*, to proceed to the next; happen
We went on to Buffalo after stopping in Rochester.
The war went on for two years.

*keep away*, to stay at a distance
Children should keep away from dangerous places.

*keep on* + (verb) + *-ing*, to continue with the same
The teacher urged us to keep on trying.

*show off*, to attract attention by flaunting an ability or a possession
He showed off his new red convertible.

*show up*, to arrive
Jose showed up at five o'clock.

*watch out*, to be careful
If you drive at night, you should watch out for stray dogs.

## EXERCISE 11.2

## PHRASALS WITH NO OBJECTS

Fill in each blank with the appropriate particle.

*Example:*  After the climb, she couldn't go _____*on*_____ with the hike.

1. When the teacher is sick, he doesn't show _____ for the class.

2. Keep _____ from squirrels.

3. When you finish Exercise 2, go _____ to Exercise 3.

4. Some rich kids show _____ their money and possessions.

5. Tonight I'll go _____ to the school for practice.

6. She came _____ to my house yesterday.

7. At crosswalks, it's important to watch _____ for cars.

8. When I went _____ to my country, everything seemed different.

9. She told us to keep _____ studying for the exam.

10. I usually get _____ at 6:00 A.M.

### Three-word combinations

These verbs use two particles.

*drop out of*, to leave school, leave a course before finishing
She dropped out of high school.

*get along with*, to have a good relationship with
Elmer gets along with his parents.

*get rid of*, to free oneself from something undesirable
I got rid of that old car and bought a new one.

*get through with*, to finish
I can't wait to get through with my math.

*keep up with*, to maintain the same pace or level
She can keep up with the boys when running.

*look forward to*, to anticipate with pleasure
We are looking forward to our summer vacation.

*look/think back on*, to remember past events
When I see that picture, I always think back on my childhood days.

*make sure of*, to check, verify
The clerk makes sure of the receipts.

*run out of*, to exhaust the supply of, finish
Zora ran out of money before she finished shopping.

*talk back to*, to answer impolitely
Never talk back to the teacher.

## EXERCISE 11.3

## THREE-WORD PHRASAL VERBS

**A.** Fill in each blank with the appropriate particle.

*Example:* We ran ____*out*____ ____*of*____ sugar at dinner.

1. The boy was angry and talked _____ _____ his mother.

2. I couldn't get _____ _____ my old aches and pains.

3. The car ran _____ _____ gas half-way home.

4. I like to think _____ _____ my high-school days.

5. Because of illness, she had to drop _____ _____ the class.

6. I always keep _____ _____ the work in math.

7. When I got _____ _____ the laundry, I started the cleaning.

8. When you do the homework, make _____ _____ the spelling and punctuation.

9. We all get _____ _____ our instructor.

10. I look _____ _____ seeing you.

**B.** Change each expression in italics to a three-word phrasal verb.

*Example:*   He *was impolite to* the teacher.

*He talked back to the teacher.*

1. The teacher forbids food in class, so we have to *remove* it.

2. I won't finish my homework if I *exhaust* all the time.

3. Many students *don't finish* high school.

4. If you get sick, you may not be able to *maintain the same pace with* the rest of us.

5. Some students *respond impolitely* to the teacher.

6. Do you *have a good relationship with* your parents?

7. When we *finish* the course, we'll know a lot more about American history.

8. Always *check* the total when you are adding a long column of figures.

9. He likes to *remember* his childhood days.

10. Before your father comes home, you'll have to *remove* that garbage.

## 2 | Separable combinations

There are hundreds of separable phrasal verb combinations. The following is a list of some common ones. Refer to the master list at the end of the chapter for a more complete listing.

Remember, if the particle is separable, a direct object or complement may come between the verb and the particle. The separation is obligatory when the direct object is a pronoun. In general, the shorter and simpler the direct object is, the more likely it is for the verb and particle to be split.

*bring up*, to suggest; raise a question.
He always brings up the past in arguments.

*bring up*, to raise children
He brought them up as if they were his own children.

*call off*, to cancel
He wondered if they called off the game.

*call up*, to telephone
She told me to call her up tonight.

*do over*, to repeat a job
I told her to do her homework over.

*fill out*, to complete an application or a form
He told me to fill out the application.

*fill up*, to fill to capacity
When my car's tank is empty, I fill it up with unleaded gas.

*give back*, to return something
After reviewing the essays, the teacher always gives them back to us.

*hand/turn in*, to submit an assignment
Did you hand the test in?
Yes, I turned it in to the teacher.

*hang up*, to put on a hanger or a hook
When we arrived, we hung our coats up.

*have on*, to be wearing
He has on a beautiful gold wristwatch.

*hold up*, to delay
Sometimes that red light holds up traffic.

*leave out*, to omit
He left the answer out by mistake.

*look over*, to examine, check
He told us to look the test over and then to answer all the questions.

*look up*, to search for in a listing
When you want to know the spelling of a word, look it up in a dictionary.

*make up*, to do work missed
When you miss an assignment, you must make it up promptly.

*make up*, to invent a story, lie
Sometimes when I'm late, I make up an excuse.

*pick out*, to choose, select
Looking through the seed catalogs, we picked out some varieties for planting.

*point out*, to call attention to
The instructor points out our most blatant mistakes.

*put off*, to postpone
They put off their appointment until ten o'clock.

*put on*, to dress oneself with
She bought the shoes and put them on in the store.

*put out*, to extinguish
If you have a cigarette, put it out before entering the classroom.

*read over*, to check for accuracy, review
Before sending the letter, he read it over one last time.

*take/write down*, to note on paper
I can tell you his number; take/write it down.

*take off*, to remove clothing
When my shoes are muddy, I take them off in the hallway.

*talk over*, to discuss
When we have a problem, we talk it over among ourselves.

*try on*, to put on clothing to see if it fits
When I buy a new suit, I try it on for size.

*try out*, to test
Did you try out the new model of that car?

*turn down*, to lower the volume
When the phone rings, I turn down the TV.

*turn off*, to switch off the electricity
When leaving a room, I always turn off the lights.

*turn on*, to switch on the electricity
She asked me to turn on the radio.

*use up*, to consume completely
I used up all the soap.

## EXERCISE 11.4

### SEPARABLE PHRASAL VERBS

Some particles are common and consistent in their meaning. For example, *up* gives a sense of completion in *tear up, mix up, wind up, cut up, break up, chop up, chew up, eat up, clean up, dress up,* and *tie up.* The same is true of *out, off,* and *down*—they give a sense of completion and finality in *wear out, fade out, turn out, burn down, run down, call off, cut off,* and *turn off.*

Fill in each blank with the correct verb from the ones listed. Be sure it is in the correct tense.

*Example:*   She was so angry that she _____*tore*_____ the paper up.

1. That old building _____ down in a fire many years ago.

2. Jose _____ off the TV when he went to bed.

3. We wanted to _____ up the job by Saturday.

4. After a few years, his favorite shoes _____ out.

5. At dusk, the light gradually _____ out, and it becomes dark.

6. The field was wet, so they _____ off the game.

7. The boys were so hungry that they _____ up all the food.

8. She _____ up the entire mess.

9. When eating, it's best to _____ up the food completely.

10. He used a hammer to _____ up the wall entirely.

## EXERCISE 11.5

### SEPARABLE PHRASAL VERBS

Fill in each blank with the correct form of one of the verbs listed.

*Example:*   My old sneakers were _____ *worn out* _____

1. (*pick out, try on, take off, put on, wear out*)

I wear sneakers so often, they tend to _____ _____. So before the new school year began, I went to the store and _____ _____ a few pairs of sneakers from the rack. Then I sat down to _____ them _____. First I _____ _____ my old shoes. Then I _____ _____ three different pairs of new sneakers. I bought some white ones.

2. (*call up, hang up, pick up*)

Last night, I _____ _____ my friend Elmer to get the football scores. After three rings, he _____ _____ the phone and answered. I asked him for the scores. After he gave them to me, I _____ _____ the telephone.

## EXERCISE 11.6

## PHRASAL VERBS

**A.** Rewrite each sentence, replacing the words in italics with a phrasal verb. Use the verbs *look into, look up, put on, read over, take down, take off, turn on,* and *turn off.*

1. Sasha decided to *study* the history of a certain disease.

2. She went to her adviser, who told her to *find* more information *in a special book* at the library.

3. Sasha *placed* her hat and coat *on her body* and walked across campus.

4. When she arrived at the library, she *removed* her coat.

5. She went to the reference room, *operated* the light, and got the book.

6. In a few minutes, she *made a quick review of* all of the information.

7. She *noted* some of the information *on paper*.

8. When she left the room, she *extinguished* the light.

**B.** Rewrite each sentence, replacing the words in italics with a phrasal verb. Use the verbs *clean up* or *straighten up*, *drive off*, *pack up*, and *put out*.

1. Be sure to *rearrange* the campsite *neatly*.

2. If you built a fire, be sure to *extinguish* it.

3. Then *neatly gather* all the equipment and load it in your car.

4. *Depart in your vehicle* before the gates close at dark.

**C.** Fill in each blank with a phrasal verb. Use the verbs *bring up*, *call up*, *fill out*, *leave out*, *look over*, *point out*, *put off*, *read over*, *talk over*, and *turn in*. Some verbs may be used more than once.

In April, all taxpayers have to _____

_____ a 1040 form for income taxes. Before you

_____ it _____, _____

the instructions _____ carefully. Answer all the

questions, and don't _____ _____

any information.

You may _____ _____ the Inter-

nal Revenue Service if you have any questions. Or you may want

to _____ _____ your tax concerns

with an accountant. _____ your questions

_____ with the accountant. The accountant should

be able to _____ _____ ways to save

you money. After the accountant _____

_____ the form for you, _____ it

_____ before you sign.

Remember, you must _____ _____

your income tax return by midnight on April 15. Don't

_____ it _____ until the last minute!

## EXERCISE 11.7

## MORE PHRASAL VERBS

Rewrite each sentence correctly, incorporating the phrasal verb
and noun or pronoun combinations indicated. Remember that the shorter
the direct object, the more likely it is that the phrasal verb is separated.

*Example:* Look at this picture; I just (*it, come across*) in the library.

*Look at this picture; I just came across it in the library.*

1. Take this hammer and (*it, put away*); just (*it, hang up*) on the wall.

2. Please come in, (*your coat, take off*), and (*this smock, put on*).

3. He asked me to (*the form, look over*) and help him (*it, fill out*).

4. He (*two pairs of shoes, pick out*), (*them, try on*), and paid for them.

5. He (*Veronica, call up*), but she didn't answer, so he (*the phone, hang up*).

6. Gerald (*the information, look up*) and (*it, write down*) on a piece of paper.


## EXERCISE 11.8

## FORMS OF PHRASAL VERBS

Rewrite each sentence, using the correct phrasal verb idiom for each italicized verb, changing other words as necessary. If the phrasal verb is separable, write the sentence in two ways.

*Examples:* John *used* all his time; he had no time left.

*John ran out of time.*

John *found* the new word in his dictionary.

*John looked up the new word in his dictionary.*

*John looked the new word up in his dictionary.*

1. I will *investigate* the matter for you.

2. Do you want to *remove* your overcoat?

3. We *used* our water completely yesterday; we had no more left.

4. That child *invents* unusual stories.

5. I want to know the movie schedule; I will *find* the schedule in my newspaper.

6. If you don't pay your bill, the telephone company will *make* your telephone *stop*.

7. I will *note* your telephone number *on paper* because I don't want to forget it.

8. I want to watch a program. Please *make* the TV *start* working.

9. The teacher *reviewed* my composition quickly.

10. You should *cover your body with* a raincoat when it rains.


## EXERCISE 11.9

## PHRASAL VERBS AND OBJECTS

In each sentence, replace the direct object noun phrase in italics with the appropriate pronoun.

*Example:*   Hand the homework in on time.

*Hand it in on time.*

1. Take *the assignment* down.


2. Look *your paper* over carefully.


3. Don't leave *the students* out.


4. The professor will ask you to do *your homework* over.


5. Talk *your questions* over with an adviser.


6. The teacher will give *your papers* back.


7. Look *the new words* up in the dictionary.


8. Make *an assignment* up if you are absent that day.


9. Look *your schedule* over.


10. Call *the teacher* up if you will miss more than one class.

# LIST OF PHRASAL VERBS AND IDIOMS

An asterisk (*) indicates that the phrasal is separable.

| IDIOM OR PHRASAL VERB | MEANING |
|---|---|
| above all | mainly, especially |
| according to | agreeing with, on the authority of |
| all at once | suddenly, without warning |
| all day | continuously throughout the day |
| all in all | everything taken into account, all things considered |
| all of a sudden | abruptly, without warning |
| all right | yes, satisfactory, correct |
| as a matter of fact | in fact, really |
| ask for | to bring something bad upon oneself |
| as soon as | just after, when |
| as to | concerning, with reference to |
| as usual | as always, customarily |
| as yet | up to the present time, as of now |
| at all | to any degree, in the least (used in a negative sense with *not* or *hardly*) |
| at first | originally, in the first instance |
| at last | finally, after a long time |
| at least | a minimum of, no fewer or less than |
| at once | immediately, right away |
| at times | sometimes, occasionally |
| back and forth | backward and forward |
| back out | to withdraw, fail to fulfill a promise or an obligation |
| back up* | to put a car in reverse, drive or move backward |
| be about to | to be at the point of, ready to |
| bear in mind | not to forget, remember |
| be a steal | to be a bargain |
| beat around the bush | to approach indirectly |
| be better off | to be in a more favorable or improved condition or situation |
| be bound to | be certain to, sure to |
| be carried away* | to be greatly affected by a strong feeling |
| become of | to happen to |
| be cut out for | to be designed for, have talent for |
| be cut out to be | to be designed for, have talent for |
| be had | to be victimized or cheated |
| be in | to be currently popular and fashionable |
| be in charge of | to manage, be responsible for |
| be into* | to have as an interest, particularly a study or style |
| believe in | to accept as true, have faith in the existence of |

| IDIOM OR PHRASAL VERB | MEANING |
|---|---|
| be looking up | to be improving |
| be mixed up | to be confused |
| be named after | to be given the same name as someone else |
| be out | to be no longer fashionable or popular |
| be out of the question | to be impossible, unthinkable |
| be over | to be finished, ended |
| be rained out | to be postponed or called off on account of rain |
| be set | to be ready, prepared to do something |
| be the matter | to be wrong or troubling |
| be up | to be ended (said only of time) |
| be up for grabs | to be on the open market and available to the highest bidder |
| be up to (someone) | to depend on the decision or responsibility of someone |
| be up to (something) | to be planning or plotting something, scheming |
| be used to | to be accustomed to |
| be well off | to be rich |
| be with (someone) | to understand or follow another person's conversation or ideas |
| big deal | very important (usually said scornfully or sarcasticllay) |
| bite off* more than one can chew | to take on too great a responsibility |
| blow out | to explode, go flat (said generally of tires) |
| blow up* | to destroy by explosion, explode |
| bow out | to remove oneself from a situation, quit |
| break down | to stop working; to lose one's composure |
| break in* | to adopt something new and stiff through use; to train a new employee |
| break into | to enter by force |
| break loose | to become free, escape |
| break off* | to terminate, put an end to; to remove (a piece or section of something) |
| break out | to occur suddenly |
| break up* | to crumble into many small pieces |
| bring about* | to cause to happen |
| bring back* | to return |
| bring out* | to produce, present |
| bring up* | to raise from childhood; to present for attention or consideration |
| bug | to annoy or disturb |
| build up* | to increase, make stronger |
| burn down* | to burn to the ground |
| burn up* | to burn completely |
| burst out crying | to begin suddenly to cry |
| burst out laughing | to begin suddenly to laugh |
| buy it | to accept or approve of an idea |

| IDIOM OR PHRASAL VERB | MEANING |
| --- | --- |
| buy out* | to buy a business |
| buy up* | to buy the complete stock of |
| by heart | by memory |
| by oneself | alone; independently |
| by the way | incidentally |
| | |
| call for | to go and get; to require |
| call it a day | to stop work on any activity for the day |
| call off* | to cancel |
| call on | to visit; to pick (someone) to answer a question |
| call up | to telephone |
| can't help (but) | be compelled to, unable to avoid |
| carry on | to continue as before; to behave in an uncontrolled manner |
| carry out* | to accomplish, execute |
| catch cold | to become sick |
| catch fire | to begin to burn |
| catch on | grasp the meaning |
| catch up | to bring up to date |
| change one's mind | to alter one's decision |
| check in | to register at a hotel |
| check out | to pay one's hotel bill and leave |
| check (up) on | to examine, inspect |
| cheer up* | to make happier |
| clear up* | to become clear |
| clue (someone) in | to give one information |
| come about | to happen |
| come across | to meet or find unexpectedly |
| come from | to originate in |
| come to | to regain consciousness |
| come to an end | to cease |
| come true | to prove to be true or correct |
| cop out on | to withdraw from or abandon |
| count on | to depend on |
| cover a lot of ground | to discuss several matters |
| cover for | to take responsibility for another person's duties |
| cover up | to conceal |
| crack a book | to study |
| cross out* | to cancel |
| cut in | to interrupt |
| cut off* | to terminate abruptly; to shorten by cutting |
| cut out* | to stop doing something; to remove by cutting |
| cut short* | to make shorter; to interrupt |
| cut up* | to cut into pieces |
| | |
| day after day | daily |
| day in and day out | every day |

| IDIOM OR PHRASAL VERB | MEANING |
| --- | --- |
| die down | to lessen in intensity |
| dish out* | to distribute in large quantity |
| do a snow job | to deceive someone |
| do over* | to repeat |
| do without | to get along without |
| draw up* | to prepare documents or legal papers |
| dream up* | to invent |
| drive up to | to approach by driving |
| drop in (on) | to visit unexpectedly |
| drop off | to fall asleep |
| drop off* | to take to and leave at a certain location |
| drop out of | to cease attending |
| drop (someone) a line* | to write briefly to someone |
| dry out* | to become dry gradually |
| dry run | rehearsal |
| dry up* | to dry completely |
| ease (someone) out | to discharge (an employee) gently |
| eat in | to eat at home |
| eat out | to eat in a restaurant |
| eat up* | to eat everything |
| every now and then | occasionally |
| every so often | occasionally |
| face to face | looking directly at someone |
| fade away | to diminish gradually |
| fall behind | to fail to keep up, lag |
| fall in love | to begin to love |
| fall off | fall from; to decrease in volume |
| fall through | to collapse, fail to happen |
| feel like | to have the desire to |
| feel sorry for | to pity |
| fifty-fifty | divided or split in two equal portions |
| figure out* | to study carefully in order to understand |
| fill in | to supply what is missing |
| fill in* | give background information |
| fill out | to gain weight |
| fill out* | to complete (paperwork) |
| find fault with | to criticize |
| find out | to learn, discover |
| fix up* | to repair or put in order; to arrange a date for another person |
| fool around | to spend time foolishly |
| for good | forever |
| for sure | without doubt |
| for the time being | for now |
| fringe benefit | something valuable that an employee gets in addition to salary |
| get along with | to not argue or fight with |
| get a rise out of | to provoke anger in |

| Idiom or phrasal verb | Meaning |
|---|---|
| get away | to leave, escape |
| get away with | to escape without punishment |
| get back* | to return |
| get better | to improve |
| get busy | to become busy |
| get carried away* | to be affected by a strong feeling |
| get even with | to take revenge on |
| get into the swing of things | to adapt to a new environment |
| get in touch with | to communicate with |
| get lost | to lose one's direction; to leave at once |
| get mixed up* | to become confused |
| get off | to descend from |
| get on | to advance |
| get (one's) own way | to obtain what one wishes |
| get on (someone's) nerves | to annoy |
| get out from under | to recover from debt |
| get out of line | to disobey |
| get over | to recover from an illness or sorrow |
| get rid of | to become free of |
| get stuck with | to be burdened with |
| get the better of | to gain the advantage over |
| get through | to finish |
| get through to | to communicate with |
| get to | to arrive |
| get up | to arise (from bed) |
| get used to | to become accustomed to |
| give a big hand | to clap hands enthusiastically |
| give a break | to give a chance |
| give birth to | to bring forth a child |
| give in | to surrender |
| give off | to release, produce |
| give out* | to distribute |
| give (someone) a call* | to telephone |
| give up* | to surrender |
| glance over* | to read quickly from beginning to end |
| go around | to be sufficient for everyone |
| go in for | to have an interest in |
| go off | to explode; to wander away |
| go off the deep end | to do something hastily or rashly |
| goof off | to neglect one's duties |
| go on | to continue, proceed |
| go out | to leave; to cease burning |
| go through | to endure, experience |
| go through channels | to make a request or a complaint through the proper procedure |
| go through with | to put into effect |
| go to town | to do something elaborately |
| go up to | to approach |

**11b/Phrasal Verbs    339**

| IDIOM OR PHRASAL VERB | MEANING |
|---|---|
| go with | to keep company with, date |
| go without | to get along without |
| go without saying | to be obvious |
| go wrong | to turn out badly |
| grow out of | to outgrow |
| had better | is advisable to |
| hand in* | to submit, turn over |
| hang up* | to place on a hook or a hanger; to replace the telephone in its cradle |
| hard of hearing | partly deaf |
| have a good time | to enjoy oneself |
| have a voice in | to have some say in |
| have got* | to possess |
| have got to | must |
| have it in for | to dislike or hold a grudge against |
| have it out with | to quarrel |
| have on* | to be wearing |
| have one's heart set on | to desire greatly |
| have one's way | to do what one wishes |
| have something going | to be successful in some undertaking |
| have time off | to have free time |
| have to do with | to have some connection with |
| have two strikes against one | to be at a disadvantage |
| have what it takes | to be successful |
| hear from | to receive news from |
| hear of | to learn about |
| hold off | to delay |
| hold on | to keep a tight hold; to pause |
| hold out | to continue in supply |
| hold over* | to continue, prolong |
| hold still* | to remain quiet without moving |
| hold up* | to rob at gunpoint; to delay |
| in a hurry | in a rush |
| in case | if it happens that |
| inside out | with the inner surface turned to the outside |
| in the long run | after a long time |
| in the way | causing inconvenience by obstructing |
| in the worst way | very much |
| in time | soon enough |
| in vain | useless |
| it figures | it seems likely |
| keep an eye on | to watch carefully |
| keep away from* | to stay away from |
| keep good time | to be accurate (said of timepieces) |
| keep in mind* | to remember |
| keep in touch with | to continue communicating with |
| keep off* | to stay off |

| Idiom or phrasal verb | Meaning |
| --- | --- |
| keep on | to continue |
| keep one's head | to remain calm under stress |
| keep out* | to stay out |
| keep track of | to keep a record of |
| keep up* | to continue at the same speed or level |
| keep up with | to maintain the same speed as |
| kick a habit | to end or change a habit |
| kick (something) around | to discuss informally |
| knock off* | to stop doing something objectionable |
| knock out* | to render unconscious with a strong blow |
| know by sight* | to recognize |
| land on one's feet | to recover safely from a bad situation |
| lay off* | to discharge from a job due to lack of work |
| leave alone* | to stay away from |
| leave open* | to defer a decision until after further discussion |
| let alone* | not to mention |
| let go* | to release |
| let on | to reveal what one knows |
| let slide* | to neglect a duty |
| let up | to lessen in intensity |
| lie down | to recline |
| line up* | to stand on line |
| little by little | gradually |
| live in | to live in the home where one works as a servant |
| live it up | to live in luxury |
| live up to | to fulfill, carry out |
| look after | to take care of |
| look at | to watch |
| look down on | to regard as less important |
| look for | to search for |
| look forward to | to anticipate with pleasure |
| look into | to examine carefully |
| look out | to be careful |
| look out on | to face, overlook |
| look over* | to examine |
| look up* | to search for in a book |
| look up to | to admire |
| lose one's cool | to get excited or angry |
| lose one's head | to lose one's self-control |
| lose one's touch | to decline in a skill |
| make clear* | to explain |
| make do | to manage with an inferior substitute |
| make faces | to show a scornful or unpleasant expression |
| make friends with | to get acquainted with |
| make fun of | to laugh at |
| make good | to succeed |

| IDIOM OR PHRASAL VERB | MEANING |
|---|---|
| make good time* | to travel at high speed |
| make no difference | to be unimportant |
| make out | to succeed; to kiss passionately |
| make out* | to decipher |
| make room for | to create space for |
| make sense | to be reasonable, logical |
| make (someone) tick | to motivate |
| make sure of | to be certain of |
| make the best of | to accept a bad situation cheerfully |
| make up | to become reconciled after a quarrel |
| make up* | to compensate for an absence; to tell a story or an untruth; to apply cosmetics |
| make up one's mind | to decide |
| make waves | to create a disturbance |
| meet (someone) halfway | to compromise |
| mind the store | to be in charge |
| miss the boat | to lose an opportunity |
| mix up* | to confuse |
| more or less | approximately |
| never mind | don't worry about it |
| no matter | regardless |
| not on your life | absolutely not |
| now and then | occasionally |
| of course | in the natural order of things |
| off and on | occasionally |
| once and for all | definitively |
| once in a while | occasionally |
| on hand | available |
| on purpose | intentionally |
| on the ball | attentive |
| on the double | quickly |
| on the whole | in general |
| on time | exactly at an appointed time |
| out of | away from |
| out of date | no longer available or in use |
| out of order | not working |
| over and over | repeatedly |
| pass out | to lose consciousness |
| pass out* | to distribute |
| pay attention* | to listen or observe carefully |
| pick out* | to choose, select |
| pick up* | to take |
| pick up the tab | to pay for someone else's purchase |
| pin (something) on (someone) | to fix responsibility on, accuse |
| play by ear* | to play music that one has heard without having to read the music; to see what happens before acting |

| Idiom or phrasal verb | Meaning |
|---|---|
| play tricks on | to tease |
| play up to | to flatter in order to gain approval |
| point out* | to indicate |
| pull off* | to succeed at something difficult |
| pull together | to get control of |
| put an end to | to end |
| put away* | to return to its proper place |
| put down* | to suppress; to ridicule |
| put off* | to postpone |
| put on* | to dress oneself in; to mislead |
| put on weight* | to gain weight |
| put out* | to extinguish |
| put together* | to assemble |
| put up* | to construct |
| put up with | to tolerate |
| quite a few | many |
| read over* | to read quickly from beginning to end |
| right away | immediately |
| right here | in this very spot |
| right now | at this very moment |
| right there | at that very spot |
| rule out* | to remove from consideration |
| run across | to find unexpectedly |
| run away | to leave without notice |
| run into | to meet unexpectedly |
| run out of | to exhaust the supply of |
| run over | to pass over with a moving vehicle |
| run up to | to approach |
| save one's breath | to waste no words |
| say nothing of | not to mention |
| screw up* | to spoil |
| see about | take care of |
| see off* | to accompany to a departure point |
| sell out* | to sell completely |
| serve one's purpose | to suit one's needs |
| serve someone right | to receive one's just punishment |
| set fire to* | to cause to burn |
| set out | to begin to move toward a destination |
| shake hands | to greet by clasping hands |
| show off* | to attract attention by flaunting an ability or possessions |
| show up | to appear |
| shut off* | to stop (a flow) |
| shut up* | to stop talking |
| sit down | to take a seat |
| sit in (on) | to participate as a member (of) |
| slow down* | to go more slowly |

| Idiom or phrasal verb | Meaning |
|---|---|
| snow job | deception |
| snow (someone) | to deceive |
| so far | up to the present time |
| stand a chance | to have the possibility |
| stand for | to represent; to tolerate |
| stand out | to be conspicuous |
| stand to reason | to be clear and logical |
| stand up | to rise from a seated position |
| stand up* | to leave someone waiting at an appointment |
| stand up for | to defend, support |
| stand up to | to withstand |
| stay in | to remain at home |
| stay out | to remain away from home |
| stay up | to remain awake |
| step down | to retire from or resign a top position |
| step out of line | to disobey or violate orders |
| stick around | to stay where one is |
| stick out* | to protrude |
| stick (someone) | to cheat |
| stick to | to adhere to, persevere at |
| stick up* | to protrude |
| stir up* | to arouse, incite |
| | |
| take advantage of | to use an opportunity; to profit at the expense of another person |
| take after | to resemble (a parent or relative) |
| take a look at | to look at |
| take apart* | to disassemble |
| take a seat | to sit |
| take a walk | to go for a walk |
| take back* | to return |
| take (someone) by surprise | to surprise |
| take care of* | to watch carefully |
| take down* | to remove; to write what is said |
| take for granted | to assume as a given |
| take hold of | to grasp |
| take in* | to alter an item of clothing in order to make it smaller; to deceive |
| take into account* | to consider a fact |
| take off | to leave the ground (said of airplanes) |
| take off* | to remove (clothes) |
| take on* | to employ, hire |
| take one's time | to work or go slowly |
| take out* | to remove, extract |
| take over* | to assume direction or control of |
| take pains | to work carefully |
| take part in | to participate, join |
| take pity on | to feel sympathy for |

| IDIOM OR PHRASAL VERB | MEANING |
|---|---|
| take place | to happen, occur |
| take (someone) for | to mistake for someone else |
| take (someone's) word | to believe |
| take (something) up with* | to consult |
| take the bull by the horns | to be bold or determined |
| take time off | not to work |
| take turns | to alternate |
| take up* | to adopt, take an interest in |
| talk back | to speak disrespectfully |
| talk over* | to discuss |
| taste of | to have the same flavor as |
| tear down* | to demolish |
| tear off* | to remove a piece by tearing |
| tear up* | to shred |
| tell apart* | to distinguish between |
| tell one from the other | to distinguish between the two |
| tell time | to be able to read a timepiece |
| think of | to have an opinion about |
| think over* | to consider carefully |
| think up* | to create, invent |
| throw away* | to discard |
| throw out* | to eject by force |
| throw (someone) a curve | to mislead |
| throw the book at | to give the full penalty |
| throw up* | to vomit |
| tie up* | to immobilize; to monopolize |
| tired out* | extremely weary |
| top (something) | to surpass something previously said or done, outdo |
| trade in* | to exchange an old article for a new one |
| try on* | to put clothes on before buying |
| try out* | to test or examine |
| turn around* | to move so as to face in the opposite direction |
| turn down* | to reduce in brightness or volume; to reject |
| turn off* | to stop |
| turn on* | to start; to attract or interest |
| turn out | to become |
| turn over* | to place upside down; to transfer from one person to another |
| upside down | inverted |
| up to date | aware of the present situation |
| used to | did at one time, formerly did |
| wait for | to expect |
| wait on | to serve |
| wait up for | to stay up late to meet (someone) |
| wake up* | to awaken |

| Idiom or phrasal verb | Meaning |
|---|---|
| walk up to | to approach |
| want out | to want to be relieved of an obligation |
| waste one's breath | to gain nothing by speaking |
| watch out for | to look out for |
| wear away*/wear down*/ wear through* | to reduce gradually through the process of wear |
| wear out* | to become shabby |
| what with | because of |
| work out | to exercise |
| work out* | to develop in a favorable manner |
| would rather | to prefer |

CHAPTER 12

# Modals and Periphrastic Modals

## 12a Modals

A modal is a special type of auxiliary (helping verb).

### 1 Form

Modals can be distinguished from other auxiliary verbs in two ways.

1. Modals do not have verb endings (*-s, -ed, -ing*).

   He can go.

   They may arrive soon.

   The normal rules of tense and number agreement do not apply. Thus modals do not require subject-verb agreement, and this type of verb may be described as basically tenseless.

2. Modals are followed immediately by the base (simple) form of the verb. If an infinitive follows a modal, *to* is omitted. Thus the following are incorrect:

   * He can to go.

   * She should to stop.

### 2 Negatives

We make a modal negative with *not*, as with other verbs.

He cannot go.

They couldn't wait.

### 3 Questions

To make a yes/no question, the modal is placed before the subject. A short answer may be given.

Can he go?
Yes, he can (go).

May I ask a question?
No, you may not.

An information question is similiar; the modal is placed before the subject.

What should we do?

How can I help you?

## 4   Continuous

A modal may be made continuous with *be* + present participle (*-ing* form).

She may be reading.

They must be eating.

## 5   Past

Some modals may be given past meaning by using modal + *have* + past participle.

I should have eaten dinner.

We could have helped her.

## 12b   Periphrastic modals

Some modals have *periphrastic* (multiword) counterparts. These periphrastic modals end in *to* and function much like true modals.

| MODAL | PERIPHRASTIC MODAL |
|---|---|
| can | be able to |
| will | be going to, be about to |
| must | have to, have got to |
| should, ought to | be to, be supposed to |
| may | be allowed to |

She
$$\begin{cases} \text{is able to} \\ \text{is going to} \\ \text{is about to} \\ \text{has to} \\ \text{has got to} \\ \text{is to} \\ \text{is supposed to} \\ \text{is allowed to} \end{cases}$$
leave tonight.

## 1   Form

The periphrastic modals do not exhibit the same formal properties as the true modals in that the subject-verb agreement rule must be applied, and all the periphrastic modals require that an infinitive with *to* precede the main verb.

He is going to be my friend.

They are allowed to play here.

## 2 Negatives

The negative of a true modal and the negative of the corresponding periphrastic modal usually have the same meaning.

I can't do it. / I am not able to do it.

You should not cheat. / You are not supposed to cheat.

## 3 Usage

Generally, the use of the true modal is more formal than the use of the corresponding periphrastic modal, especially in its phonologically reduced form.

COMPARE

The students must study the chart.
The students have to ("hafta") study the chart.
The students have got to ("gotta") study the chart.

This experiment will end soon.
The experiment is going to ("gonna") end soon.

## EXERCISES 12.1

## ERROR CORRECTION

Each sentence contains an error in the form of the modal. Rewrite the sentence correctly.

*Example:* He shoulds be here.

*He should be here.*

1. He cans hear it.

2. She can to hear it.

3. He can smells the grass.

4. She can smelled it too.

5. They don't can find it.

6. Do you can find it?

7. Yuko must to speak Japanese.

8. He can should eat now.

9. He could used to be a fireman.

10. She is going to be about to leave.

## EXERCISE 12.2

## PERIPHRASTIC MODALS

Substitute the correct periphrastic modal for the modal given.

*Example:* He ought to be on time.

*He's supposed to be on time.*

1. She can ride a horse well.

2. Will she go away to school next year?

3. His father said he may go out tonight.

4. They must arrive before we leave.

5. Everyone should bring a towel.

## 12c  The meaning of modals

Modals have two basic areas of meaning: social and logical.

### 1  Social interaction

The social meaning of modals (see Table 12.1) involves permission and requests, suggestions and advice, and commands.

You may leave the room.

May I leave the room?

You should see a doctor.

You had better fix that.

You must be in by midnight.

#### Making requests and asking permission

GENERAL REQUESTS

Will
Would
Can
Could
} you help me with my car?

SPECIFIC PERMISSION

May
Might
Can
Could
} I go to the movies?

The etymologically past-tense forms (*could, would*) are generally considered a more polite and softer way of making requests than the present forms (*can, will*).

Table 12.1
## SOCIAL MEANING OF MODALS AND PERIPHRASTIC MODALS

| MEANING | PRESENT | FUTURE | PAST |
|---|---|---|---|
| Suggestion | — | can | could have |
| | — | could | — |
| Advice | should | should | should have |
| | ought to | ought to | ought to have |
| | had better | had better | — |
| | be supposed to | be supposed to | be supposed to |
| Necessity | must | must | — |
| | have to | have to | have to |
| Nonnecessity | not have to | not have to | not have to |
| Prohibition | must not | must not | — |
| Promise | — | will | — |
| Polite offer | — | will | — |
| Refusal | won't | won't | — |
| Request | would | would | — |
| | could | could | — |
| | will | will | — |
| | can | can | — |
| | would you mind* | would you mind* | — |
| Command | must | must | — |
| | have to | have to | have to |
| Invitation | would like | would like | — |

*  *Yes, I mind* means "no." It is usually said in anger. To be agreeable, one says, "No, I don't mind" or "Not at all."

Would you kindly help me with my car?

The present forms are used in responses to avoid a conditional response.

Yes, I will help you.

*May* is considered the most polite form for requests and permission. The greater the formal authority of the person being addressed, the more likely it is that *may* will be used in the request.

The permission sense of *might* is used only in questions and is considered archaic.

### Polite requests with *I* as the subject

REQUESTS

FORMAL         May I (please) see that camera?

               Could I see that camera (please)?

INFORMAL       Can I (please) have one of those?

Yes, you may.

                       No, you may not.

Sure.

                       OK.

## EXERCISE 12.3

## POLITE REQUESTS WITH *I* AS THE SUBJECT

Fill in the blanks with the correct forms.

*Example:*    ___*May*___ (formal)    I ___*please*___ borrow
your car?

        Yes, ___*you may*___ (formal).

1. _____ (formal) I _____ borrow a piece of
paper?

    Yes, _____ (formal).

2. _____ (informal) ask you a question?

    _____ (informal).

3. _____ (formal) I borrow your pen for a minute,

    _____?

    Yes, _____ (formal).

4. _____ (informal) I _____ bother you for a cigarette?

_____ (informal).

5. _____ (formal) I borrow your dictionary _____?

Yes, _____ (formal).

6. _____ (formal) I _____ borrow a pencil?

Yes, _____ (formal).

### Polite requests with *you* as the subject

| | |
|---|---|
| **REQUESTS** | |
| **FORMAL** | Would you pour the milk (please)? |
| | Will you (please) pour the milk? |
| | Could you pour the milk (please)? |
| **INFORMAL** | Can you pour the milk? |
| **RESPONSES** | |
| **FORMAL** | Yes, I'd be happy/glad to. |
| | Certainly. |
| **INFORMAL** | Sure. |
| | OK. |

## EXERCISE 12.4

## POLITE QUESTIONS WITH *YOU*

Using *you* as the subject, write a formal and an informal polite question and response as indicated.

*Example:*   Ask a friend for a favor.

(*formal*)

*Would you do me a favor, please?*
*Certainly.*

(*informal*)

*Can you do me a favor?*
*Sure.*

1. Ask someone to pass the newspaper.

   (*formal*)


   (*informal*)


2. Ask another student to come pick you up.

   (*formal*)


   (*informal*)


3. Ask the teacher permission to leave early.

   (*informal*)


   (*formal*)

4. Ask to have some gas put in your car.

(*formal*)

(*informal*)

5. Ask for a phone number of a friend.

(*formal*)

(*informal*)

### Would you mind?

**PERMISSION**

Would you mind if I borrowed a book? (formal, written)

Would you mind if I borrow a book? (informal, spoken)

NOTE: The verbs in the *if* clauses are in the simple past and present, but both have a present or future meaning after *would you mind*. (See Table 12.1 on page 352.)

**REQUESTS**

Would you mind closing the door?

Would you mind sitting here?

Not at all.

No, I don't mind.

No, I'd be happy/glad to.

NOTE: *Yes, I mind!* means "no."

## EXERCISE 12.5

## REQUESTS AND PERMISSION WITH *WOULD YOU MIND?*

Fill in the blanks with the correct form of the verb. Use *if I* + past, or use the present participle.

*Examples:* It's early in the day. Would you mind _*leaving*_ (leave) a little early?

Answer (negative) *Yes, I would mind.*

I'm broke. Would you mind *if I borrowed* (borrow) some money?

Answer (affirmative) *No, I don't mind.*

1. It's late. Would you mind _____ (go) now?

   Answer (affirmative)

2. I didn't hear you. Would you mind _____ (repeat) that?

   Answer (affirmative)

3. Tomorrow is Tuesday. Would you mind _____ (drive) you to the station a little earlier than usual?

   Answer (affirmative)

4. Would you mind _____ (use) your pen?

Answer (negative)

5. This movie is bad. Would you mind _____ (walk out) now?

Answer (negative)

## EXERCISE 12.6

## REQUESTS

---

A. Choose the correct modal from the options in parentheses.

*Example:* Dad, (⟨may⟩, *should*) I stay out until midnight tonight?

"Dad, (*may, should*) I borrow the car tonight?"

"Sorry, son. You (*shouldn't, can't*); the boss just called, and he said we have to work tonight."

"Well, if that's the case, (*would you mind, can you*) driving me to the movies?"

"No, I (*shouldn't, wouldn't*) mind at all. Let's go now. The boss asked me to be near the phone after eight."

The next day, the son asks, "Hey, Dad, did you get that work done?"

"Yes."

"Then (*will, could*) I please borrow the car tonight?"

"Yes, you (*may, shall*)."

**B.** In the space below, write a letter to the dean requesting permission to use the cafeteria for an international festival.

### Suggestions, advice, obligation, and commands

Making suggestions, giving advice, expressing obligation, and giving commands are the other social uses of modals. The greater the speaker's authority or the greater the urgency of the message, the greater the intensity of suggestion, advice, or obligation.

$$\text{You} \begin{Bmatrix} \text{might} \\ \text{could} \\ \text{should} \\ \text{ought to} \\ \text{had better} \\ \text{must} \end{Bmatrix} \text{see the teacher.}$$

### Necessity or obligation

*Must, have to* ("hafta"), and *have got to* ("gotta") all express necessity. *Must* is stronger than *have to*, which is used more commonly in everyday speech because it is less urgent.

I have to go shopping for a new dress.

The doctor says I must get plenty of rest.

*Have got to* is informal and is primarily spoken.


## EXERCISE 12.7

## NECESSITY OR OBLIGATION

**A.** Write a short essay on one of the following topics.

1. What a student must do to succeed.
2. What a business must do to be profitable.
3. What a teacher must do to retain the respect of the students.

**B.** In your notebook, make a list of all the things you have to do this week. After listing five to ten, choose one item, and write about it for ten minutes in your notebook.

**C.** Read "The Boy Who Cried Wolf." What three morals or lessons would you give this tale? Use *must* and *have to* in your reply.

### THE BOY WHO CRIED WOLF

Once there was a boy who lived with his family on a farm in the countryside near a small village. This boy's job was to help tend the sheep while his father worked on the farm. The boy did his job every day and was alone with the sheep much of the time.

One day, he decided to have some fun and excitement. Even though there was no danger, he cried out, "The wolf is coming! The wolf is coming!" He knew this would bring some elders to protect the sheep and drive off the wolf. And so it did. First his father arrived armed with a sickle, and then other men and women came running from the fields and the small village. Some people had farm implements with them; others had brooms or sticks they had picked up along the way. One man had a gun. They all wanted to protect the boy and his sheep.

When his father and the other people asked the boy where the wolf was, he replied, "The wolf did not come. I called out because I was bored and lonely, and I wanted some excitement." Most of the other people just smiled to themselves and walked away. But his father was annoyed and said, "You have disturbed me and the other people from our work. Please don't do this again." The little boy said he was sorry, and everyone went back to work.

A few days later, the boy had forgotten what his father had said. He was lonely and full of mischief. And so again he called out loudly, "The wolf is coming! The wolf is coming! Please help!" Once again, his father and many people from the surrounding fields and the small village came running. Again they came with what weapons they had to protect the boy and his flock of sheep. But again, there was no wolf and no danger. And this time some of the other people murmured and shook their heads and walked away without saying goodbye. This time the boy's father was angry. He said, "Never do this again, or I will punish you severely." The boy apologized, and this time he meant it. He knew that his father was truly angry, and he was sorry for what he had done.

The next day, he was wandering the hills above the town with his flock of sheep when a big wolf suddenly appeared out of the forest. The boy, with real fear in his voice, cried, "The wolf is coming! The wolf is coming!" This time, nobody came to his aid, the people in the fields shook their heads and muttered, and in the little town, people just frowned and went about their business. The boy's father kept on working too, and he became really angry when he heard the boy cry out, "Oh, help me, please help me!" before giving a bloodcurdling scream.

Moral:  1.



2.



3.



## Negation

*Must not* can be a form of severe warning, a prohibition. And though *must* and *have to* often mean the same thing in the affirmative, they are quite different in meaning in the negative. *Not have to* is weaker, suggesting a lack of necessity. Note the difference:

You must not eat sugar—you're a diabetic.

I don't have to do my homework tonight; it's Friday.

# EXERCISE 12.8

## MUST AND HAVE TO

**A.** Write two statements about each subject, the first expressing obligation and the second stating lack of necessity.

*Example:* A waitress

*A waitress must serve the food.*
*A waitress doesn't have to sweep the floor.*

1. A child

2. A student

3. She

4. A truck driver

5. I

**B.** Use the phrases given to express obligation or lack of necessity, as appropriate.

*Example:*   written homework, reading homework

*We must do the written homework for tomorrow. But we don't have to do the reading assignment until next week.*

1. pay taxes, vote

2. respect our parents, pay them

3. go to school, go to the movies

4. sleep, play soccer

5. eat dinner, eat dessert

## EXERCISE 12.9

### FREEWRITING

Study Table 12.1 on page 352. Then freewrite in your notebook for ten minutes, using as many of the modals listed in the table for necessity, nonnecessity, prohibition, refusal, and commands as you can.

### Advice or expectation

Giving advice is another major social function of modals. *Should* and *ought to* mean the same thing; they express advisability. Though similar in meaning, *had better* is a little stronger; it often expresses a warning or threat.

*Be supposed to* is similar to *should*, but *be supposed to* suggests that someone expects, requires, or requests a certain behavior.


## EXERCISE 12.10

## GIVING ADVICE

---

Write sentences that use *should*, *ought to*, and *had better* in the main clause to give advice.

*Example:*   avoiding splinters

*If you want to avoid splinters, you should wear shoes on the boardwalk.*

1. being tired


2. cooking dinner


3. being homesick


4. feeling ill


5. being warm


6. crossing the street


7. entering politics

8. having the hiccups

9. having the flu

10. writing an essay

## EXERCISE 12.11

## EXPECTATION

Tell what is expected of you in each situation.

*Example:*   You are invited to dinner.

*If you are invited to dinner, you are supposed to arrive on time.*

1. You take a taxi.

2. You accidentally bump into someone.

3. You fail to understand someone clearly.

4. You are in a library.

5. You meet someone for the first time.

## ERROR ANALYSIS

**A.** Find and correct the errors.

*Example:* They had sho̶uld better do that homework.

*They had better do the homework.*

1. He has better do that homework.

2. You must to eat all of the vegetables.

3. The clerk supposed to open the shop every morning.

4. What must he does to get a good grade?

5. He ought for to see his parents.

6. They should do not walk on the grass.

7. At the meeting, I suppose to say a few words.

8. I told him he had better went to see the dean.

9. Lawrence has supposed to be here at seven.

10. I ought get a haircut.

**B.** Look up the word *prohibition* in your dictionary. Write an essay in your notebook on the things you think people should or must not do.

### Belated advice

*Should have* and *ought to have* express belated advice. They are usually said after someone has done something wrong or badly.

You failed the test? You should have studied last night.

You had an accident? You ought to have been more careful.

## EXERCISE 12.13

## BELATED ADVICE

Write a sentence about the situation described using *should have* or *ought to have*.

*Example:*    She left the door open, and the dog ran away.

*She should have closed the door.*

1. Joe was sick, but he didn't see a doctor. Now he's sicker.

2. You missed yesterday's quiz because you went to the beach.

3. I had a party and forgot to invite Mary. Now she is mad at me.

4. I signed that contract without reading it. Now I have to pay them more money.

5. I was late for work again today. I forgot to set the clock.

**EXERCISE 12.14**

**ADVICE AND EXPECTATION**

Use one of the modals *must, have to, ought to, should, be supposed to,* and *should have* to complete each statement. The verbs may be used more than once.

As you know, Jonah, all students _____ be on time for class, just as we all _____ pay our taxes. Lateness will not be tolerated unless there is a good excuse, and it _____ be in writing. Otherwise, the rules say I _____ (not) waive the punishment. You _____ thought of this ahead of time.

You _____ wake up earlier, and you _____ ask your roommate to call you too. Now, because you have been late five times, I _____ send you to the dean, and he will send a letter to your parents. So from now on, you _____ try harder, and that _____ fix the problem.

**EXERCISE 12.15**

**MODALS**

Underline the modals and periphrastic modals in the following fable.

There once was a young elephant who lived in a big herd. All his life, he listened to things he should and shouldn't do. His elders were always warning, reminding, and advising him.

"You should watch out for splinters," he thought he remembered his mother saying when he was very little. "And you ought to eat all your vegetables if you want to grow up big and strong."

The brother-in-law elephant also had advice. "You should always eat your greens," he often said. He followed this by saying, "And you had better get plenty of sleep, too." The elephant could still hear him saying these things.

Dad always said, "You had better be good," somewhat sarcastically. Sometimes he said it to others. The young elephant heard him say it a lot, especially at the gas station. "You had better change the oil, too" and "You had better fill it up."

In the house, Mary the elephant had a big sign; it said NO SMOKING. Some of the other elephants smoked; they said it was a habit. "But you shouldn't smoke," said Mary. "It's bad for your health; you ought to quit. And if you must smoke, do it outside. You should not smoke around others." Once the little elephant heard her say to another young elephant, "You had better not smoke in my house."

Sister Alice always said we should not put our feet on the couch. She said, "You're supposed to keep it clean." She also told us that we had better not watch so much TV. "It will make you cross-eyed," she warned.

This fable has several morals:
You should eat well.
You ought to get enough sleep.
You had better not smoke.
You are supposed to listen to your elders.

# EXERCISE 12.16

## SOCIAL MODALS OF ADVICE AND WARNING

Fill in each blank with the correct modal.

"Students, for the state board examinations, you _____ memorize this chart. To do this, you _____ read the chapters first; then you will be able to understand all the numbers. You _____ also write an essay, so you _____ do the written exercises at the end of the chapter."

"Excuse me, Ma'am. _____ I please ask you a question? _____ I do all of the exercises on page 67? And do you think I _____ do some other assignments?"

"Beside all that you _____ do, you may want to do the exercises in the workbook, and you _____ do this sheet of exercises too. If you do all of this, you _____ quite well on the test."

## 2 ∎ Logical probability

The logical use of modals (see Table 12.2) usually deals with an inference or a prediction that can range from possibility through probability to certainty. As with the suggestion, advice, and command uses, the logical use allows for a hierarchy with increasing certainty or degree of probability regarding the inference.

The phone is ringing. That $\begin{cases} \text{could} \\ \text{might} \\ \text{may} \\ \text{should} \\ \text{ought to} \\ \text{must} \\ \text{will} \end{cases}$ be Tran.

Table 12.2

## LOGICAL MEANING OF MODALS AND PERIPHRASTIC MODALS

| Meaning | Present | Future | Past |
|---------|---------|--------|------|
| Certainty | can | can | could |
| | | could | |
| Possibility | may | may | may have |
| | might | might | might have |
| | could | could | could have |
| Impossibility | couldn't | — | couldn't have |
| Potential | — | can | could have |
| | — | could | — |
| Deduction | must | — | must have |
| Certainty | must | must | — |
| Uncertainty | must not be | must not be | — |

Adjectives and adverbs such as *possible* and *certainly* can often be used to paraphrase the logical (but not the social) use of a modal.

It might rain tomorrow (Rain is possible.)

It should rain tomorrow. (Rain is probable.)

It will rain tomorrow. (Rain is certain.)

Expressing degrees of certainty in the present can range from absolute certainty (*is*) to doubtful guessing (*could*).

Why is the teacher absent?

He is sick (100%)

He must be sick. (95%)

He may be sick. (50%)

He might be sick. (50% or less)

He could be sick. (50% or less)

## EXERCISE 12.17

## PROBABILITY

**A.** Complete each sentence using *must, may, might,* or *could.*

*Example:* He has always driven a truck.

He _____*must*_____ like it.

1. He has always worn a beard.

   He _____ like it.

2. Ali bought a Mercedes for his wife.

   Wow, he _____ be rich.

3. What is that man doing over there?

   I can't really see; he _____ be just waiting for someone.

4. Hello, may I speak to Vic?

   Sorry, you _____ have the wrong number.

5. She's got a low fever and a pain in the stomach.

   She _____ have a cold, or it _____ just be an upset stomach.

6. Give this dress to Mary.

   It _____ be too small for her, but it _____ fit Sally.

7. I haven't seen my mother in two years.

   You _____ miss her.

8. Can you lend me ten thousand dollars?

   You _____ be kidding!

9. Where can I get a new notebook?

   You _____ try the store on the corner.

10. I wonder what that costs.

    It _____ be very expensive; it's imported.

**B.** Express each prediction by using a sentence with a predictive modal.

*Example:* A fifteen percent chance of rain tomorrow

*It might rain tomorrow.*

1. A thirty percent chance of snow on Tuesday

2. The probability of a major earthquake in California

3. A seventy-five percent chance of rain tomorrow

4. The possibility of a woman becoming President of the United States in the next twenty years

5. The probability of a manned spaceship reaching the other planets in the next hundred years

6. The possibility of life on Mars

7. A fifty percent chance that we will win the tennis match

8. The probability that school will be canceled because of the snow

9. The certainty that I will be punished for my mistake

10. A ninety percent chance of rain tomorrow

C. Watch and observe the weather portion of a televised newscast. Then prepare a five-day weather report similar to the one given on TV.

*Example:*

On Monday, it will be sunny in the morning, but it may cloud up in the afternoon....

**D.** Fill in the blanks with an appropriate modal. The first one has been done for you as an example.

Each week, millions of people buy lottery tickets, thinking that they ____*will*____ win the prize. Some people are so sure that they _____ win that they plan how they _____ spend the money.

Some people buy only one ticket because they feel that anyone _____ win. Others buy ten, twenty, or more tickets, thinking that they _____ have a better chance of winning. They _____ be right.

One thing is for certain: Eventually, someone _____ win.

### Negation

Significant differences in meaning occur when the logical modals are negated.

This _____ be the answer.

| AFFIRMATIVE | | NEGATIVE |
|---|---|---|
| will | 100% | can't, couldn't, won't |
| | 99 | won't |
| must | 95 | must not |
| should | | shouldn't |
| may | 50 | may not |
| could, might | | might not |

*Can* is infrequently used to express logical probability in affirmative sentences, yet it is often used in negative sentences.

It can rain tomorrow. (rare)

That can't be the answer.

Whereas the logical probability of *can* and *could* in affirmative sentences is quite low, in negative sentences it is quite high. To say, for example, "That can't be the answer" means that it is a virtual impossibility.

The contracted forms *can't, couldn't,* and *shouldn't* are frequently used in sentences of logical probability, but *may* and *must* are rarely contracted.

## EXERCISE 12.18

## NEGATIVE PROBABILITY

Give a reason using the negative modal in parentheses.

*Example:*　I think she's with her mother. (couldn't)

*She couldn't be; I just saw her mother.*

1. I think Mary has quit her job. (may not)

2. I think Joe is hungry. (shouldn't)

3. See that bird? I think it's a dodo. (can't)

4. Was that an elephant? (couldn't)

5. I think he's driving his father's car. (might not)

6. I think Oskar lives on the west side of town. (may not)

7. I think the baby is tired. (shouldn't)

8. A dinosaur ate those bushes. (can't)

9. I think she is going to marry him. (won't)

10. They will be here soon. (might not)

### Degrees of certainty: past tense

As with the present tense, a range of degrees of certainty can be expressed in the past. Note the differences between the affirmative and the negative.

Was that Naomi I just saw?

It _____ her.

| AFFIRMATIVE | | NEGATIVE |
|---|---|---|
| was | 100% | wasn't |
| | 99 | couldn't have been |
| must have been | 95 | must not have been |
| may have been | 50 | may not have been |
| might have been, could have been | | |

## EXERCISE 12.19

## PAST PROBABILITY

Fill in each blank with the appropriate affirmative or negative form of the past modal.

"Kyu was absent yesterday, wasn't he, Mel?"

"Oh, he _____ been sick."

"No, he was at the library later, so he _____ been that sick."

"Well, he _____ had an appointment with the dentist, or he _____ been helping Dean Delaney in his office."

"He _____ been; I stopped there on my way to class."

"Well, he _____ forgotten to go to class."

"He's late today."

"He _____ missed his bus."

## EXERCISE 12.20

## NEGATIVE PAST PROBABILITY

**A.** Supply a reason for each statement.

*Example:*   Gordon couldn't have been hungry.

*He already ate.*

1. Joe must not have been here.

2. Nola couldn't have been happy.

3. Louise might not have been scared.

4. Ted may not have been injured.

5. Larry couldn't have been there.

**B.** Circle the correct modal of each pair in parentheses.

*Example:*   Joe didn't call me last night.

He (*must*, *should*) not have been home.

1. Larry took the video.

   Oh, it (*couldn't, may not*) have been him; he's in Europe.

2. Per ate all the cake.

   He (*should, may*) not have; the crumbs are by Martine's place.

3. Anna is angry with you.

   She (*may, should*) not be; I just made her dinner.

4. Marisol missed that question.

   She (*may not, couldn't*) have been paying attention.

5. He didn't call Barry last night.

   He (*will not, must not*) have been home.

## EXERCISE 12.21

## POSSIBILITIES

Read "Eveline" by James Joyce. Then write a paragraph explaining what you think might have happened if she had decided to go to America with Frank.

### EVELINE

She sat at the window watching the evening invade the avenue. Her head was leaned against the window curtains and in her nostrils was the odour of dusty cretonne. She was tired.

Few people passed. The man out of the last house passed on his way home; she heard his footsteps clacking along the concrete pavement and afterwards crunching on the cinder path before the new red houses. One time there used to be a field there in which they used to play every evening with other people's children. Then a man from Belfast bought the field and built houses in it—not like their little brown houses but bright brick houses with shining roofs. The children of the avenue used to play together in that field—the Devines, the Waters, the Dunns, little Keogh the cripple, she and her brothers and sisters. Ernest, however, never played: he was too grown up. Her father used often to hunt them in out of the field with his blackthorn stick; but usually little Keogh used to keep *nix* and call out when he saw her father coming. Still they seemed to have been rather happy then. Her father was not so bad then; and besides, her mother was alive. That was a long time ago; she and her brothers and sisters were all grown up; her mother was dead. Tizzie Dunn was dead, too, and the Waters had gone back to England. Everything changes. Now she was going to go away like the others, to leave her home.

Home! She looked round the room, reviewing all its familiar objects which she had dusted once a week for so many years, wondering where on earth all the dust came from. Perhaps she would never see again those familiar objects from which she had never dreamed of being divided. And yet during all those years she had never found out the name of the priest whose yellowing photograph hung on the wall above the broken harmonium beside the coloured print of the promises made to Blessed Margaret Mary Alacoque. He had been a school friend of her father. Whenever he showed the photograph to a visitor her father used to pass it with a casual word:

—He is in Melbourne now.

She had consented to go away, to leave her home. Was that wise? She tried to weigh each side of the question. In her home anyway she had shelter and food; she had those whom she had known all her life about her. Of course she had to work hard both in the house and at business. What would they say of her in the Stores when they found out that she had run away with a fellow? Say she was a fool, perhaps; and her place would be filled up by advertisement. Miss Gavan would be glad. She had always had an edge on her, especially whenever there were people listening.

—Miss Hill, don't you see these ladies are waiting?

—Look lively, Miss Hill, please.

She would not cry many tears at leaving the Stores.

But in her new home, in a distant unknown country, it would not be like that. Then she would be married—she, Eveline. People would treat her with respect then. She would not be treated as her mother had been. Even now, though she was over nineteen, she sometimes felt herself in danger of her father's violence. She knew it was that that had given her the palpitations. When they were growing up he had never gone for her, like he used to go for Harry and Ernest, because she was a girl; but latterly he had begun to threaten her and say what he would do to her only for her dead mother's sake. And now she had nobody to protect her. Ernest was dead and Harry, who was in the church decorating business, was nearly always down somewhere in the country. Besides, the invariable squabble for money on Saturday nights had begun to weary her unspeakably. She always gave her entire wages—seven shillings—and Harry always sent up what he could but the trouble was to get any money from her father. He said she used to squander the money, that she had no head, that he wasn't going to give her his hard-earned money to throw about the streets, and much more, for he was usually fairly bad of a Saturday night. In the end he would give her the money and ask her had she any intention of buying Sunday's dinner. Then she had to rush out as quickly as she could and do her marketing, holding her black leather purse tightly in her hand as she elbowed her way through the crowds and returning home late under her load of provisions. She had hard work to keep the house together and to see that the two young children who had been left to her charge went to school regularly and got their meals regularly. It was hard work—a hard life—but now that she was about to leave it she did not find it a wholly undesirable life.

She was about to explore another life with Frank. Frank was very kind, manly, open-hearted. She was to go away with him by the night-boat to be his wife and to live with him in Buenos Ayres where he had a home waiting for her. How well she remembered the first time she had seen him; he was lodging in a house on the main road where she used to visit. It seemed a few weeks ago. He was standing at the gate, his peaked cap pushed back on his head and his hair tumbled forward over a face of bronze. Then they had come to know each other. He used to meet her outside the Stores every evening and see her home. He took her to see *The Bohemian Girl* and she felt elated as she sat in an unaccustomed part of the theatre with him. He was awfully fond of music and sang a little. People knew that they were courting and, when he sang about the lass that loves a sailor, she always felt pleasantly confused. He used to call her Poppens out of fun. First of all it had been an excitement for her to have a fellow and then she had begun to like him. He had tales of distant countries. He had started as a deck boy at a pound a month on a ship of the Allan Line going out to Canada. He told her the names of the ships he had been on and the names of the different services. He had sailed through the Straits of Magellan and he told her stories of the terrible Patagonians. He had fallen on his feet in Buenos Ayres, he said, and had come over to the old country just for a holiday. Of course, her father had found out the affair and had forbidden her to have anything to say to him.

—I know these sailor chaps, he said.

One day he had quarrelled with Frank and after that she had to meet her lover secretly.

The evening deepened in the avenue. The white of two letters in her lap grew indistinct. One was to Harry; the other was to her father. Ernest had been her favourite but she liked Harry too. Her father was becoming old lately, she noticed; he would miss her. Sometimes he could be very nice. Not long before, when she had been laid up for a day, he had read her out a ghost story and made toast for her at the fire. Another day, when their mother was alive, they had all gone for a picnic to the Hill of Howth. She remembered her father putting on her mother's bonnet to make the children laugh.

Her time was running out but she continued to sit by the window, leaning her head against the window curtain, inhaling the odour of dusty cretonne. Down far in the avenue she could hear a street organ playing. She knew the air. Strange that it should come that very night to remind her of the promise to her mother, her promise to keep the home together as long as she could. She remembered the last night of her mother's illness; she was again in the close dark room at the other side of the hall and outside she heard a melancholy air of Italy. The organ-player had been ordered to go away and given sixpence. She remembered her father strutting back into the sickroom saying:

—Damned Italians! coming over here!

As she mused the pitiful vision of her mother's life laid its spell on the very quick of her being—that life of commonplace sacrifices closing in final craziness. She trembled as she heard again her mother's voice saying constantly with foolish insistence:

—Derevaun Seraun! Derevaun Seraun!

She stood up in a sudden impulse of terror. Escape! She must escape! Frank would save her. He would give her life, perhaps love, too. But she wanted to live. Why should she be unhappy? She had a right to happiness. Frank would take her in his arms, fold her in his arms. He would save her.

She stood among the swaying crowd in the station at the North Wall. He held her hand and she knew that he was speaking to her, saying something about the passage over and over again. The station was full of soldiers with brown baggages. Through the wide doors of the sheds she caught a glimpse of the black mass of the boat, lying in beside the quay wall, with illumined portholes. She answered nothing. She felt her cheek pale and cold and, out of a maze of distress, she prayed to God to direct her, to show her what was her duty. The boat blew a long mournful whistle into the mist. If she went, to-morrow she would be on the sea with Frank, steaming towards Buenos Ayres. Their passage had been booked. Could she still draw back after all he had done for her? Her distress awoke a nausea in her body and she kept moving her lips in silent fervent prayer.

A bell clanged upon her heart. She felt him seize her hand:

—Come!

All the seas of the world tumbled about her heart. He was drawing her into them: he would drown her. She gripped with both hands at the iron railing.

—Come!

No! No! No! It was impossible. Her hands clutched the iron in frenzy. Amid the seas she sent a cry of anguish!

—Eveline! Evvy!

He rushed beyond the barrier and called to her to follow. He was shouted at to go on but he still called to her. She set her white face to him, passive, like a helpless animal. Her eyes gave him no sign of love or farewell or recognition.

**Degrees of certainty: future**

Degrees of certainty may also be expressed in future time. Observe the following:

Bo will do well on the test. (absolutely certain)

He should/ought to do well on the test. (probable)

He may/might/could do well on the test. (possible)

# EXERCISE 12.22

## DEGREES OF CERTAINTY IN THE FUTURE

**A.** Use *will, should, ought to, may, might,* or *could* to express a degree of certainty about a future event.

*Example:* "Anne seems angry."

"She ___*should*___ be; her wallet was stolen."

1. "Hello, is Jack there?"
    "No, but he'll be home later."
    "What time do you expect him?"

    "He's usually home for dinner, so he _____ be here by seven."

2. "Hello, is Jack there?"
    "No, but he'll be home later."
    "What time do you expect him?"

    "He _____ be home around ten."

3. "Hello, is Jack there?"
    "No, but he'll be home later."
    "What time do you expect him?"

    "I really don't know. It _____ be anytime tonight."

4. "Hello, is Jack there?"
    "No, but he'll be home later."
    "What time do you expect him?"

    "He just called and said he _____ be home at five."

5. "I want you to be here by eleven!"

    "Yes, sir, I _____ be here at eleven."

Table 12.3
## OTHER MEANINGS OF MODALS AND PERIPHRASTIC MODALS.

| MEANING | PRESENT | FUTURE | PAST |
|---|---|---|---|
| Ability | | | |
|    Learned | can | — | could |
| | be able to | be able to | be able to |
|    Physical | can | — | could |
| Preference | would rather | would rather | would rather have |
| Opportunity | — | — | could have |
| Habit | would | would | would have |
| Want | — | would like | — |

## 12d Other uses of modals

Modals can also be used to express ability, desire, offer, preference, and habit (see Table 12.3).

### 1 Ability

Ability is expressed by *can* and *be able to*. *Could* is used in the past tense.

I can speak Japanese.

I am able to swim.

Once I could run like the wind.

*Can* combines the ideas of possibility and ability. For physical ability, *be able to* is the same as *can*. For learned abilities, *know how to* means the same as *can*. *Be able to* is commonly used with other auxiliaries.

I will be able to see you tomorrow.

I used to be able to speak Chinese fluently, but I can't anymore.

### EXERCISE 12.23

### Ability

Rewrite each sentence, changing *can* to *be able to*.

*Example:* A baby can crawl.

*A baby is able to crawl.*

1. A monkey can climb well.

2. A dog can fetch sticks.

3. A fish can't walk.

4. How fast can you swim?

5. My mother can't ride a bike.

**B.** Rewrite each sentence, changing *can* to *know how to*.

*Example:* He can ride a horse.

*He knows how to ride a horse.*

1. I can play the piano.

2. I can write Chinese.

3. He can't translate from Spanish.

4. She can drive a car.

5. Can you speak Japanese?

**C.** Write a short paragraph on each topic.

1. Why I can swim

2. Why I can't dance

3. Why I am able to play my favorite sport

4. Why I know how to speak my native language

**Ability in the past**

*Could* in the affirmative usually means "used to be able to." In the negative, it means "was not able to."

When I was a child, I could run all day.

When I was a child, I could not drive a car.

## EXERCISE 12.24

## ABILITY IN THE PAST

Think of your childhood; write a series of sentences telling what you could and couldn't do.

*Example:* When I was a child, I couldn't drive a car, but I could ride a bicycle.

**2** **Desire**

Desire is expressed by *would like to.*

I would like to go to the movies.

I would like to go to Japan.

## EXERCISE 12.25

## DESIRE

---

If you could do anything, what would you do? Write a list of ten sentences starting with "I would like to . . ." Then choose one of those sentences, and write about it for ten minutes in your notebook.

**3** | **Offer**

An offer is expressed by *would . . . like* in the form of a question.

Would you like a soda?

Would they like me to drive?

## EXERCISE 12.26

## OFFER

---

Write a sentence offering to perform each activity.

*Example:* bake the bread

*Would you like me to bake the bread?*

1. wash the car


2. clean the house

3. help with your homework

4. think of a good gift

5. make the coffee

**4** **Preference**

*Would rather* can replace *prefer*. In a question, we use *or* between the options; in an answer, *than* is used instead.

Would you rather have coffee or tea?

I would rather have coffee than tea.

## EXERCISE 12.27

## PREFERENCE

Write a question with the words given; then write a response.

*Example:*   eat Greek food, Korean food

*Would you rather eat Greek food or Korean food?*
*I would rather eat Greek food than Korean food.*

1. work alone, work with other people

2. live in a big city, live in a small town

3. live in the United States, live in your native country

4. work during the day, work at night

5. eat a hot lunch, eat a cold lunch

## 5 | Habit

Habit is expressed by *would* and *used to*. *Would* is used only for regularly repeated actions in the past. *Used to* may replace *would* in this sense.

In high school, I would go bowling with my friends.

In high school, I used to go bowling with my friends.

However, when *used to* refers to uninterrupted situations from the past, *would* may not replace it.

I used to be a doctor.

Not  *I would be a doctor.

## EXERCISE 12.28

## *WOULD* AND *USED TO*

---

**A.** Fill in the blanks with *would* or *used to*.

*Example:* When I was a kid I _____*used to*_____ live in California.

WHERE I _____ LIVE

When I was a kid, I _____ live in California,

and every summer, I _____ go to summer camp. I

**392    Modals and Periphrastic Modals**

_____ be very shy, and so I hid from the counselors and the other kids. They _____ look for me for hours, but they couldn't find me because I _____ hide under the bed or up in a tree. I _____ like to do this every day.

**B.** Write for ten minutes in your notebook on the topic "things I used to do."

### Used to and be used to

It is possible to confuse *used to* and *be used to*. *Used to* expresses a habit, activity, or situation that existed in the past but no longer exists.

Mary used to be a teacher. Now she is a doctor.

*Be used to* means "be accustomed to." Notice that *be used to* is followed by a gerund or gerund phrase (see Chapter 13).

I am used to living in a city.

He is used to being in charge.

## EXERCISE 12.29

## USED TO AND BE USED TO

Add a form of *be*, if necessary. Put an X in the blank if *be* is not needed.

*Examples:* I _____*am*_____ used to living there.

I _____X_____ used to live there.

1. I have lived in Texas for ten years, and now I

_____ used to living there.

2. I _____ used to live in Denver, Colorado.

3. I _____ used to eating here; I've done it for two years.

4. I _____ used to sit there, but now I have moved over here.

5. People _____ used to believe in politicians.

6. When I was a child, I _____ used to play a lot of silly games.

7. Jones is a pilot; he _____ used to flying all over the world.

8. The railroad _____ used to run through this town, but the tracks were removed in 1972.

9. They've lived here for years, and they _____ used to the weather.

10. He _____ used to play tennis with his neighbor.

## EXERCISE 12.30

## MODAL REVIEW

**A.** Rewrite each sentence correctly.

1. I used to fell down once last year.

2. We supposed to bring some cake.

3. May you please drive us to the corner?

4. When you go to a concert, you should gave the ticket to the man.

5. A policeman must has his wits about him.

6. When I was a child, I can saw all my cousins and other relatives every Sunday.

7. If you have the time, you can traveled around the country.

8. When you want to leave, you must to ask permission.

9. Every Christmas, my parents would bought me some presents.

10. Many people would rather to travel by themselves than go on a tour.

11. If you take a taxi, you can supposed to tip the driver.

12. Be you able to help me move my furniture next Sunday?

13. Should I ask you a question, please?

14. He's in the hospital now; he did have called the doctor.

15. He had better should fix that rear tire.


**B.** For each sentence, circle the letter of the option that correctly fills the blank.

1. Would you rather have coffee _____ tea?
   a. than   b. that   c. or

2. Next year, I will _____ to save some money.
   a. can   b. be supposed to   c. be able to

3. You _____ better be careful when you talk to him.
   a. had   b. should   c. would

4. I _____ rather have tea than coffee.
   a. can   b. should   c. would

5. You _____ be quiet in the library.
   a. are able to   b. are supposed to   c. are allowed to
6. I heard a shout. The neighbors must _____ a fight.
   a. be having   b. are having   c. having
7. You failed the test. You _____ studied harder.
   a. ought to   b. should have   c. must
8. Like some other drugs, alcohol _____ be addictive.
   a. must   b. would   c. can
9. If the oil embargo continues, there _____ not be enough oil
   for everyday use.
   a. might   b. must   c. should
10. She couldn't speak Japanese last year, but she _____ now.
    a. can be able   b. can   c. can do
11. When I was a child, I _____ drive a car.
    a. can't   b. couldn't   c. might not
12. Next year, I will _____ take a vacation.
    a. can   b. able to   c. be able to
13. Police officers _____ be careful on the job.
    a. may   b. should   c. might
14. He's so quiet; he _____ be very shy.
    a. will   b. would   c. must
15. A monkey _____ learn to read.
    a. wouldn't   b. ought not to   c. can't
16. That politician _____ known better.
    a. would have   b. should   c. should have
17. You _____ drive through a stop sign.
    a. couldn't   b. don't have to   c. must not
18. You _____ wear your seat belt, or you might get hurt.
    a. might   b. had better   c. may
19. I would rather eat apples _____ oranges.
    a. than   b. or   c. then
20. That couldn't _____ George; he's out of town.
    a. has been   b. have been   c. been

C. Rewrite each sentence substituting an appropriate periphrastic
   modal for each modal.

   1. Can you swim well?

2. She will be here soon.

3. The runners will begin the race.

4. Larry must learn to be more subtle.

5. Joe ought to read the whole chapter.

6. Mary should bring her pass every time she comes.

7. Jane got permission, so she may leave tonight.

8. George can lift more than two hundred pounds by himself.

9. We must leave soon, or we'll miss the boat.

10. Should Lena be bringing the sandwiches?

# CHAPTER 13

# Infinitives and Gerunds

## 13a Verbals

**Verbals** are words formed from verbs but used as different parts of speech. There are three types of verbals: infinitives, gerunds, and participles (see Section 10a).

An **infinitive** is one of the four principal parts of a verb. It is formed with *to* + the base form of the verb.

| | | |
|---|---|---|
| to read | to be | to think |
| to write | to walk | to feel |

To make an infinitive negative, we put *not* before *to*.

I decided not to read the book.

It was not to be.

A **gerund** is formed by adding *-ing* to the base form of the verb.

| | | |
|---|---|---|
| reading | being | thinking |
| writing | walking | feeling |

Gerunds are used as nouns and may be used as subjects, direct objects, or objects of a preposition.

Swimming is my favorite sport.

I like swimming.

You can't get to the raft without swimming.

It is important to distinguish between the gerund and the present participle form of a verb. The gerund has only noun functions. The present participle, however, can follow the auxiliary *be* to form the present continuous and may also function as an adjective.

Walking makes me feel good. (gerund as subject)

He is walking to the beach today. (present participle forming the present continuous)

He is wearing his walking shoes. (present participle as adjective)

A gerund is often preceded by a possessive form.

> She complained about his smoking.

> The coach commented on her running.

## 13b Infinitives

A sentence with an infinitive actually represents two sentences. One sentence is embedded as a complement within the other. For example, *It's time for them to leave* is actually two sentences:

> It's time.

> They leave.

Infinitive use ocurs when a hypothetical, future, or unfulfilled sense is being expressed. For example, in *It's time for them to leave*, they have not left yet.

An **infinitive phrase** is made up of an infinitive plus modifiers or complements. Infinitive phrases may be used as nouns, adjectives, and adverbs.

> To cook that dish without salt is virtually impossible. (infinitive phrase as subject)

> I want to give you a gift. (as direct object)

> The route to be taken is specified on the map. (as adjective)

> To be sure of a good result, protect your neck. (as adverb)

### 1 Infinitive following the verb

The most common use of the infinitive is as the direct object after certain verbs. The most common of these verbs are *hope, plan, decide, promise, agree, refuse, seem, appear, ask, expect, want,* and *need*.

> I want to leave early tomorrow.

> He agreed to stop annoying her.

> They hope to visit Canada.

> George and Luka need to study more science.

> Elvin decided to sit in the balcony.

## VERBS FOLLOWED BY AN INFINITIVE

| | | | | |
|---|---|---|---|---|
| agree | consent | have | offer | shoot |
| aim | continue | hesitate | ought | start |
| appear | dare | hope | plan | stop |
| arrange | decide | hurry | prefer | strive |
| ask | deserve | intend | prepare | swear |
| attempt | detest | leap | proceed | threaten |
| be able | dislike | leave | promise | try |
| beg | expect | like | propose | use |
| begin | fail | long | refuse | wait |
| care | forget | love | remember | want |
| choose | get | mean | say | wish |
| condescend | happen | neglect | | |

It is important to note that in such sentences, the subject of the main sentence is also the subject of the infinitive.

In answering questions with verb + infinitive form, the second verb may be omitted, but the *to* is retained.

Do many people study yoga?
Some people choose to, but some do not even think about it.

Do people quit their jobs?
Some promise to; others threaten to, and still others refuse to.

## EXERCISE 13.1

## VERB + INFINITIVE

**A.** Fill in each blank with an appropriate infinitive.

*Example:*  I want ___*to live*___ in Seattle some day.

1. Herbert agreed _____ harder from now on.

2. We prefer _____ by the beach.

3. Jill expects _____ by the end of the week.

4. Clare hopes _____ in the communications field.

5. They needed _____ for a much larger crowd.

6. They plan _____ to North Carolina from Washington, D.C.

7. I promised _____ next Monday morning.

8. She wants _____ in the next year.

9. Yoshio wishes _____ a nice apartment.

10. Babies learn _____ before they learn _____.

**B.** Answer each question with a complete sentence.

*Example:* Why do you want to learn English?

*I want to learn English to improve my job prospects.*

1. Why did you leave your native country?

2. What would you agree to do for a good grade?

3. What did you need to do to get a passport?

4. What do you hope to accomplish after you finish school?

5. Where did you learn to write in English?

6. Why did you decide to come to this school?

7. What do you want to do tonight?

8. Do you want to get a permanent visa?

9. Have you ever failed to be where you were expected?

10. Have you ever threatened to quit your job?

## 2　Verb + object + infinitive

Some verbs are followed by an infinitive plus an object. Among the most common are *tell, advise, invite, warn, require, ask*, and *expect*.

I expect you to do it.

He asked them to read more science books.

Marisa bought a mix to make a chocolate cake.

In these sentences, the subject of the main clause is not the subject of the infinitive.

---

### VERB FOLLOWED BY AN OBJECT AND AN INFINITIVE

| | | | | |
|---|---|---|---|---|
| advise | choose | have | love | remind |
| allow | command | hire | motivate | require |
| ask | dare | instruct | order | send |
| beg | direct | invite | pay | teach |
| bring | encourage | lead | permit | tell |
| build | expect | leave | persuade | urge |
| buy | forbid | let | prepare | want |
| challenge | force | like | promise | warn |

Note that some of these verbs may also be used without an object, as indicated in the box on page 400.

---

## EXERCISE 13.2

## VERB + OBJECT + INFINITIVE

**A.** Answer each question with an appropriate complete sentence.

*Example:* What did you advise him to do?

*I advised him to take the exam and to apply to graduate school.*

1. What was he allowed to do?

2. Where did she ask him to drive her?

3. Who reminded them to bring their books?

4. Who promised you to do the work?

5. What did she tell him to do?

6. What were they prepared to do?

7. What did the police officer command them to do?

8. What do you want to do in the future?

9. What are some people forced to do in order to survive?

10. Did the teacher remind them to do the assignment?

**B.** Fill in the blanks with the appropriate form of the verb and pronoun in parentheses.

*Example:* She begged _____*us*_____ _____*to forgive*_____ (we, forgive) her.

"Class, next week is the state licensing exam. Can anyone tell me how many parts you will be asked to complete? Dan."

"The examiners will ask _____

_____ (we, answer) four different parts."

"Are _____ prepared _____ (you, answer) all four parts?"

"I would like _____ _____ (he, skip) the last part, but I don't think he will."

"What do _____ expect _____ (you, happen) after the test?"

"After the exam, it will be time for the students to relax. I will urge _____ _____ (they, celebrate) at the campus restaurant."

"Well, I hope that I have taught _____

_____ (you, expect) almost anything on the test."

"You have done a great job! You've instructed _____ _____ (we, be) ready for all possibilities."

"Well, I encourage _____ _____ (you, sleep) well the night before the exam."

"I agree, and I hope they will allow _____ _____ (we, rest) during the exam. It lasts all day."

**C.** Fill in each blank with the appropriate form of the verb or pronoun in parentheses.

*Example:* They ____*asked*____ (ask) ____*me*____

____*to explain*____ (me, explain) how to fly a kite.

Last year, I was _____ (invite) by a Chinese university _____ (teach) English to graduate students in science. They _____ (want) _____ (I, teach) them how to write on an advanced level.

At first, when I _____ (ask) my school adminis-trators for a leave, they _____ (refuse) _____ (give) me permission. But I _____ (ask) _____ _____ (they, reconsider), and finally they _____ (allow) _____ (I, go). I had always _____ (want) _____ (travel) to China, and I _____ (expect) _____ _____ (it, be) a wonderful experience.

It was. I _____ (teach) _____ _____ (they, write) better in English, and I _____ (urge) _____ _____ (they, try) to visit the United States. They were such a wonderful group that I would _____ (hire) _____ _____ (they, be) my assistants anytime. I

_____ (think)   I _____ (motivate)

_____   _____ (they, do) their best.

**3** **Infinitive with *to* omitted**

The infinitive with *to* omitted forms a phrase that is used as the direct object of such verbs as *do, help, observe, feel, let, see, hear, make,* and *watch*.

I let him sail the small boat.

She heard them come in last night.

The nurse felt the patient's heart rate increase.

The infinitive without *to* may also be used as the object of a preposition such as *besides, except,* or *but*.

She would do nothing but cry.

They could do nothing besides sympathize.

## EXERCISE 13.3

### INFINITIVE WITH *TO* OMITTED

Complete each sentence using an appropriate infinitive or infinitive phrase with *to* omitted.

*Example:*   She watched . . .

*She watched the plants grow taller each day.*

1. She helped me . . .


2. He let them . . .


3. They did nothing besides . . .


4. Aaron heard . . .

5. The teacher makes us . . .

6. I observed the moon . . .

7. They watched the cat . . .

8. He would do nothing but . . .

9. The doctor felt . . .

10. We saw . . .

**Gerunds**

A gerund or gerund phrase may be used as the object of a verb or the object of a preposition to express something real, vivid, and fulfilled. In the negative, *not* precedes the gerund.

We enjoy watching old movies.

They enjoy swimming.

We spoke about watching old movies.

He excels at swimming.

They considered not swimming because the lifeguard was off duty.

He resents not having a car.

| VERBS FOLLOWED BY A GERUND | | | | |
|---|---|---|---|---|
| admit | delay | finish | permit | resist |
| advise | deny | forbid | postpone | resume |
| appreciate | detest | get through | practice | risk |
| avoid | dislike | have | quit | spend (time) |
| can't help | enjoy | imagine | recall | suggest |
| complete | escape | mind | report | tolerate |
| consider | excuse | miss | resent | waste (time) |

## EXERCISE 13.4

## GERUNDS

**A.** Use a gerund or gerund phrase to complete each sentence.

*Example:* When Joe had worked three hours, he quit

_working_.

1. Mark detests ——————— so much he actually avoids

   ———————.

2. Do you permit ——————— in the lobby?

3. I enjoy ——————— after a big meal.

4. The teacher advises ——————— before the final.

5. When Nabil tells a joke, the class can't stop

   ———————.

6. That teacher is so dull that I can't resist ———————
   during his lessons.

7. She said she can't help ——————— the whole house
   every week.

8. The security officer asked me to stop, but I just kept

   ———————.

9. Many restaurants permit ——————— in a certain section.

10. They suggest ——————— after a long run.

**B.** Write a complete sentence telling whether your instructor permits or doesn't permit each activity. Then give a reason.

*Example:* studying in the classroom

*Mr. Nelson permits studying in the classroom. He says it may help our grades.*

1. smoking in the classroom

2. reading the newspaper during class

3. sleeping in class

4. borrowing someone's dictionary

5. doing other students' homework for them

**C.** Finish each sentence with an appropriate gerund or gerund phrase.

*Example:* I dislike *taking tests* .

1. I enjoy _____

2. I avoid _____

3. I always finish _____

4. I practice _____

5. I regret _____

## 1  Verb + preposition

Many verbs in English are followed by a preposition (*on, up, about, in, to, of*). Some of these two- and three-word verbs are usually followed by the gerund form.

Note that a verb following a preposition is always in the gerund form.

He succeeded in calming the angry crowd.

They talked about saving money.

Irina admits to liking chocolate.

The morning was so beautiful that he felt like singing.

### VERBS FOLLOWED BY A PREPOSITION AND A GERUND

| | | |
|---|---|---|
| admit to | depend on | plan on |
| approve of | disapprove of | prevent (someone) from |
| argue about | discourage from | refrain from |
| believe in | dream about | succeed in |
| care about | feel like | talk about |
| complain about | forget about | think about |
| concentrate on | insist on | worry about |
| confess to | object to | |

## 2  Phrasal verbs

A large number of verbs followed by prepositions in English are called *phrasal verbs* and are considered idiomatic. That is, the meaning of the verb + preposition (particle) is not the same as the component parts. (See Chapter 11.) Some of these verbs are frequently followed by a gerund. For example, the combination *look forward to* means "to expect or anticipate, usually pleasantly." Other idiomatic verbs followed by gerunds are *keep on* (meaning "to continue"), *put off* ("to postpone"), *give up* ("to stop"), *get used to* ("to become accustomed to"), and *be used to* ("to be accustomed to").

Some verbs follow the pattern verb + object + preposition. If such a verb is followed by another verb, the second verb must be in gerund form. These verbs include *apologize to someone for, blame someone for, thank someone for,* and *warn someone about.*

## 3    Adjectives and nouns followed by prepositions

Some adjectives are followed by prepositions. When a verb is used after these adjective phrases, it must be in gerund form. Some common adjective + preposition combinations are *afraid of, guilty of, proud of, tired of, concerned about, worried about, accustomed to, famous for,* and *responsible for.*

There is also a series of common noun + preposition combinations that are frequently followed by a gerund or gerund phrase.

He is in charge of running the store.

They are in danger of failing because they are not attending class.

Norbert had reasons for quitting his job.

---

### NOUN + PREPOSITION COMBINATIONS

| | | |
|---|---|---|
| difficulty in | in favor of | problem in |
| experience in | in place of | reason for |
| impression of | in return for | requirement for |
| in addition to | interest in | technique for |
| in charge of | in the middle of | the point of |
| in danger of | need for | |

---

## EXERCISE 13.5

## VERB + PREPOSITION

---

**A.** Complete each sentence with an appropriate gerund or gerund phrase.

*Example:* The instructor asked me if I was worried about

> *failing the course.*

1. She is afraid of _____

2. I apologized to the teacher for _____

3. The suspect is accused of _____

4. He is in danger of _____

5. The boy complains about _____ because they don't fit.

6. George said he was thinking about _____

7. I warned the children about _____

8. The supervisor explained the need for _____

9. We were told to concentrate on _____

10. Mother said the clothes were not appropriate for _____

**B.** Supply the correct objective form and gerund phrase for each sentence.

*Example:* He suspected ___*them*___ of *stealing his watch* (they, steal).

1. Mother forgave _____ for _____ (we, break).

2. The student apologized to _____ for _____ (I, step).

3. The government warned _____ about _____ (he, cheat).

4. We prevented _____ from _____ (they, take).

5. She devotes _____ to _____ (herself, practice).

6. I blame _____ for _____ (you, fail).

7. Because he suspected _____ of _____ (she, take), he accused _____ of _____ (she, steal).

8. The boss blames _____ for _____ (himself, lose).

9. I reprimanded _____ for _____
   (they, lie).

10. I forgive _____ for _____ (she, slap).

**C.** Fill in each blank with an appropriate preposition and the verb in gerund form.

*Example:* Lee took pride *in speaking* (speak) perfect English.

Isaac was proud _____ (look) good. He always dressed well. He was fond _____ (wear) the newest styles in sneakers and jeans. Whenever he went to the mall, he couldn't refrain _____ (buy) something new.

At school, he was famous _____ (appear) in a new outfit quite regularly. Some people accused him _____ (be) conceited. And his mother warned him _____ (lose) the respect of others, but she never prevented him _____ (do) what he wanted. She said, "You work part time and make a salary, so you're in charge _____ (spend) that money as you see fit. I don't blame you _____ (want) to look good, but you ought to care _____ (do) well in school, too."

Isaac always concentrated _____ (study). He was good _____ (read and write). So he succeeded _____ (pass) all his courses. He was happy about this. And he always looked forward _____ (wear) new clothes.

## 4  *Go* + gerund

The verb *go* is followed by a gerund in some idiomlike expressions. These usually refer to recreational actions.

Do you go fishing often?

I went swimming yesterday.

They go jogging every morning.

---

### COMMON ACTIVITIES IN *GO* + GERUND FORM

| | | |
|---|---|---|
| go bowling | go hiking | go sailing |
| go camping | go hunting | go shopping |
| go dancing | go jogging | go sightseeing |
| go fishing | go running | go swimming |

---

### EXERCISE 13.6

### *GO* + GERUND

Write a complete sentence using each expression.

*Example:*  go dancing

*She likes to go dancing every weekend.*

1. go fishing


2. go shopping


3. go skiing


4. go swimming


5. go hunting

6. go jogging

7. go sailing

8. go driving

9. go skating

10. go running

**5**  **Possessive + gerund**

A possessive noun or pronoun is used to modify a gerund.

The teacher complained about their arriving so late.

The teacher talked about Eric's writing.

He didn't like her taking the car.

## EXERCISE 13.7

## POSSESSIVE MODIFYING A GERUND

Fill in each blank with the appropriate possessive + gerund forms of the words in parentheses.

*Example:*  We were excited by *his winning* (he, win) the race.

1. His parents are proud of _____ (she, make) the team.

2. She was mad about _____ (not, he, want) to go out.

3. I couldn't understand _____ (they, feel) that way.

4. Everyone was shocked by _____ (we, win) the award for neatness.

5. I object to _____ (you, speak) out of turn.

6. He complained about _____ (we, have) such bad seats.

7. They all resented _____ (Nora, manipulate) them like that.

8. He greatly appreciated _____ (we, lend) him the car.

9. They should take advantage of _____ (the expert, be) here today.

10. You don't understand _____ (not, I, want) to do it.

## 13d Using infinitives and gerunds

### 1 Verbs followed by infinitives or gerunds

While there are some verbs that can be followed only by infinitives and some that can be followed only by gerunds, there are other verbs that can be followed by either infinitives or gerunds. Sometimes there is no difference in meaning.

> It began to snow.
> It began snowing.

> I started to study.
> I started studying.

Verbs that have little or no difference in meaning with either construction include *begin, start, continue, like, prefer, can't stand, hate, love,* and *can't bear.*

> With other verbs, there is a marked difference in meaning.

> I stopped to call my friend.

> I stopped calling my friend.

*Stop* + infinitive means "to stop for a reason, to do something." *Stop* + gerund means "to quit, to discontinue an action."

It helps to remember that in general, infinitives imply something for the future, something as yet unfulfilled.

> He stopped to smoke.

Gerunds, conversely, express something real and already fulfilled.

> He stopped smoking.

Verbs that express a difference in meaning when followed by an infinitive or a gerund include *stop*, *remember*, *forget*, *regret*, and *try*.

## EXERCISE 13.8

## VERBS FOLLOWED BY INFINITIVES OR GERUNDS

**A.** Complete each sentence with an appropriate infinitive, infinitive phrase, gerund, or gerund phrase using the verb in parentheses. In some sentences, either solution is possible.

*Example:* I remember ___*eating*___ (eat) Grandma's famous stew.

1. I stopped _____ (smoke) last year.

2. She stopped _____ (smoke) before she came into the party.

3. If you're tired while driving, stop _____ (have) a cup of coffee.

4. If you're very sleepy, stop _____ (drive) and pull over.

5. It began _____ (rain) late last night.

6. She loves _____ (sleep) late.

7. Last year, I tried _____ (stop) smoking, but I couldn't.

8. She can't stand _____ (sit) in the bleachers.

9. It started _____ (snow) while we were walking home.

10. She is trying _____ (learn) French in her spare time.

11. He was cold, so he tried _____ (close) the window, but it didn't help.

12. Sean always remembers _____ (lock) the door.

13. Sean remembers _____ (run) with his pet dog.

14. I regret _____ (lend) them the money.

15. I prefer _____ (leave) early in the evening.

**B.** Fill in each blank with the correct verb tense for the first verb and an infinitive, infinitive phrase, gerund, or gerund phrase for the second verb. In some sentences, either is appropriate.

*Example:* Doris *regretted leaving* (regret, leave) her old school.

Last year, Rose _____ (consider, go) to a high

school downtown, but she finally _____ (decide, at-

tend) the one in her neighborhood. She _____

(prefer, stay) close to home. Some of her friends, however,

_____ (choose, leave) the neighborhood.

Each day on the bus, she _____ (enjoy, talk) to

her friends. She _____ (expect, meet) her two best

friends at the bus stop each morning. They _____

(appreciate, see) each other and always sit together if they can.

They _____ (like, share) the school gossip and

_____ (try, avoid) arguing about anything.

Rose _____ (remember, have) these friends for-

ever.

**C.** Fill in each blank with an infinitive or a gerund. Only one or the other is correct in each case.

*Example:* Gregory couldn't resist _*adopting*_ the adorable
puppy.

In the future, Maria hopes _____ her degree in marketing. At first, she wanted _____ biology, but she found out that she disliked _____ about plants and cells, and she couldn't deny _____ the sight of blood. She worked as an intern at a marketing company one summer and discovered that she loved _____ this kind of work. Therefore, she has decided to avoid _____ courses in science. She would like _____ a career in marketing.

**2** **Adjective + infinitive**

Sometimes an infinitive is used after an adjective.

She is so happy to be here.

I'm sad to see you so ill.

### ADJECTIVES FOLLOWED BY AN INFINITIVE

| | | | | |
|---|---|---|---|---|
| afraid | delighted | happy | proud | stunned |
| amazed | determined | hesitant | ready | stupid |
| anxious | eager | likely | relieved | surprised |
| ashamed | foolish | lucky | reluctant | upset |
| astonished | fortunate | motivated | sad | willing |
| careful | free | pleased | shocked | wrong |
| content | glad | prepared | sorry | |

## EXERCISE 13.9

## ADJECTIVES FOLLOWED BY INFINITIVES

Complete each sentence with an appropriate infinitive or infinitive phrase.

*Example:*   I am glad . . .

*I am glad to be here.*

1. She was sorry . . .

2. Zarus was upset . . .

3. They were prepared . . .

4. Mother is anxious . . .

5. The class is motivated . . .

6. I am determined . . .

7. Lydia is afraid . . .

8. He said he would be delighted . . .

9. The team is proud . . .

10. I would be happy . . .

11. She was sad . . .

12. We were relieved . . .

13. The child was lucky . . .

14. Father is content . . .

15. He was ashamed . . .

**3**   **Infinitives with *too* and *enough***

An infinitive is often used with *too* and *enough*.
*Too* precedes an adjective or an adverb and implies a negative result.

That box is too heavy to lift.

We are too late to be admitted to the theater.

*Too much* and *too many* are used for quantities.

We had too much food to eat.

There were too many people to feed.

*Enough* follows an adjective or an adverb to imply sufficiency. It may also be used with nouns.

We had enough to eat.

He is tall enough to touch the ceiling.

She has enough talent to be the next president.

The infinitive may be preceded by *for* + an object.

The food is too hot for us to eat.

The line was short enough for us to arrive on time.

## EXERCISE 13.10

## INFINITIVES WITH *TOO* AND *ENOUGH*

Write two sentences using each word. Make one a negative sentence with *too* and the other a positive sentence with *enough*.

*Example:* busy

*I'm too busy to go.*
*She is just busy enough to feel useful.*

1. late

2. young

3. cold

4. difficult

5. tired

6. expensive

7. heavy

8. easy

9. big

10. small

**Gerunds and infinitives as subjects**

Both a gerund or gerund phrase and an infinitive or infinitive phrase can be the subject of a sentence. The gerund form as subject is much more common.

Dancing is my favorite pastime.

Sleeping in a tent can be fun.

To dance is a pleasure.

To sleep in a tent is fun.

*It* can be used for a delayed subject in a general sentence. (See also Chapter 9.) *For* + an object may be used to provide a specific subject for the infinitive.

It is fun to sleep in a tent.

It is fun for us to get together.

## EXERCISE 13.11

## GERUNDS AND INFINITIVES IN THE SUBJECT POSITION

**A.** Complete each sentence.

*Example:* Making a cake *requires the right ingredients.*

1. Taking care of a baby _____

2. Writing to my mother _____

3. Learning to ski _____

4. Not understanding how to do something _____

5. Living in a big city _____

**B.** Complete each sentence with a gerund or a gerund phrase.

*Example:* _____*Driving while drunk*_____ is very dangerous.

1. _____ is bad for your health.

2. _____ is the right thing to do.

3. _____ is good for your nerves.

4. _____ is illegal.

5. _____ is not very smart.

**C.** Combine each pair of sentences, using a gerund or gerund phrase as the subject.

*Example:*   I play ball with my friends. It is often exhausting.

*Playing ball with my friends is often exhausting.*

1. I wash dishes at the restaurant. It is very boring.

2. I study chemistry. It is interesting.

3. I study physics. It is difficult.

4. I play the violin. It takes a lot of practice.

5. I go camping with my friends. It is a nice change of pace.

6. I study literature. It involves a lot of reading.

7. I run a small business. It is time-consuming.

8. I read the census reports. It is hard on the eyes.

9. I drive a truck. It can be uncomfortable after a while.

10. I study chemical engineering. It takes serious concentration.

**D.** Complete each sentence with a delayed infinitive subject.

*Example:*   It is bad for us ___ *to be late for class.* ___

1. It is difficult for them _____

2. It is easy for you _____

3. It is fun for her _____

4. It is frightening for children _____

5. It is important for us _____

**E.** Make an existential sentence with the words given.

*Example:* difficult, child

*It is difficult for a child to learn patience.*

1. fun, boy

2. important, children

3. hard, parents

4. necessary, students

5. boring, children

## 5   Past and passive forms of infinitives and gerunds

The infinitive and gerund forms may use auxiliaries and the past participle to indicate tense and voice.

**PAST**

**INFINITIVE:** *to have* + past participle

**GERUND:** *having* + past participle

The argument appears to have ended in a draw.

She forgets having fallen down the stairs.

Note that the past infinitive or gerund expresses something that happened before the time of the main verb.

**PASSIVE**

**INFINITIVE:** *to be* + past participle

GERUND: *being* + past participle

He didn't expect to be distracted by the noise.

Lola enjoyed being invited to the party.

PAST PASSIVE

INFINITIVE: *to have been* + past participle

GERUND: *having been* + past participle

I am lucky to have been allowed to teach the class.

She appreciated having been given a chance.

## EXERCISE 13.12

## PAST AND PASSIVE INFINITIVES AND GERUNDS

**A.** Fill in each blank with the appropriate infinitive or gerund form of the verb in parentheses.

*Examples:*   He doesn't appreciate ___*being told*___ (told) to go home.
She was angry at me for ___*having taken*___ (take) the money without asking her.

1. I regret _____ (answer) your letter so late.

2. He appears _____ (gain) control over his emotions.

3. The class expects _____ (invite) to the teacher's house.

4. I keep on _____ (interrupt) by that woman.

5. Jane wished _____ (spare) these difficulties.

6. He recollects _____ (tell) that he had been in an accident.

7. It is quite easy _____ (trick) by all the details.

8. She didn't appreciate _____ (not, encourage) to participate.

9. She doesn't recall _____ (hit) by the flying glass.

10. They agreed _____ (not, involve) in the entire project.

11. I am angry at _____ (push) aside by the bully.

12. Eli is happy _____ (give) the chance to prove his ability.

**B.** Complete each sentence, using a past, passive, or past passive infinitive or gerund.

*Example:* Helen avoids *being seen* (see) in a bathing suit.

1. I don't think I know him, and I don't recall ever _____ (meet).

2. This package has _____ (sent) today. People are waiting for it.

3. He was ill, but he appears _____ (recover).

4. Dino appreciates _____ (have) the use of the computer for two weeks.

5. I'm not sure where he's from, but I think he said something about _____ (live) in Central America.

6. Margot is camera shy; she always avoids _____ (photograph).

7. We were very happy _____ (see) you.

8. Being on a tight budget, he appreciates _____ (invite) to dinner.

9. She complained about _____ (not, tell).

10. The boss expects _____ (inform).

## 13e  *That* complements

Both the infinitive and the possessive + gerund constructions are what are known as **complements.** The complement construction allows the embedding of a sentence within another sentence. For example, the sentence *It's time for them to leave* is really two sentences:

It's time.

They leave.

The sentence *Kevin's studying pleases me* is really these two sentences:

Kevin studies.

It pleases me.

A third common complement is called a **clausal complement,** which is usually introduced by *that*. The complementizer *that* is distinct from the relative pronoun *that*; it cannot be replaced by *who* or another relative pronoun.

### 1  Three types of clausal complements

1. Clausal complements (*that* clauses) follow certain verbs, including *wish, say, hope, believe, know, guess, feel, trust, think,* and *acknowledge.*

   Junji says that he will return to his country.

   Mark thinks that he will get a job soon.

   Robert knows that Rhonda will help him.

2. *That* clauses also follow specific nouns dealing with information or ideas, including *news, fact, opinion, conclusion, announcement, statement, idea, theory, claim, decision,* and *feeling.*

   The news that her baby was well pleased us all.

   The announcement that a storm was coming scared the children.

3. A final type of *that* clause occurs as the delayed subject in an existential sentence (see Chapter 9).

   It surprises me that she cheated on the exam.

   This type of complement may also appear (much less frequently) in the subject position.

   That she cheated on the exam surprised me.

## 2 Omission of *that*

*That* in a *that* clause may be omitted if it introduces a noun clause and if no misunderstanding can result.

| | |
|---|---|
| ACCEPTABLE | He knows the delivery will arrive at noon. |
| CONFUSING | He knows the students in his class will arrive at noon. (On first reading, *the students in his class* is taken for the direct object, whereas in fact it is the subject of a relative clause.) |
| IMPROVED | He knows that the students in his class will arrive at noon. |

## EXERCISE 13.13

## CLAUSAL COMPLEMENTS: *THAT* CLAUSES

A. Complete each sentence with a *that* clause.

*Example:* He trusts . . .

*He trusts that his boss will pay him.*

1. She believes . . .

2. Pol guesses . . .

3. Johnny acknowledged . . .

4. I wish . . .

5. The teacher says . . .

6. Everyone here hopes . . .

7. I should have known . . .

8. In my heart, I feel . . .

9. She trusted . . .

10. One should always think . . .

B. Complete each sentence with an appropriate *that* clause.

Example: The news _*that he was unhurt*_ relieved me.

1. The feeling _____ scared me.

2. The news _____ was a pleasant surprise.

3. The decision _____ invigorated him.

4. The fact _____ frightened them.

5. He disputed the claim _____.

6. She expressed the opinion _____.

7. He came to the conclusion _____.

8. The statement _____ was erroneous.

9. The idea _____ was expressed by everyone.

10. He is researching the theory _____.

C. Underline each *that* clauses from which *that* has been omitted.

Example: The fact <u>the woman was alive</u> surprised me.

1. Gert hopes the gift is a pair of shoes.

2. The idea the cell is immortal is foolish.

3. She wishes she had never met him.

4. They believe he just left town.

5. We all had the feeling the storm was coming.

6. Mack trusts the teacher will pass him.

7. Jason knows the mail comes after noon each day.

8. He disputed the conclusion he stole the money.

9. I object to the idea they are racists.

10. She always acknowledges they helped her a lot.

**D.** Write a complete sentence with an appropriate *that* clause.

*Example:* It surprises me . . .

*It surprises me that meat is so cheap and plentiful in America.*

1. It shocks me . . .

2. It annoys me . . .

3. It angers me . . .

4. It makes me happy . . .

5. It amazes me . . .

# CHAPTER 14

# More About Complex Sentences

**14a** **Adverb clause movement**

For added emphasis or for sentence variety, some adverb clauses can be moved from the end to the beginning of a sentence. These include adverb clauses of cause, condition, frequency, and time.

She was late because her car broke down.
Because her car broke down, she was late.

We will go after the last person leaves.
After the last person leaves, we will go.

She will be the winner if she scores twenty-five points.
If she scores twenty-five points, she will be the winner.

When the adverb clause is at the beginning of a sentence, it is followed by a comma.

Some adverb clauses, like comparison clauses, cannot be moved and are said to have a fixed order. The following sentences cannot be changed by moving the subordinate clause:

Lon seems as mature as his brother.

He works harder than I do.

## EXERCISE 14.1

## ADVERB CLAUSE MOVEMENT

Whenever possible, change these sentences by moving the adverb clause to the front of the sentence and use a comma. If no such change is possible, write *NA* (not applicable).

*Examples:*   You'll be fired because you are always late.

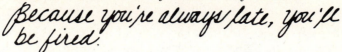

*Because you're always late, you'll be fired.*

Sean's drawing is not as attractive as Kevin's.

*NA*

1. He was tired out after his long walk.

2. Julia waited while I packed the lunch.

3. The apple tree is not as tall as the maple tree next to it.

4. He was smiling even though he had lost the race.

5. He waited for us until he had to go to work.

6. June always gets more sleep than I do.

7. Eduardo will give us some help even if he is busy.

8. I love it when the weather is cool.

9. They will go to China if the school invites them.

10. The boat continued to circle in the water while we dived down below.

## 14b Reduced adverb clauses

When logical relationships are expressed in a sentence, two full clauses are not always necessary. Redundancy and repetition are usually avoided in discourse unless there is a specific reason for them.

As with adjective clauses, some adverb clauses may be reduced to modifying phrases, and the changes are made in the same way.

1. When the subject of the adverb clause and the subject of the main clause are the same, the subject and a form of the verb *be* in the dependent clause may be omitted.

   While he was running to school, he noticed his sneaker was ripped.

   While running to school, he noticed his sneaker was ripped.

2. If there is no form of *be* in the dependent clause, the subject may be omitted and the verb changed to the *-ing* form.

   Before she left town, she called her mother.

   Before leaving town, she called her mother.

No change is possible if the subject of the main clause is different from the subject of the dependent clause. For example, *While she was packing, they left for the beach* cannot be rewritten. The two subjects are not the same.

Adverb clauses beginning with *after, while, before,* and *since* can be changed to modifying phrases.

   Since Loris came to the United States, he has had many jobs.
   Since coming to the United States, Loris has had many jobs.

   Alberto was hurt while he was walking to school.
   Alberto was hurt while walking to school.

## EXERCISE 14.2

## REDUCING ADVERB CLAUSES OF TIME TO MODIFYING PHRASES

Whenever possible, change the adverb clauses to modifying phrases. If no change is possible, write *NA*.

*Examples:* Before I left for the beach, I got some food.

*Before leaving for the beach, I got some food.*

While she was ironing last night, the kids played ball outside.

*NA*

1. Since you came to school, everyone has gotten to know you.

2. I have learned a lot of English since I came here.

3. Before I visited Washington State, I had never seen a really big mountain.

4. Clare rented a car before she drove to New York.

5. While I was trying to study, a fly kept annoying me.

6. After he took his shower, he ate his breakfast.

7. Alice went home after she finished her shopping.

8. The Chens have experienced many changes in their lives since they moved from China.

9. When I was living in Brazil, I enjoyed the food very much.

10. Always watch the road while you are driving.


## 1   Reducing *while* clauses

In addition to reducing a clause to a phrase by omitting the repeated subject and a form of *be*, the subordinating word may also be omitted. Sometimes *while* (meaning "during, at the same time") is omitted at the beginning of a sentence. The *-ing* phrase gives the sentence the same meaning. The following three sentences mean the same thing.

While he was walking to school, Alberto was hurt.

While walking to school, Alberto was hurt.

Walking to school, Alberto was hurt.

## 2    Reducing cause-and-effect clauses

*Because* may be omitted from a cause-and-effect clause in three instances:

1. When an *-ing* phrase at the beginning of the sentence gives the meaning of *because*

    Because he wanted some time to complete the job, Mel took a day off from school.

    Wanting some time to complete the job, Mel took a day off from school.

2. When *having* + past participle give the meaning of *because*

    Because I took that test earlier, I don't need to take it now.

    Having taken that test earlier, I don't need to take it now.

3. When a form of *be* is changed to *being* to express a cause-and-effect relationship

    Because they were unable to catch the early flight, they stayed an extra night.

    Being unable to catch the early flight, they stayed an extra night.

    This sentence may be further reduced:

    Unable to catch the early flight, they stayed an extra night.

## 3    Reducing *when* clauses

An adverb clause introduced by *when* may be reduced to a modifying phrase beginning with *upon* + *-ing*.

When I turned 20, I bought my first car.

Upon turning 20, I bought my first car.

## 4    Reduced clauses of comparison

Adverb clauses of comparison (using *than* and *as*) have two distinctive characteristics:

1. Part or all of the verb, though needed grammatically, is usually not expressed.
2. When an action verb is reduced from the subordinate clause, an appropriate form of the auxiliary verb *do* is often used, even though it does not occur in the main clause.

    Silver is more valuable than copper (is).

    Her house is not as big as yours (is).

Tom worked harder than his brother did.

Ryuko earns more money than I do.

## EXERCISE 14.3

## REDUCED ADVERB CLAUSES

**A.** Reduce the adverb clause in each sentence.

*Example:* While I was running in the park, I saw some of my friends parking their car.

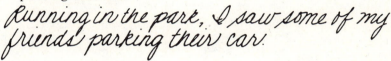
*Running in the park, I saw some of my friends parking their car.*

1. Because I was in shape, I could do the exercises.

2. Because he did not want to disturb his father, he tried to be quiet.

3. Because I had forgotten to pay the bill, I received a late notice.

4. Because he is sick, he can't come to the meeting.

5. While I was traveling across China, I was amazed at the number of people living there.

6. While I was studying in my room, I heard a loud noise in front of the building.

7. Because he lacked the proper license, he did not get the job.

8. Because she needed some extra credits, she took a summer course.

9. While I am driving on the highway, I always use my mirrors.

10. Because she was totally surprised by the idea, she didn't know what to say.

**B.** Reduce the adverb clause in each sentence by using *having* + past participle or *upon* + *-ing* where appropriate.

*Examples:*  Because I had eaten dinner already, I left before the rest of the group.

*Having eaten dinner already, I left before the rest of the group.*

When I reached the store, I parked my car.

*Upon reaching the store, I parked my car.*

1. I almost fell when I walked past your house.

2. Because she had paid the bill on time, she refused to pay the interest.

3. When Van crossed the finish line, he knew he had won a medal.

4. Bring your notebook up to the teacher's desk when you finish writing.

5. I felt nervous when I met my future in-laws.

**C.** Complete each sentence appropriately. Add commas where necessary.

*Example:*  Before I left work . . .

*Before I left work, I cleared my desk.*

1. After driving for three hours . . .

2. Having failed the driver's test . . .

3. Upon finishing his lunch . . .

4. Since arriving in the city . . .

5. Before going to work . . .

6. Upon hearing an explosion down the block . . .

7. Having been told not to enter . . .

8. After arriving late for the show . . .

9. Being the largest store in town . . .

10. Driving to school yesterday . . .

## 14c Expressing cause or reason

### 1 Expressing cause or reason by combining ideas

The decision to coordinate or subordinate clauses by combining them into one sentence is made to improve logical clarity or to avoid a series of short, choppy sentences. Either way, the writer is combining two or more ideas that could be written as separate sentences; for example:

He wanted to work. He quit school.

These sentences could be combined using *because, since, so,* or *therefore.* The following sentences all mean the same thing.

He quit school because he wanted to work.

He quit school since he wanted to work.

He wanted to work, so he quit school.

He wanted to work; therefore, he quit school.

To combine sentences effectively calls for a grasp of sentence structure as well as an understanding of the intended meaning.

Using coordination (either the coordinating conjunctions or the conjunctive adverbs) shows that the ideas expressed in each assertion are equal grammatically and logically. Note that we use the semicolon (;) before *therefore* and follow it with a comma (,) because it is a conjunctive adverb. We put a comma before *so* because it is a coordinating conjunction. The conjunctive adverbs (also called *transitionals*) are always more formal than the coordinating conjunctions. They are used in speeches, formal reports, and other serious compositions.

Using subordination (combining the clauses with a subordinating conjunction or a relative pronoun) shows that there is a marked difference between the clauses: One is dependent on the other. There are a main idea and one or more subordinate ideas. We set off a subordinate clause at the beginning of a sentence with a comma.

*Because* is a word that directly expresses cause or reason. It answers the question *why?*

Why was John late?
He was late because his car broke down.

Why did Greta get an *A*?
Greta got an *A* because she studied a lot.

The ideas in these sentences can also be related by using the word *therefore*, which also expresses cause or reason.

His car broke down; therefore, he was late.

Greta studied hard; therefore, she got an *A*.

We can move the *because* clause:

Because the car broke down, he was late.

This kind of movement is not possible with conjunctive adverbs like *therefore*.

*Since* can have the same meaning as *because*.

Because he didn't study, he failed the test.

Since he didn't study, he failed the test.

*Therefore* has the same meaning as *so*.

He didn't study; therefore, he failed the test.

He didn't study, so he failed the test.

## EXERCISE 14.4

## EXPRESSING CAUSE AND EFFECT

**A.** Combine each pair of sentences, first with *because* and then with *therefore*.

Example:   Hazel gets good grades. She studies very hard.

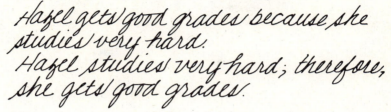

Hazel gets good grades because she studies very hard.
Hazel studies very hard; therefore, she gets good grades.

1. Carmencita goes to school. She wants an education.

2. Mother set the table. It was dinnertime.

3. Kevin ate lunch early. He was very hungry.

4. Lillian put on a dress. She wanted to look nice.

5. Tom turned on the light. It was dark.

6. Mose will study hard tomorrow. He wants to pass the test.

7. People read. They want to learn.

8. We had an accident. We were careless.

9. We drove slowly. It was snowing.

10. She went to the dentist. Her teeth hurt.

B.  Change each sentence by using the word in parentheses.

*Example:*  He quit school because he wanted to work. (so)

*He wanted to work, so he quit school.*

1. They took a break because they weren't busy. (therefore)

2. She talked to the teacher because her grades have been bad. (since)

3. He quit his job because he wanted to go to school. (so)

4. He studies hard since he wants an *A*. (so)

5. I have a lot of work, so I couldn't leave. (because)

6. We went home since it was late. (therefore)

7. Since the sun didn't shine, I didn't get a tan. (because)

8. Agnes won the race because she trained for it. (therefore)

9. Because the price was high, I couldn't afford to take the trip. (so)

10. He was tired, so he took a nap. (because)

**C.** Combine each pair of sentences, using the words given in parentheses.

*Example:* It rained tonight. The roads are very wet.

(Because) *Because it rained tonight, the roads are very wet.*

(since) *The roads are very wet since it rained tonight.*

Her computer was broken. She didn't type the statistics.

    1. (so)

    2. (Since)

    3. (because)

The boss was out of town. The meeting was canceled.

    4. (Because)

    5. (therefore)

    6. (Since)

He stayed home. It was a snowy day.

    7. (Since)

    8. (since)

    9. (Because)

    10. (therefore)

### 2   Using prepositions to show cause and reason

Another way of combining ideas is to use a prepositional phrase. *Because of* and *due to* may be used to show cause or reason.

He wanted to work. He quit school.

He quit school because of work.

He quit school due to work.

Whereas a clause contains a subject and a verb, a phrase is a preposition followed by a noun phrase. Like clauses of cause or reason, prepositional phrases of cause or reason may also be moved, and if they come at the beginning, they are set off with a comma.

Because of work, he quit school.

Due to work, he quit school.

## EXERCISE 14.5

## COMBINING IDEAS WITH PREPOSITIONS

**A.** Use the idea in parentheses to complete each sentence.

*Example:* (It was very rainy there.) The trees and grass grew quickly

because of _____ *the rain* _____.

1. (Mrs. Smith has done a lot of gardening.) Due to _____,
we have a beautiful view out this window.

2. (Lon's teacher is absent.) Lon will go home early today because of

_____.

3. (It was cold there.) We all wore our jackets and gloves due to

_____.

4. (The traffic was light.) Because of _____,
we were able to stop and relax for a while.

5. (It was very hot here.) I couldn't work in the attic because of

_____.

**B.** Using *because of* + a noun phrase, combine the situation and the reason to make one sentence.

*Example:* People are careful crossing this street.
Reason: many accidents have occurred here

*People are careful crossing this street because of the many accidents that have occurred here.*

1. People are doing more exercise.
   Reason: the health benefits

2. The buses are always crowded.
   Reason: the increasing number of passengers

3. She was angry at him.
   Reason: their recent argument

4. Many people who smoke cigarettes are quitting.
   Reason: the danger to their lungs

5. Prices have increased a lot.
   Reason: inflation

## 3 Words that express cause, reason, and purpose

If you look up *because, so,* and *therefore* in the dictionary, you will find some other words that mean the same thing. The accompanying box summarizes connecting words used to express cause, reason, and purpose.

---

### WORDS USED TO EXPRESS CAUSE, REASON, AND PURPOSE

**COORDINATING CONJUNCTIONS:** *so, for*

Use a comma before a conjunction because it comes between two complete ideas.

**SUBORDINATING CONJUNCTIONS:** *because, since, as*

The adverb clause may come before or after the independent clause. Use a comma if the adverb clause comes first.

**CONJUNCTIVE ADVERBS:** *therefore, consequently, accordingly, hence*

This formal connector is used with independent clauses. It shows the relationship of the second main clause to the first main clause. The conjunctive adverb may be moved only within the second clause. Since the clauses are independent, they may be treated as separate sentences. To make a compound sentence, use a semicolon (;). If the adverb precedes its clause, it is set off with a comma.

---

> **PREPOSITIONS:** *because of, due to*
>
> A preposition forms a prepositional phrase with an object; it has no subject or verb. If the prepositional phrase precedes the subject and verb, it is usually set off with a comma.

## EXERCISE 14.6

## EXPRESSING CAUSE, REASON, AND PURPOSE

**A.** Use the words *consequently, because of, so, since, due to, therefore,* and *as* to fill in the blanks. Use each word only once.

The mayor said that _____ the recent economic downturn, he had to cut the budget. The cuts will be in many areas. _____ the Board of Education has the largest budget, it will be cut the most. There will be many layoffs of teachers, aides, and other personnel _____ it is their salaries that make up most of the educational budget. When asked about the impact of his cuts on the future of the city, the mayor said, "_____ circumstances beyond our control, we have to do this. By law, I have to balance the budget; _____, we have to cut back our spending." The head of the teachers' union was shocked and said, "This budget shortchanges education; _____, future generations will suffer. We need well-funded education for the city to thrive." One man on the street said, "The politicians don't have the money, _____ the people have to suffer."

**B.** Write a paragraph explaining why you deserve a good grade, why something happened, or why you are in school. Use connectors listed in the box on page 445.

## 14d Expressing opposition, contrast, and unexpected result

### 1 Conjunctions

*While, although, even though,* and *though* are subordinating conjunctions that show opposition. These words express a direct contrast between the two clauses in the sentence. The coordinating conjunctions *but* and *yet* and the conjunctive adverbs *however, nonetheless,* and *nevertheless* also express a direct difference between the first clause and the second. All of the following sentences mean the same thing.

He didn't see her, but she was there.

He didn't see her; however, she was there.

Although she was there, he didn't see her.

He didn't see her even though she was there.

Though he didn't see her, she was there.

Note that adverb clauses with *although* and *even though* may be moved, whereas clauses with coordinating conjunctions and conjunctive adverbs may not. Remember that the conjunctive adverbs (*however, nevertheless*) always sound more formal than the other connectors.

## EXERCISE 14.7

## CONJUNCTIONS EXPRESSING OPPOSITION, CONTRAST, AND UNEXPECTED RESULT

**A.** Complete each sentence with an appropriate clause, using the connecting word in parentheses. Be sure to punctuate your sentence correctly.

*Examples:*   Jim worked very hard yesterday (but)

*Jim worked very hard yesterday, but he didn't accomplish much.*

Jim worked very hard yesterday (however)

*Jim worked very hard yesterday; however, he didn't accomplish much.*

Jim worked very hard yesterday (though)

*Though Jim worked very hard yesterday, he didn't accomplish much.*

1. Arasam has a big house and a new car (even though)

2. Kevin went to the beach (but)

3. Zack drives an old car (nevertheless)

4. Maria is Esperanza's good friend (yet)

5. George is a handsome man (although)

6. Gilbert is a fine mechanic (nevertheless)


7. My room is small (yet)


8. He studied for a long time (nonetheless)


9. She is a very pretty girl (although)


10. We went to the mall (but)


**B.** Transform each sentence, using the words given in parentheses. Be sure to punctuate your sentences correctly.

*Example:* She wanted to act on stage, but she was afraid.

(however) *She wanted to act on stage; however, she was afraid.*

(Although) *Although she wanted to act on stage, she was afraid.*

(though) *She wanted to act on stage though she was afraid.*

She loves her husband, but he has many problems.
1. (nevertheless)


2. (Even though)


3. (While)

Although Maria likes to eat breakfast before going to work, she is often too late to do so.

4. (but)


5. (although)


6. (nevertheless)


They were in a hurry, but the car kept overheating.

7. (though)


8. (yet)


9. (Although)


He went to see her, but she wouldn't talk to him.

10. (Although)


11. (however)


12. (although)


Although he really wanted to do well, he failed the final exam.

13. (although)


14. (but)


15. (however)

**C.** Combine the ideas in each pair of sentences using each of the connectives given.

    *Example:* We wanted to go to the beach. It was raining. (*even though, yet, however*)

        *Even though it was raining, we wanted to go to the beach.*

        *We wanted to go to the beach, yet it was raining.*

        *We wanted to go to the beach; however, it was raining.*

1. Her grade was high. She did not get an *A.* (*although, but, nonetheless*)

2. My room is small. It is very comfortable. (*even though, however, but*)

3. She drove very fast. She missed her flight. (*while, but, nevertheless*)

4. They went to the park. It was snowing. (*even though, yet, nonetheless*)

5. His high-school record was poor. He got into college. (*although, but, however*)

2 **Prepositions**

The prepositions *despite* and *in spite of* may be used to express an unexpected result.

We went to the beach despite the rain.

In spite of the rain, we went to the beach.

## EXERCISE 14.8

## PREPOSITIONS EXPRESSING OPPOSITION, CONTRAST, AND UNEXPECTED RESULT

**A.** Complete each sentence appropriately. Be sure to punctuate your sentences correctly.

*Example:*   Despite her poor health . . .

*Despite her poor health, she became an accomplished harpist.*

1. In spite of his low scores . . .

2. He won the race despite . . .

3. Despite . . . he has been able to pay his bills.

4. He is very popular in spite of . . .

5. Louis lost the race despite . . .

**B.** Fill in each blank with an appropriate connector. Use *although, because, though, despite, however, while, due to, consequently, but,* and *even though.* Use each only once.

Some people think we should explore the Alaskan wilderness

for oil, _____ others do not agree. The advocates

say the most important reason is economic _____

oil is a precious commodity. _____ they admit there

are risks of harm to the environment, they feel that the risks are

worth taking.

_____ this, many people are opposed to the

idea. These people feel that _____ there is a need

for oil, the environment should come first. _____,

_____ the pressure of the oil companies and others,

the project is going forward. _____, don't count the

**14d/Expressing Opposition, Contrast, and Unexpected Result**    **453**

environmentalists out, _____ the search for oil seems to be the winner. The environmentalists have a lot of support and energy; _____, they will be heard from in the future.

## 14e  Expressing conditions

Conditional sentences are used to express inferences and hypothetical ideas. They specify under what conditions something is or is not possible. Conditional sentences are also used to express emotion, make exclamations, and give advice.

A factual conditional sentence in the present tense has two clauses. One is an adverb clause of condition (an *if* clause), which presents possible conditions; the other is the main clause in the sentence, which expresses result.

If you study, you will pass the exam.

If it rains tonight, I will stay home.

An *if* clause expresses a situation or an event that might happen, might be happening, or might have happened. The order of the two clauses may be reversed.

You will pass the exam if you study.

I will stay home if it rains tonight.

The verb in the *if* clause is in the simple present or present continuous tense. The main clause verb is either a simple modal, the present or future tense, or a command.

## EXERCISE 14.9

## EXPRESSING CONDITIONS

Write a complex sentence expressing the consequences of each possibility. Use an *if* clause.

*Examples:* It may be raining tomorrow.

*If it is raining tomorrow, the game will be canceled.*

You might not wake up.

*If I don't wake up, I will miss the bus.*

1. It may snow on Sunday.

2. You may miss the bus.

3. The teacher may be absent on Friday.

4. You might forget your key.

5. Your car might break down.

6. You may get sick.

7. Maybe the sun will be shining tomorrow.

8. Maybe I will have that day off.

9. It may be very cold tomorrow.

10. Maybe we will win the lottery.

### 1 Using *even if* and *whether . . . or not*

An *if* clause is followed by an expected result.

If it rains, the game will be canceled.

A clause with *even if* is followed by an unexpected result. *Even if* has an emphatic tone.

Even if it rains, the game will not be canceled.

You should be there even if you don't want to be.

*Whether . . . or not* is close in meaning to *even if. Whether . . . or not* expresses the ideas that neither condition matters; that is, the conditions are irrelevant, and the result will be the same.

Whether it rains or not, the game will not be canceled.

You should be there whether you want to be or not.

## EXERCISE 14.10

## UNEXPECTED RESULT

---

**A.** Transform each sentence, using the words in parentheses.

*Examples:* If it rains, I will not go out tonight. (even if)

*Even if it rains, I will go out tonight.*

If he is on time, he will get the job. (whether . . . or not)

*Whether he is on time or not, he will get the job.*

1. If it snows, the school will be closed. (even if)

2. If he is sick, he will quit school. (whether . . . or not)

3. If things get worse, we will have to leave. (even if)

4. If you pass the exam, the teacher will give you a good grade. (whether . . . or not)

5. If it is hot tomorrow, we will go to the beach. (whether . . . or not)

**B.** Fill in each blank with an appropriate clause.

Examples: Whether ___*he likes it*___ or not, I will be going.

Even if ___*he doesn't want me to go*___, I will be going.

1. Whether _____ or not, the game will be played.

2. Even if _____, the game will be played.

3. Whether _____ or not, you are responsible.

4. Even if _____, you are responsible.

5. Whether _____ or not, she will pass the course.

6. Even if _____, she will pass the course.

## 2   Using *unless*

*Unless* is often used to give an ultimatum or a warning. *Unless* can often mean "if . . . not." It expresses an exception; the condition is exclusive. The main clause may be in the form of an imperative or a command. Though the following pairs of sentences mean almost the same thing, *unless* is stronger than *if . . . not*.

Unless you apologize, I won't forgive you.
If you don't apologize, I won't forgive you.

Unless you pay me, I won't deliver the materials.
If you don't pay me, I won't deliver the materials.

Unless you can work a lot of hours, don't open a retail store.
If you can't work a lot of hours, don't open a retail store.

## EXERCISE 14.11

## USING *UNLESS*

**A.** Rewrite each sentence, using *unless*.

Example: You can't get a good grade if you don't study.

*You can't get a good grade unless you study.*

1. If you don't enrich the soil, your garden will not prosper.

2. If you do not pay the rent, you will be evicted.

3. He loses money if he does not work.

4. I always get hungry in class if I don't eat breakfast.

5. If the weather does not change, the game will be canceled.

**B.** Complete each sentence with a conditional clause. Be sure to punctuate your sentences correctly.

*Example:* He will fail to get there unless . . .

*He will fail to get there unless his car begins to run better.*

1. Unless . . . he will lose the race.

2. Julia will do well in school unless . . .

3. Kevin's plant will grow tall if . . . not . . .

4. The students will all be happy unless . . .

5. Unless . . . the party will be canceled.

**C.** Write five different appropriate clauses to complete the sentence "You will do well in school unless . . ."

*Example:* *You will do well in school unless you stop studying.*

1.

2.

3.

4.

5.

**D.** For each expression, use *unless* in a negative imperative to warn another student. Follow the example.

*Example:* accept a job during the day

*Don't accept a job during the day unless school is on vacation.*

OR *Unless school is on vacation, don't accept a job during the day.*

1. accept a job at night

2. apply for admission to medical school

3. go out the night before a final exam

4. open a retail store

5. play with matches

**Affirmative implications of *unless***

Although *unless* is often used with negative implications, it can also be used with affirmative implications. It is usually used when discussing plans to express the idea that something could intervene.

I'll see you next week unless my car breaks down.

Unless she has a problem, she will be here soon.

## EXERCISE 14.12

## USING *UNLESS* WITH POSITIVE IMPLICATIONS

For each statement of intent, write a sentence using an *unless* clause.

*Example:*   I'll be there Monday night.

> *Unless I have to work, I'll be there Monday night.*
>
> OR
>
> *I'll be there Monday night unless I have to work.*

1. I'll see you next week.

2. Jill will go to Spain next January.

3. She will pass the chemistry final.

4. Maria will work as a hostess.

5. We'll see you tomorrow.

**3** **Using *only if* or *provided that* to express one condition only**

*Only if* and *provided that* mean that there is only one condition that will cause a particular result.

The experiment will work only if you use salt. (If you use water, oil, pepper, or any other substance, the experiment won't work.)

The car will start provided that you use gasoline. (If you use water, electricity, steam, or some other fuel, the car won't start.)

When an *only if* clause begins a sentence, the subject and verb of the main clause are inverted.

Only if you use salt will the experiment work.


## EXERCISE 14.13

## ON ONE CONDITION

**A.** For each statement, write a sentence using *only if* or *provided that*.

*Example:*   A B.A. degree requires completion of 120 credits.

> *Only if students complete 120 credits will they receive a B.A. degree.*
>
> OR *Provided that students complete 120 credits, they will receive a B.A. degree.*

1. Student admission requires a fee of fifty dollars.

2. A license is granted when the test is passed.

3. A final grade requires the completion of seven papers.

4. All the work must be complete before payment is made.

5. You need a visa to enter that country.

**B.** Complete each sentence so that it makes sense. Be sure to use correct punctuation.

*Example:* I . . . only if . . .

*I will do the work only if you pay me.*

1. He . . . provided that . . .

2. Only if . . . will he . . .

3. Laura . . . only if . . .

4. Provided that . . . Steve . . .

5. Only if . . . will Nicolette . . .

**4** **More ways of expressing condition**

The conjunctive adverb *otherwise* and the coordinating conjunction *or* (or *or else*) may also be used to express conditions. They both mean "if the opposite is true, this result is possible."

I always chain my bike to the fence; otherwise, it might be stolen.

I always chain my bike to the fence, or else it might be stolen.

Because they are conjunctions, *otherwise* and *or* (or *or else*) cannot be moved within the sentence, whereas adverb clauses of conditions (*if* clauses) can.

COMBINING IDEAS: SUMMARY

|  | REASON, PURPOSE, CAUSE | CONTRAST, OPPOSITION | CONDITION |
|---|---|---|---|
| **COORDINATING CONJUNCTIONS** | so | but, yet | or |

Used to combine main clauses to form compound sentences (see Section 4c).

|  | REASON, PURPOSE, CAUSE | CONTRAST, OPPOSITION | CONDITION |
|---|---|---|---|
| **COORDINATING CONJUNCTIONS**<br><br>*Punctuation:* comma + conjunction (semicolon if conjunction is omitted)<br>*Clause movement:* none permitted | so | but, yet | or |
| **CONJUNCTIVE ADVERBS**<br><br>Used to combine main clauses to form compound sentences (see Section 4c).<br>*Punctuation:* semicolon + adverb + comma<br>*Clause movement:* none permitted, but adverb may be moved within the second clause. | therefore, consequently, accordingly, hence | however, nonetheless, nevertheless | otherwise |
| **SUBORDINATING CONJUNCTIONS**<br><br>Used to join one main (independent) clause and one or more dependent (subordinate) clauses to form complex sentences (see 4c and Chapter 14).<br>*Punctuation:* none; if subordinate clause precedes main clause, set off with comma<br>*Clause movement:* permitted | because, since, as | although, though, even though, whereas, while | if, even if, only if, unless, whether . . . or not, provided that, in case, in the event that |
| **PREPOSITIONS**<br><br>Used to introduce a noun phrase as part of a main clause (see Chapter 8).<br>*Punctuation:* none; if prepositional phrase precedes main clause, set off with comma<br>*Clause movement:* permitted | because of, due to | despite, in spite of | in case of, in the event of |

**14e/Expressing Conditions**     463

## EXERCISE 14.14

## CONDITIONS WITH *OTHERWISE, OR,* AND *OR ELSE*

Rewrite each sentence, using *otherwise* and then *or* or *or else* to express the same meaning.

*Example:*   If you don't pay the rent, you will be evicted.

*Pay the rent; otherwise, you will be evicted.*
*Pay the rent, or else you will be evicted.*

1. If you don't hurry, you will be late for class.

2. If I don't do the wash now, I won't have any clothes for work tomorrow.

3. Only if you work hard will you be promoted.

4. If Dennis doesn't start to study, he will not pass the final.

5. If you don't sleep tonight, you will be tired in the morning.

6. You can't enter the country unless you have a visa.

7. Unless you hand in the reports, you won't get a good grade.

8. If you don't have a ticket, they can't give you a seat.

9. He will play soccer only if his father gives permission.

10. Unless you practice often, you won't become an expert player.

## EXERCISE 14.15

## USING VARIOUS CONNECTORS

**A.** Complete each sentence about work with an appropriate clause or phrase. Correct punctuation and capitalization as necessary.

*Example:* I didn't get to work because . . .

*I didn't get to work because I missed the bus.*

1. Because I had to work . . .

2. I worked extra hours because . . .

3. Although I worked . . .

4. I worked overtime although . . .

5. I did not work however . . .

6. I worked for eight hours nevertheless . . .

7. Even though I worked for eight hours . . .

8. I started working at noon but . . .

9. Although I was late for work . . .

10. I was late for work yet . . .

11. I didn't work so . . .

12. I worked late therefore . . .

13. Since I worked late . . .

14. Though I was on time for the bus . . .

15. The boss was angry as . . .

16. Because of . . . I worked overtime.

17. I was on time for work despite . . .

18. In spite of . . . I was early for work.

19. If . . . I will work overtime.

20. I will not work overtime even if . . .

21. I will not come in to work tomorrow unless . . .

22. The boss has to give me a ride otherwise . . .

23. The boss has to give me a raise or . . .

24. I worked hard yet . . .

25. Since I have been working there . . .

**B.** Write complex sentences, adding punctuation where necessary.

*Example:* If he makes a lot of money . . .

*If he makes a lot of money, he will buy a new car.*

1. Because she is . . .

2. Even though the house is new . . .

3. Because the woman who . . .

4. Since the school where we . . .

5. He is happy although he is the man who . . .

6. Unless the car that . . .

7. Only if she is the one who . . .

8. She is in school now although she said . . .

9. Though I didn't hear what . . .

10. Because the hotel where . . .

C. Rewrite each sentence, correcting the errors.

*Example:* Unless I fail the exam, I certainly won't pass the course.

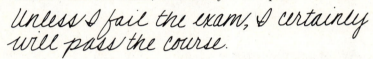

*Unless I fail the exam, I certainly will pass the course.*

1. Even if I work overtime, the boss will appreciate what I've done.

2. Only if I study all night will I fail the exam.

3. I always pay my bills on time however my credit is bad.

4. Although he is a good driver, but he had an accident last week.

5. Because he wants to be a successful doctor; therefore, he works long hours.

6. If he wants to win the game, so he plays very hard.

7. In spite of the wind is blowing hard, so he won't take the boat out now.

8. He always makes money because of he works long hours.

9. Since he has the time, because he like to garden.

10. Even if he pays the other bills, unless the rent is still due.

## 14f Verb tense and conditionals

Choosing the correct verb tenses in the clauses of a conditional sentence presents many options. It requires a firm grasp of the English tense and aspect system and the modal auxiliaries, as well as an understanding of sentence structure and shades of meaning.

There are three major types of conditional sentences: factual conditionals, future (predictive) conditionals, and imaginative conditionals.

### 1 Factual conditionals

Factual conditionals are the most common in everyday English, and the category includes generic, habitual, and inferential sentences.

#### Generic and habitual conditionals

The generic type is frequent in scientific and technical writing and is used to state physical laws. The verbs in both clauses are in the simple present tense.

If water reaches one hundred degrees Celsius, it boils.

If water boils, it evaporates.

The habitual is similar to the generic in that it also states a relationship between the clauses that is not bounded in time, but the relationship is based on habit instead of physical law. Frequent in conversation, habitual conditional sentences may be in the present or the past, with both clauses having the same verb tense.

If I cook, she clears the table.

If he told his son to do something, the boy did it.

*When* or *whenever* may also be used with a generic or habitual conditional.

When water boils, it evaporates.

Whenever I cook, she clears the table.

## EXERCISE 14.16

## GENERIC AND HABITUAL CONDITIONALS

**A.** Match the actions in the left column with their consequences in the right column. Then write a factual conditional sentence for each.

*Example:* _____e_____ boil water

*If you boil water, it evaporates.*

_____ 1. pour oil on water

_____ 2. add lemon juice to milk

_____ 3. fly from west to east

_____ 4. expose water to temperatures below zero degrees Celsius

_____ 5. put salt in water

a. it freezes

b. it floats

c. it curdles

d. it dissolves

e. it evaporates

f. you lose time

1.

2.

3.

4.

5.

**B.** Use each statement to make a conditional sentence of habit. Use *if,* *when,* or *whenever.*

*Examples:* stay up late

*If I stay up late, I am tired the next day.*

eat too much

*Whenever I eat too much, I feel sick.*

1. can't sleep

2. get mad

3. feel angry

4. think about my mother

5. think about my native country

6. meet someone new

7. drink too much water

8. make a mistake in English

9. go to sleep early

10. get tired

**C.**  Complete each statement with an imperative in the main clause.

*Example:*  If your feet are sore, . . .

*If your feet are sore, take off your shoes and rub your toes.*

1. If you see a red light, . . .

2. If your car skids on the ice, . . .

3. If you have a flat tire, . . .

4. Whenever a teacher asks you a question, . . .

5. When you see an accident, . . .

6. Whenever you have a bad fall, . . .

7. If you witness a crime, . . .

8. Whenever the roads are very slippery, . . .

9. When you feel sick, . . .

10. If your ear aches, . . .

### Factual conditionals of inference

Factual conditionals of inference make wider use of tenses and auxiliaries than generic and habitual conditionals, though they do tend to have the same tense or modal in both clauses.

If you will bring something to eat, I will bring something to drink.

If she can be reached, she can be convinced.

Explicit factual conditionals of inference, however, do not have strict parallelism of tense, aspect, or modals in both clauses. Because the *if* clause is used to make an explicit inference, the result clause contains an inferential modal, usually *must* or *should*.

If someone is at home, it must be mother.

If anyone could afford it, it would be Uncle George.

## EXERCISE 14.17

## FACTUAL CONDITIONALS OF INFERENCE

Study the salesman's schedule. Then make explicit inferences with
*must* or *should,* based on the schedule.

LEO THE SALESMAN'S DAY

| | |
|---|---|
| 6:00 | Get up |
| 6:00–6:30 | Read newspaper |
| 6:30–7:30 | Exercise |
| 7:30–8:15 | Shower and eat breakfast |
| 8:15–9:00 | Travel to work |
| 9:00–12:00 | Make appointments and do paperwork |
| 12:00–1:00 | Eat lunch |
| 1:00–3:00 | Call on clients |
| 3:00–5:00 | Make deliveries |
| 5:00–6:00 | Travel home |
| 6:00–7:00 | Eat dinner |
| 7:00–10:00 | Relax, watch TV, read |
| 10:00 | Go to bed |

*Example:* 6:00 A.M.

*If it's 6:00 A.M., Leo must be getting out of bed.*

1. 7:00 A.M.


2. 8:30 A.M.


3. 9:15 A.M.


4. 11:00 A.M.


5. 12:30 P.M.


6. 2:00 P.M.

7. 4:30 P.M.


8. 6:30 P.M.


9. 9:30 P.M.


10. 11:30 P.M.


### 2  Future (predictive) conditionals

Another common conditional is the future or predictive conditional. Future conditional sentences explain the conditions for future plans or contingencies. They answer the question *what if*. The normal verb pattern is present tense in the *if* clause, future tense (*will* or *be going to*) in the main clause.

Sometimes the future outcome expressed in the result clause is not certain and *will* and *be going to* are too strong. In this case, a weaker modal of prediction, such as *may* or *should*, can be used. The prediction scale for modals (outlined in Chapter 12) applies here: *will* = absolutely certain, *should* = probable, *may* and *might* = possible.


## EXERCISE 14.18

## FUTURE CONDITIONALS

Read the paragraphs; then complete the sentences that follow them.

Astrophysicists say that a collision with an asteroid big enough to destroy large portions of the planet Earth is possible. The odds of an individual's dying by such a catastrophic event vary from 40,000 to 1 to 400,000 to 1, depending on the scientific source. But all scientists agree that if an Earth-asteroid collision happens, there will be catastrophic results changing the lives of millions of people.

The scientists point to recent studies that claim that the extinction of the dinosaurs may have been caused by just such an event. Some people hypothesize that about one million years ago, a huge asteroid collided with Earth, causing so much damage and so many profound environmental changes (such as loss of sunlight due to dust, leading to massive plant and animal distress) that many life forms around at the time, like dinosaurs, could not survive under the conditions. These scientists feel that if an asteroid of the same size that killed the dinosaurs comes, all creatures living on the planet will have to be worried.

1. If there is an Earth-asteroid collision of significant size, the results will

be _____.

2. If there is an Earth-asteroid collision of significant size, it will

change _____.

3. If Earth collides with an asteroid of significant size, _____

_____ will have to be worried.

4. If Earth collides with an asteroid of significant size, the odds that an

individual will die are _____.

5. If there is an Earth-asteroid collision similar to the one that killed

_____, many life forms will again be threatened.


## EXERCISE 14.19

## MORE FUTURE CONDITIONALS

**A.** Complete each statement. Use the future or a modal in the main clause.

*Examples:* If I study three hours a day, . . . (future)

*If I study three hours a day, I will pass the final.*

If I study three hours a day, . . . (modal)

*If I study three hours a day, I should pass the test.*

1. If I don't study every day, . . . (future)


2. If I pass the final test, . . . (modal)

3. If she doesn't have the money, . . . (future)

4. If she gets a visa, . . . (modal)

5. If the rain stops, . . . (modal)

**B.** Complete each statement with an appropriate *if* or *unless* clause in the present tense.

*Examples:* I might fail the test if . . .

*I might fail the test if I don't study.*

I am not going to go to college unless . . .

*I am not going to go to college unless I have the money.*

1. I'll pass this course if . . .

2. I won't pass this course unless . . .

3. She will complain to us if . . .

4. You won't get a good grade unless . . .

5. The driver will come to pick you up if . . .

**C.** Transform each statement into a *what if?* question; then supply a future conditional answer.

*Example:* I'm going to the beach tomorrow.

*What if there is a storm tomorrow?*
*If there is a storm, I will stay home.*

1. I have to be in the office at nine tomorrow.

2. I have to finish this project by the end of the month.

3. David says he does not have any time to study this week.

4. I wrote a four-hundred-word essay.

5. Trisha says she can't afford car insurance.

**D.** Using this scale, fill in an appropriate predictive modal to complete each sentence.

*will, must* = certain
*should* = probable
*may, could, might* = possible

*Example:* If it gets cold tonight, it _____*will*_____ snow tomorrow. (certain)

1. If it gets hotter tonight, it _____ rain tomorrow. (probable)

2. If it gets colder tomorrow, it _____ snow. (possible)

3. If it gets cooler, it _____ snow tomorrow. (possible)

4. If the snow is heavy, they _____ close the school. (probable)

5. If the cool air meets the hot air, it _____ rain. (certain)

**3**    **Imaginative conditionals**

Imaginative conditionals express hypothetical (possible) or counterfactual (impossible) states or events in the *if* clause; the main clause expresses the result.

If she had the time, she would go to Paris. (In reality, she does not have the time now, but she might in the future.)

If Moses were alive today, he would be appalled at some behaviors. (In reality, Moses is not alive and will never be.)

**Present tense**

To express imaginative or unreal conditions with a present meaning, a past form is used in the *if* clause, and *would* + the base form is used in the main clause.

REAL       I don't have a car. I can't take the job.
IMAGINATIVE   If I had a car, I would take the job.

REAL       I don't have a job. I can't make any money.
IMAGINATIVE   If I had a job, I would make some money.

The modals *might* and *could* may also be used in the main clause.

REAL       It's late. He can't make it.
IMAGINATIVE   If it weren't late, he could make it.

For the verb *be*, the subjunctive form, *were*, is used in the *if* clause with all persons, singular and plural.

If he were king of the world, we would all be better off.

# EXERCISE 14.20

## IMAGINATIVE CONDITIONALS IN THE PRESENT

**A.** Complete each sentence with an appropriate main clause.

*Example:* If I worked harder, . . .

*If I worked harder, I might get better grades.*

1. If I were the boss, . . .

2. If I were very rich, . . .

3. If I could live another hundred years, . . .

4. If I studied more, . . .

5. If I ran faster, . . .

6. If I looked like a movie star, . . .

7. If I could be a child again, . . .

8. If I were of the opposite sex, . . .

9. If I were the principal of the school, . . .

10. If I didn't pay the rent, . . .

**B.** Complete each sentence with an appropriate *if* clause.

*Example:* I would get better grades if . . .

*I would get better grades if I studied more.*

1. I would be rich if . . .


2. I wouldn't be working if . . .


3. If . . . , I would return to my country.


4. I would do better at math if . . .


5. I would be poor if . . .


6. If . . . , I would work more.


7. I would be very sad if . . .


8. If . . . , I would be very happy.


9. His life would be much better if . . .


10. I would study more if . . .

**C.** Imagine that you are one of the animals or objects indicated. Write three counterfactual conditional sentences about each.

*Example:* a tree

*If I were a tree, I would have many leaves. If I were a tree, I would have roots under the ground. If I were a tree, I would be happy in springtime.*

1. an elephant

2. a house

3. a can of soda

**D.** Complete each sentence by giving advice to the person described in parentheses.

*Example:* (noisy student)

If I were you, I would _____ *keep quiet* _____.

1. (failing student)

   If I were you, I would _____.

2. (tardy student)

   If I were you, I would _____.

3. (student with the highest grades)

   If I were you, I would _____.

4. (student athlete)

   If I were you, I would _____.

5. (impatient student)

   If I were you, I would _____.

### Past tense

   To talk about imaginary conditions in the past, the past perfect is used in the *if* clause, and *would/might/could have* + a past participle is used in the main clause.

   If Columbus hadn't sailed to the New World in 1492, he would have done something else.

   If I had passed last term, I might have finished my degree.

   If I had done my job right, I would not have failed.

## EXERCISE 14.21

## IMAGINATIVE CONDITIONALS IN THE PAST

**A.** Fill in the blanks, using the words in parentheses.

   *Example::*  If you __*had told*__ (tell) me the news, I would have alerted the boss.

1. If she _____ (read) the entire chapter, she would have passed the test.

2. If I _____ (take, not) physics, I would have made the dean's list.

3. If you _____ (pay) last month's rent, you would not have been evicted.

4. If you _____ (come) to class today, you would have heard the news.

5. If I _____ (live) here all my life, I would be fluent in English.

**B.**   Complete each sentence appropriately.

*Example:*   I would have come home earlier if . . .

*I would have come home earlier if the car had not broken down.*

1. I would have stayed in my country if . . .

2. She would have done better in school if . . .

3. The judge would have explained the case again if . . .

4. My mother would have been disappointed if . . .

5. I would have stayed later at work if . . .

**C.**   Imagine being each of the famous people from history listed. State what you would or would not have done.

*Example:*   Christopher Columbus

*If I had been Columbus, I would have kept on exploring.*

1. Julius Caesar

2. Martin Luther King, Jr.

3. George Washington

4. Harriet Beecher Stowe

5. Amelia Earhart

## 14g Wishes

The verb *wish* creates sentences similar to counterfactual or imaginative conditional sentences. *Wish* is used to express the idea that the speaker or writer wants reality to be different from what actually is.

REALITY    He won't hire me.
WISH       I wish (that) he would hire me.

REALITY    She won't be here.
WISH       I wish (that) she were going to be here.

REALITY    She didn't come to visit.
WISH       I wish (that) she had come to visit.

NOTE: *That* in such constructions is optional and may be omitted.

### 1 Verb tense

Wish sentences are like conditionals in verb tense.

**Present tense**

For present meaning, the past is used in the *that* clause.

I don't understand math.

I wish that I understood math.

*Were* + present participle is used for a wish about now.

It's snowing now.

I wish that it weren't snowing now.

Future wishes follow the same pattern.

He is not going to be there.
I wish that he were going to be there.

She can't arrive next week.
I wish that she could arrive next week.

**Past tense**

For a past meaning, the past perfect (*had* + past participle) is used in the *that* clause.

Anya didn't come to the party.
I wish that Anya had come to the party.

He fired me.
I wish that he had not fired me.

If the verb is *could* or *would*, it is followed by *have* + past participle.

John wouldn't work for me.
I wish that he would have worked for me.

Maria couldn't come.
I wish that Maria could have come.

## 2  Questions and short answers

Frequently, questions in the present tense are answered with a *wish* reply.

Are all Americans happy?
No, they're not happy, but they wish they were happy.

Do all Americans own houses?
No, they don't own houses, but they wish they did own houses.

These answers are usually shortened.

No, they're not, but they wish they were.

No, they don't, but they wish they did.

## EXERCISE 14.22

## WISHES

---

**A.**  Complete each sentence appropriately.

*Example:*   I wish I could . . .

*I wish I could fly like a bird.*

1. I wish I were . . .

2. I wish I had . . .

3. I wish I could speak . . .

4. I wish I owned . . .

5. I wish I could go . . .

6. I wish I knew how . . .

7. I wish I could hear . . .

8. I wish I could cook . . .

9. I wish I could sing . . .

10. I wish I could be . . .

**B.** Answer each question with a short answer.

*Example:* Will all the athletes be selected for the team?

*No, they won't be, but they wish they could be.*

1. Will we all become rich?

2. Will all of them be able to buy a house?

3. Are all the students happy?

4. Are all the students graduating this year?

5. Do all the students speak perfect English?

**C.** Fill in each blank with an appropriate verb in the correct tense.

*Example:* My house doesn't have a fan. I wish that it ___*had*___ *I wish*
one. *it did.*

*he would*

1. He won't tell me the answer. I wish that he _____
tell me.

2. I didn't go to the bank. I wish I _____ to the bank.

3. Ron didn't come to our house. I wish that he
_____.

4. She wouldn't tell him about it. He wishes she
_____.

5. I don't know how to sail a boat. I wish I _____
how to do it.

6. The sky is cloudy, but I wish that the sun _____
now.

7. Our house doesn't have a basement. I wish our house
_____ a basement.

8. I will not be able to go next week. I wish that I
_____ with you.

9. You haven't met my girlfriend. I wish that you
_____ her.

10. Ray couldn't make the big meeting last night. I wish that he
_____ the meeting; it was important.

**D.** Write two sentences about what is wrong with each item and what you wish were different.

*Example:*   your car

*My car doesn't have a tape player.*
*I wish my car had a tape player.*

1. your school




2. your house




3. your wardrobe




4. your friends




5. your job

**E.** Write a paragraph about things that you wish you could change in your native country. Then write a paragraph about things that you wish you could change in the United States.

## CHAPTER 15

# Punctuation

## 15a End marks of punctuation

Punctuation is a set of graphic symbols. Punctuation is used by writers as a visual aid to distinguish separate sentences and paragraphs. Ponsot and Deem say it well: "All the graphics of punctuation are intended to enhance the reader's sense of whole structures."†

Since by definition a sentence contains an unsubordinated subject and its verb, each sentence expresses a complete idea. The most important job of the writer in terms of punctuation is to show the reader where one complete idea begins and ends. The beginning of a sentence is marked by a capital letter, and the end by a terminal mark of punctuation—a period (.), a question mark (?), or an exclamation point (!). Periods are used at the end of declarative sentences. Most of the sentences in this book fall into this category. Question marks come at the end of questions.

Who are you?

Where are they going tomorrow?

An exclamation point comes at the end of an exclamatory sentence.

Stop doing that!

Get out of here!

## 15b Sentence fragments

The biggest problem that most writers have with punctuation is writing sentence fragments. A **sentence fragment** is a phrase or clause that is not a complete idea but is punctuated as if it were. A fragment either lacks a verb or a subject or is a clause beginning with a subordinating conjunction or a relative pronoun. None of the following are sentences.

*Especially the maid. (no verb)

*Walking with a cane. (no subject; the *-ing* form of verb cannot stand alone)

†M. Ponsot and R. Deem, *The Common Sense* (Upper Montclair, N.J.: Boynton Cook, 1985), p. 45.

*Because she was a dancer. (not a complete idea; begins with a subordinating conjunction)

*Who is my brother. (not a complete idea; begins with a relative pronoun)

The last two examples represent the most common sentence fragments and the hardest to recognize. This is because clauses contain subjects and verbs and appear to be sentences. If we read them carefully, however, we can usually sense or "hear" their incompleteness.

A sentence fragment may be corrected in two ways: by attaching it to a complete sentence or by adding the missing parts.

| | |
|---|---|
| FRAGMENT | She was late. Because her car broke down. |
| COMPLETE SENTENCE | She was late because her car broke down. |
| COMPLETE SENTENCE | Because her car broke down, she was late. |
| FRAGMENT | Some of the men and most of the women. |
| COMPLETE SENTENCE | The group included some of the men and most of the women. |
| COMPLETE SENTENCE | Some of the men and most of the women were in the group. |

## EXERCISE 15.1

## FRAGMENTS AND SENTENCES

**A.** Below are eighteen fragments and two complete sentences. Revise the fragments into complete sentences. Below the two complete sentences, write *OK*.

*Example:* When the people were told not to vote.

*The problem started when the people were told not to vote.*

1. When the wind began to blow very hard.


2. The dog running by the side of the road.


3. He started and was finished yesterday.

4. A former policeman, who had a suspicious personality.

5. On a starry night just last week.

6. After the party was over.

7. Taking his sweet time to do it.

8. Run and hit the ball.

9. From above and behind him.

10. Although it was his birthday.

11. Which faded in the hot sun.

12. Having the best education possible.

13. A resident of Ohio.

14. With prices soaring to record levels.

15. The child looking for his toy.

16. Who raised the entire crop himself.

17. Because the dog was running.

18. During the big storm last night.

19. Eating on the run.

20. Despite the high temperature.

**B.** Read the following paragraphs. Insert punctuation and capital letters where necessary. The first sentence has been done for you as an example.

1. A Day in August

*A*ugust is the hottest month₀ the average temperature is over

ninety degrees fahrenheit there is hardly any rain or cool breeze the

humidity is very high after a while it just gets to you tempers flare

often during this kind of weather that's why they call it the dog days

of summer.

2. Sailing the Lake

sailing is a fun and enjoyable hobby it gets you outdoors the

exercise is good for the body it's important to learn some of the basics

before trying to sail on your own the beginner has to learn how to

rig the boat and do some simple maneuvers taking a life preserver for each person on board a sailboat is a must it's important to be

safety-conscious

3. Learning to Drive

learning to drive is also fun and enjoyable it makes life more

convenient you can get from place to place much quicker you don't

have to wait for buses or trains during the weather you will stay

dry and safe now many people learn to drive while in high school

this is a good way to learn others learn from their parents or friends

this could be dangerous since most people don't have cars equipped

properly for teaching others you may lose a friend because of hurt

feelings

C. Read the following paragraphs. Then rewrite them, correcting any fragments by supplying the missing parts or connecting them to a main clause. The first sentence has been done for you as an example.

Yoga beginning four to five thousand years ago. Before the birth

*Yoga began four to five thousand years ago, before the birth of Christ.*

of Christ. The science of the body, the mind, and the breath. Which has many postures and breathing practices. The postures are called *asanas*. Various ways of stretching the body's major parts. The body stretched backward, forward, and upside down. Which is done to tone the muscles and make the body limber.

Breathing practices to calm the mind and to prepare the mind for meditation. Because yoga practitioners believe meditating helps them come in contact with their inner selves. Leading to a sense of spirituality missing in the world.

Learning from a teacher how to do the postures and the breathing practices. Some people learn yoga by taking classes. Others by reading books. Still others learn from their families. Because yoga is such an ancient discipline. Many people studying it today for its wisdom. Concerned with their bodies, their minds, and their spirits.

## 15c Comma splices and fused sentences

### 1 Comma splices

A **comma splice** results when two or more main clauses (complete sentences) are separated only by a comma. Each complete sentence must be marked as to its beginning (a capital letter) and its end (a terminal mark of punctuation). A comma can never mark the end of a sentence. For example, the following sentences are comma splices:

*George and Marilyn went to the movies, they sat in the front row.
*Louise is a student, she attends a nearby college.

A comma splice can be corrected in a number of ways.

1. Make each sentence into a separate main clause beginning with a capital letter and ending with a period.

   George and Marilyn went to the movies. They sat in the front row.

2. Make the two clauses into a compound sentence. This may be done by inserting a semicolon for the comma, by inserting a semicolon for the comma and adding a conjunctive adverb, or by following the comma with a coordinating conjunction (see Chapters 5 and 14).

   Louise is a student; she attends a nearby college.

   Louise is a student; hence, she attends a nearby college.

   Louise is a student, and she attends a nearby college.

3. Make the two clauses into a complex sentence by beginning one of the clauses with a subordinate conjunction or a relative pronoun (see Chapters 5 and 14).

   George and Marilyn went to the movies, where they sat in the front row.

   Because Louise is a student, she attends a nearby college.

4. Reduce one of the clauses to a subordinate phrase.

   Having gone to the movies, George and Marilyn sat in the front row.

### 2 Fused sentences

A **fused sentence** is also often called a run-on sentence. This error connects two or more main clauses with no connecting word or punctuation between them. It can be corrected in the same ways as a comma splice.

<small>Fused</small> George and Marilyn went to the movies they sat in the first row.

<small>Fused</small> Louise is a student she attends a nearby college.

## EXERCISE 15.2

## COMMA SPLICES AND FUSED SENTENCES

**A.** Rewrite each sentence, correcting the comma splices and fused sentences.

*Example:* The students were tired they had worked all night.

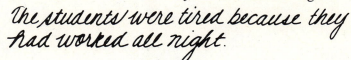

*The students were tired because they had worked all night.*

1. The governor was reelected the treasurer was not.

2. The people came to see the games, their patience was rewarded.

3. Walt Whitman wrote many great poems he is known as the father of modern American poetry.

4. Traveling to Spain was easy for them, they work for the airlines.

5. They played and daydreamed they got no work done.

6. The boy was an orphan, he lived with a distant cousin on a farm.

7. The party was on Saturday night I had to work.

8. She rested on the bed he carried in all the groceries.

9. I wanted to attend the wedding, however I was too busy.


10. She was the boss, therefore whatever she said was done.


**B.** Combine each pair of sentences in two ways as specified in parentheses.

> *Example:* The school had to close early today. The students left at 1:00 P.M.
> (comma, coordinating conjunction)
>
> *The school had to close early today, so the students left at 1:00 P.M.*
>
> (semicolon, conjunctive adverb)
>
> *The school had to close early today; therefore, the students left at 1:00 P.M.*

1. Larry moved to California in 1968. He has lived there since then. (semicolon)




(comma, coordinating conjunction)




2. I couldn't afford a big apartment on my own. I found a roommate. (comma, coordinating conjunction)




(semicolon, conjunctive adverb)

3. He liked his job. He was forced to quit.
   (semicolon, conjunctive adverb)


   (comma, coordinating conjunction)


4. He lives in the countryside. He grows his own vegetables and raises chickens.
   (relative pronoun)


   (subordinating conjunction)


5. She lost the race. She felt the pain of defeat.
   (first clause reduced to modifying phrase)


   (relative pronoun)


## 15d Nonrestrictive relative clauses

Besides its most important function—to combine two main clauses into a compound sentence in combination with a coordinating conjunction—the comma has another common function. That is to set off nonrestrictive relative clauses.

A **restrictive clause** limits the meaning of the word or words it refers to and cannot be omitted without changing the meaning. For example, the following sentences both have restrictive clauses.

All the people who were sitting in the rear could not hear.

Suggestions that she made are ridiculous.

If we omit these relative clauses, the sentences are not true.

All the people could not hear.

Suggestions are ridiculous.

A **nonrestrictive clause** adds extra but nonessential information about the word or words it modifies. The following sentences contain nonrestrictive clauses.

The museum, which opened two years ago, is located at Broadway and Seventy-second Street.

The game, which lasted two innings, was called off because of rain.

If a nonrestrictive clause is removed, the meaning of the sentence is not altered.

The museum is located at Broadway and Seventy-second Street.

The game was called off because of rain.

A nonrestrictive clause always immediately follows the head noun and is set off by commas. In nonrestrictive clauses, *who, whom,* or *whose* is used for people and *which* for things. *That* is never used in a nonrestrictive clause.

## EXERCISE 15.3

## NONRESTRICTIVE CLAUSES

**A.** Fill in each blank with an appropriate nonrestrictive clause about a place of work.

*Example:* One major change in policy, which *I heard about yesterday*, is that we can come in earlier and leave earlier.

1. The boss, who _____,
   was appointed in 1990.

2. The traditional workday, which _____,
   goes from 8:30 to 5:00, with an hour off for lunch.

3. The meeting room, which _____,
   is on the second floor.

4. All employees are eligible to serve on the safety committee, which

   _____.

5. Payday, which _____,
   is every other week.

**500    Punctuation**

**B.** Combine each pair of sentences into one sentence with a nonrestrictive clause.

*Example:* Yoga is four to five thousand years old. Yoga originated in India.

*Yoga, which originated in India, is four to five thousand years old.*

1. The typhoon raged for four hours. It caused substantial flooding.

2. The boss is in charge of management and all decisions relating to manufacturing. He graduated from Harvard.

3. The woman works in shipping and receiving. She is married to Mike.

4. Some stars are visible in the daytime. These stars are very bright.

5. The heart beats about seventy times every minute of the day. The heart is a series of valves.

6. This pen cost sixty dollars. It was made in Japan.

7. The Sears Tower has more than one hundred stories. It is located in Chicago.

8. The Hudson River runs from upstate New York into the Atlantic Ocean. The Hudson River separates New York and New Jersey.

9. Johnson City had a population of half a million people. It was founded in 1773.

10. The Great Wall took generations to build. It is four thousand miles long.

**C.** The following sentences have restrictive and nonrestrictive clauses. Insert commas where necessary.

*Example:*   The teacher, who was born in Charleston, has been at the school for seventeen years.

1. My dog who is nine years old is the only pet I have.

2. The teacher who wrote the exam is over there.

3. The students who came from Peru all speak Spanish.

4. The book which is a best seller is lying on the table.

5. That woman whose name is Marie can cook better than I.

6. New Jersey which is known as the Garden State is adjacent to New York.

7. I own a car which I use a lot.

8. I have a friend whom I go camping with.

9. Haiti which is on an island was one of the first places visited by Christopher Columbus.

10. Richard Nixon who was born in California was the only president of the United States to resign.

**D.** Read the following paragraphs. Insert commas where necessary. The first sentence has been done for you as an example.

Haiti, which is on an island in the Caribbean Sea, was one of the first places visited by Christopher Columbus and his men in 1492. Before Columbus discovered Haiti which he called Santo Domingo the island was the home of the Caribs and other native peoples. The people who inhabited the island were called Indians by Columbus. A legend which may or may not be true says that he thought he had reached India. One fact that cannot be disputed is that Columbus began a whole new era in the history of Haiti.

## 15e The apostrophe

There are two main uses for the **apostrophe**:

1. To form the possessive case of nouns and indefinite pronouns

   That is Elmer's book.

   To everyone's surprise, she was quite angry.

2. To mark the omitted letters in a contraction

   | | |
   |---|---|
   | do not = don't | could not = couldn't |
   | does not = doesn't | she is/has = she's |
   | will not = won't | I would = I'd |
   | has not = hasn't | |

   Be careful to distinguish between these pairs of contractions and possessives:

   | | |
   |---|---|
   | it's = it is | its = of it |
   | who's = who is | whose = of whom |
   | there's = there is | theirs = of them |
   | they're = they are | their = possessive pronoun or adjective |
   | you're = you are | your = possessive pronoun or adjective |

## EXERCISE 15.4

## APOSTROPHES

Insert an apostrophe wherever necessary.

*Example:* Don't do that!

1. That dog hangs on to its bones.

2. Its Tuesday, the third of July.

3. He says its his right to be at the meeting.

4. Theres a lot of love and understanding here.

5. That book is theirs.

6. I dont know whos the boss in that center.

7. Youre responsible for Maras books.

8. She said she doesnt know whose hat this is.

9. Hed rather not answer any more questions about this.

10. Hes mad at everyones indifference.


## 15f Quotation marks

Quotation marks are used to indicate three things:

1. A direct quotation

   He said, "I won't give up my rights."

2. A title of a poem, short story, or essay

   T. S. Eliot wrote "The Lovesong of J. Alfred Prufrock."

3. An expression used in some special way, usually ironic

   The "improvements" he made to the premises cost a fortune to repair.


### EXERCISE 15.5

### QUOTATION MARKS

Insert quotation marks and any other punctuation where necessary.

*Example:*   He wrote the poem «Terminal Restaurant."

1. The woman was so happy she exclaimed whoopee!

2. Be sure to fill in all the spaces on the answer sheet the teacher said at the beginning of the test.

3. He visited the Big Easy—that's New Orleans—last year.

4. He wrote an essay on thermal warming called Thermal Heat Patterns.

5. The man said I have never been accused of a crime, and I trust I never will be.

6. He wanted to ski down Deadman's Drop.

7. I regret that I have but one life to give for my country are famous heroic words.

8. He said Please do and she answered I'll think about it.

9. Did she write Hail the Conquering Hero?

10. The teacher warned us Don't skip any parts on the final exam.

# CHAPTER 16

# Pronunciation

The word *pronunciation* has two distinct definitions. One describes the act of speech in general—the way in which a word is pronounced in a language. The other is more specific, focusing on the phonetic transcription of individual words. In a sense, language consists of putting together the specific sounds of each word in the proper order with the proper stress and intonation. Sound determines meaning. So both definitions are relevant.

Native speakers are naturally fluent and articulate in their native language. They do not need to be told that *alone* has two syllables with the stress on the second syllable. They do not need any transcript of words to say them—native speakers unconsciously know the syllable breaks and the stress patterns of most words.

## 16a Phonetic alphabet

In English, the spelling of a word and its pronunciation are often quite different, and many different letters can represent the same sound. For example, look up *coffee, tough, free,* and *photograph* in your dictionary. You'll see that each has an /f/ sound, but the sound is spelled differently in each case. Many dictionaries provide a pronunciation guide for each word in a phonetic alphabet. The **International Phonetic Alphabet (IPA)** is an alphabet system in which one symbol represents one sound. It's not necessary to memorize all of the IPA symbols, but becoming familiar with them and being able to use them will help you in your goal of achieving clear and understandable pronunciation in English.

The phonetic alphabet uses most of the twenty-six letters in the English alphabet. It also uses some additional symbols. Phonetic letters and symbols are written between slash marks to distinguish them from individual letters. For example, /k/ = the sound that begins the words *keep* and *cat*; k = the letter *k*. The word *cat* is pronounced /k æ t/.

## 1 Consonants

Many phonetic symbols for consonants are the same as alphabet letters.

| PHONETIC SYMBOL | Initial | Medial | Final |
|---|---|---|---|
| /p/ | pig | upon | stop |
| /b/ | big | about | rob |
| /t/ | tip | later | hat |
| /d/ | day | candy | had |
| /k/ | cat | lake | neck |
| /g/ | get | again | beg |
| /f/ | food | before | safe |
| /v/ | victim | over | live |
| /s/ | see | lesson | bus |
| /z/ | zebra | easy | choose |
| /m/ | me | admit | home |
| /n/ | no | panic | balloon |
| /l/ | love | alive | swell |
| /r/ | read | very | bore |
| /w/ | wall | away | — |
| /y/ | yes | canyon | — |
| /h/ | house | behold | — |

Other phonetic symbols differ from the letters of the alphabet.

POSITIONS IN WHICH THE SOUND OCCURS

| PHONETIC SYMBOL | Initial | Medial | Final |
|---|---|---|---|
| /θ/ | thing | nothing | bath |
| /ð/ | the | mother | bathe |
| /ʃ/ | shot | machine | dish |
| /ʒ/ | genre | pleasure | mirage |
| /tʃ/ | child | preacher | teach |
| /dʒ/ | job | wages | cage |
| /ŋ/ | — | sinking | king |

## 2 Vowels

A vowel is a sound produced with vibrating vocal cords and a continuous unrestricted flow of air coming from the mouth.

POSITIONS IN WHICH THE SOUND OCCURS

| PHONETIC SYMBOL | Initial | Medial | Final |
|---|---|---|---|
| /i/ | each | believe | tea |
| /ɪ/ | it | hit | sunny |
| /eɪ/ | ate | take | they |
| /ɛ/ | egg | head | — |
| /æ/ | at | hat | — |
| /a/ | army | hot | Ma |
| /u/ | ooze | rule | to |

| PHONETIC SYMBOL | Initial | Medial | Final |
|---|---|---|---|
| /ʊ/ | — | book | — |
| /oʊ/ | own | boat | no |
| /ɔ/ | all | tall | paw |
| /ʌ/ | up | but | — |
| /ɝ/ | urn | first | sir |
| /aʊ/ | out | house | cow |
| /aɪ/ | I | bite | pie |
| /ɔɪ/ | oil | noise | toy |

The schwa /ə/ is sounded much like the /ʌ/, but it is unstressed (for example, *upon* and *soda*).

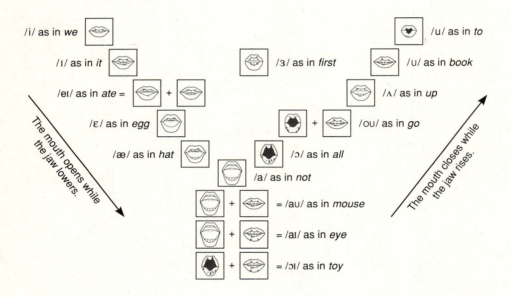

## EXERCISE 16.1

## PHONETIC SPELLING

___

**A.** Indicate the number of letters and the number of sounds in each word; then give its phonetic spelling. The first one has been done for you as an example.

| | LETTERS | SOUNDS | PHONETIC SPELLING |
|---|---|---|---|
| 1. cough | 5 | 3 | /kɔf/ |
| 2. plumb | _____ | _____ | /_____/ |

|  | LETTERS | SOUNDS | PHONETIC SPELLING |
|---|---|---|---|
| 3. food | _____ | _____ | /_____/ |
| 4. tea | _____ | _____ | /_____/ |
| 5. fix | _____ | _____ | /_____/ |
| 6. thought | _____ | _____ | /_____/ |
| 7. bath | _____ | _____ | /_____/ |
| 8. though | _____ | _____ | /_____/ |
| 9. buy | _____ | _____ | /_____/ |
| 10. hour | _____ | _____ | /_____/ |

**B.** Match each phonetic symbol with the words in which it occurs. The first one has been done for you as an example.

| | | |
|---|---|---|
| _a___ | 1. /m/ | a. happy |
| _____ | 2. /i/ | b. church |
| _____ | 3. /h/ | c. wife |
| _____ | 4. /tʃ/ | d. come |
| _____ | 5. /ŋ/ | e. tall |
| _____ | 6. /t/ | f. see |
| _____ | 7. /f/ | g. sing |
| _____ | 8. /ð/ | h. the |
| _____ | 9. /k/ | i. page |
| _____ | 10. /p/ | j. cake |

## EXERCISE 16.2

## VOWEL SOUNDS

Each of the following words contains one of four vowel sounds. Look up each word in your dictionary; then spell the word phonetically

**16a/Phonetic Alphabet**    509

and write it in the proper column according to its vowel sound. The first word has been done for you as an example.

field    /_*fild*_____/          group    /_____/

led      /_____/          ski      /_____/

clue     /_____/          move     /_____/

boot     /_____/          people   /_____/

box      /_____/          lot      /_____/

read     /_____/          said     /_____/

bury     /_____/          scene    /_____/

do       /_____/          guess    /_____/

father   /_____/          watch    /_____/

friend   /_____/          clod     /_____/

|       /i/        |       /ɛ/        |       /a/        |       /u/        |
|------------------|------------------|------------------|------------------|
| *field*          | _____ | _____ | _____ |
| _____ | _____ | _____ | _____ |
| _____ | _____ | _____ | _____ |
| _____ | _____ | _____ | _____ |
| _____ | _____ | _____ | _____ |

## EXERCISE 16.3

## CONSONANT SOUNDS

Each of the following words contains one of three consonant sounds. Look up each word in your dictionary; then spell the word phonetically and write it in the proper column according to the consonant sound. The first word has been done for you as an example.

| dice | /_*daɪs*_/ | photographer | /_____/ |
|------|------------|--------------|---------------|
| wreck | /_____/ | pseudonym | /_____/ |
| city | /_____/ | fizzle | /_____/ |
| knack | /_____/ | some | /_____/ |
| come | /_____/ | science | /_____/ |
| tough | /_____/ | queen | /_____/ |
| free | /_____/ | kick | /_____/ |
| | | laughed | /_____/ |

| /s/ | /f/ | /k/ |
|-----|-----|-----|
| _dice_ | _____ | _____ |
| _____ | _____ | _____ |
| _____ | _____ | _____ |
| _____ | _____ | _____ |
| _____ | _____ | _____ |

## 16b Other pronunciation factors

### 1 Articulators

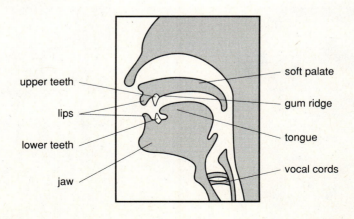

upper teeth
lips
lower teeth
jaw

soft palate
gum ridge
tongue
vocal cords

The parts of the mouth and throat that we use when speaking are the lips, the gum ridge, the tongue, the soft palate, the teeth, the vocal cords, and the jaw. These are the articulators.

The various consonant sounds are created by the position of the **articulators**, the way the air stream comes from the mouth to the nose, and the vibration of the vocal cords.

The vowel sounds are affected by the changing shape and position of the articulators. The vowels are created by the position of the tongue in the mouth, the shape of the lips, and the size of the jaw opening.

## 2 Voiced and voiceless sounds

It is very important to notice the difference between voiced and voiceless sounds. The difference between the sounds can make a difference in the meaning of a word. For example /p/ and /b/ are formed in exactly the same way, but /b/ is voiced and /p/ is not.

All vowels are voiced, so the vocal cords vibrate when they are produced.

Voiced consonants are the sounds produced when the vocal cords are vibrating. These are /b/, /d/, /g/, /v/, /z/, /ð/, /ʒ/, /dʒ/, /l/, /r/, /w/, /y/, /m/, /n/, and /ŋ/.

Voiceless consonants are the sounds produced when there is no vibration of the vocal cords. These are /p/, /t/, /k/, /f/, /s/, /θ/, /ʃ/, /tʃ/, and /h/.

## 3 Diphthongs

A **diphthong** begins as one vowel sound and ends as another. Thus it is a combination of two vowel sounds. To produce a diphthong, the articulators glide from the position of the first vowel to the position of the second. The most common diphthongs in English are /aʊ/, /eɪ/, /aɪ/, /ɔɪ/, and /oʊ/.

### PRODUCTION OF CONSONANT SOUNDS

| PLACE OF ARTICULATION | MANNER OF PRODUCTION |
| --- | --- |
| Two lips | /p/ pen <br> /b/ boy <br> Lips are closed; air builds up and releases when lips part. <br> /m/ me <br> Lips are closed; air passes out through nose. <br> /w/ wash <br> Back of tongue is high in mouth; lips are rounded. |

| Teeth and lip | /f/ face |
| | /v/ void |
| | Upper teeth contact inside of lower lip; air is forced through. |
| Tongue tip and teeth | /θ/ thin |
| | /ð/ the |
| | Tip of tongue is between teeth; air is forced through. |
| Tongue tip and upper gum ridge | /t/ tin |
| | /d/ day |
| | Tongue tip is on upper gum ridge; built-up air is released when tongue is removed. |
| | /s/ seed |
| | /z/ zoom |
| | Tongue tip is close to upper gum ridge; air is forced through narrow opening of tongue. |
| | /n/ none |
| | Tip of tongue is on upper gum ridge; air passes out through nose. |
| | /l/ like |
| | Tongue tip is on upper gum ridge; air passes over sides of tongue. |
| | /r/ real |
| | Tongue tip points to upper gum ridge; air passes over tongue. |
| Front of tongue and roof of mouth | /ʃ/ shin |
| | /ʒ/ pleasure |
| | Front part of tongue is raised toward roof of mouth; air passes over tongue; lips are rounded. |
| | /y/ yes |
| | Center part of tongue is raised toward roof of mouth; air passes over tongue. |
| | /tʃ/ church |
| | Combination of /t/ and /ʃ/, said quickly. |
| | /dʒ/ job |
| | Combination of /d/ and /ʒ/, said quickly. |
| Back of tongue and back of roof of mouth (soft palate) | /k/ kick |
| | /g/ go |
| | Back of tongue touches soft palate; air builds up and is released when back of tongue is lowered. |
| | /ŋ/ king |
| | Back of tongue touches soft palate; air passes out through nose. |
| Glottis | /h/ help |
| | Formed at the vocal folds; air passes through small opening between them. |

## 16c Other vocal features

Individual sounds can be significantly influenced by certain vocal features including stress and intonation.

### 1 Stress

**Stress** is the amount of volume a speaker gives to a sound, syllable, or word. Every word in English with more than one syllable has a syllable that is stressed. Correct use of stress is important for the proper pronunciation of words.

A **syllable** is part of a word that contains a vowel sound. Any syllable may also have one or more consonant sounds. A dictionary pronunciation guide shows the syllables in a word. The sign ˈ or ′ before a syllable means that that syllable should be stressed. For example, in the word *pronunciation*, there are five syllables or vowel sounds, and the stress comes on the fourth syllable: /prə, nʌn, siˈeɪ ʃən/.

The stress in some words depends on their part of speech. Note the following pairs of nouns and verbs; they are spelled the same, but as nouns the first syllable receives the stress; as verbs, the second.

| NOUNS | VERBS |
|---|---|
| ˈconflict | conˈflict |
| ˈconduct | conˈduct |
| ˈcontent | conˈtent |
| ˈdesert | deˈsert |
| ˈdigest | diˈgest |
| ˈcontest | conˈtest |
| ˈpermit | perˈmit |
| ˈexploit | exˈploit |
| ˈobject | obˈject |
| ˈincrease | inˈcrease |

#### Some hints about word stress

1.  Most two-syllable words are accented on the first syllable.

    ˈMonday  ˈalmost  ˈmother  ˈwindow

2.  Compound nouns are usually accented on the first syllable.

    ˈbookstore  ˈairport  ˈlighthouse  ˈbedroom

3.  Compound verbs are usually accented on the second or last syllable.

    outˈdo  upˈhold  withˈdraw  outˈrun

4. The numbers that are multiples of ten are accented on the first syllable.

'thirty   'eighty   'ninety

5. Reflexive pronouns are usually accented on the second syllable.

my'self   her'self   your'self   them'selves

It rarely helps to memorize pronunciation rules. The more you listen to and speak English, the more you will become aware of patterns like those just listed. Through practice and patient use of the dictionary, you will form habits that will enable you to pronounce most new words you encounter.

### Natural phrasing

Word stress gives meaning to the words you say. Native speakers of English do not pronounce words one at a time; instead, they link words together into phrases. Natural phrasing is made from both grammatical units and the meaning of the part of the sentence. For example, the words in the following sentence are grouped into phrases:

Being able   to read   by phrases   instead of   by single words results   from practice.

Content words—nouns, verbs, adjectives, and adverbs—are usually given the most stress in a sentence. Function words—articles, prepositions, pronouns, conjunctions, and auxiliary verbs—are usually not stressed.

## EXERCISE 16.4

## SYLLABLES AND STRESS

Look up each of the following words in your dictionary. Note the number of syllables, spell the word phonetically, and circle the stressed syllable.

*Example:*   vocabulary          5          /və(kæb)ulari/

| | SYLLABLES | PHONETIC RESPELLING |
|---|---|---|
| 1. teacher | _____ | /_____/ |
| 2. calculator | _____ | /_____/ |
| 3. medicine | _____ | /_____/ |

|  | SYLLABLES | PHONETIC RESPELLING |
|---|---|---|

4. revolutionary    _____     /_____/

5. liability    _____     /_____/

6. discover    _____     /_____/

7. understand    _____     /_____/

8. always    _____     /_____/

9. misunderstood    _____     /_____/

10. mathematics    _____     /_____/

## 2   Intonation

**Intonation** is the rise and fall of the voice. Intonation expresses feelings such as sadness or happiness, surprise, annoyance, and skepticism. There are two basic intonation patterns in English, rising and falling. The voice usually rises with the stress and falls off at the end of a sentence.

### Some hints about intonation

1. Use rising intonation when asking yes/no questions.

   Is this your book?

   Are you coming?

2. Use falling intonation with information (*wh-*) questions.

   What is it?

   How much does it cost?

3. Use rising intonation for each item in a list but falling intonation for the last item.

   I want paint, brushes, a pail, and some tape.

   He's taking math, English, history, and gym.

4. Use falling intonation with statements and commands.

   He likes it a lot.

   Come over here.

**516**    **Pronunciation**

## 16d Problem sounds

### 1 Vowels

1. Compare /i/ as in *seat* and /ɪ/ as in *sit*. Read the following pairs of pronunciation contrasts to practice the distinction between those two sounds.

| /i/ | /ɪ/ |
|-----|-----|
| eat | it |
| seat | sit |
| feet | fit |
| heat | hit |
| beat | bit |
| least | list |
| leave | live |
| leak | lick |
| sleep | slip |
| sheep | ship |

2. The /ə/ is called the **schwa** sound in English. It is a short, quick, unstressed sound made with the lips relaxed and barely moving. It is represented by many different letters. For example, the following words all have two /ə/ sounds, each represented by a different letter.

president elephant accident

A common error is to put an extra /ə/ before or after a word. Say the following list of words aloud. Be careful not to add a /ə/ to the beginning. Ask your instructor to listen to you.

| | |
|---|---|
| spelling | Spanish |
| sports | spontaneous |
| sleep | slick |
| soap | soup |

Practice saying the following words aloud. Be sure not to add a /ə/ at the end.

| | |
|---|---|
| like | tape |
| take | lake |
| hate | have |
| spike | slave |

### 2 Consonants

1. Compare /θ/ as in *thin* and /ð/ as in *then*. These sounds are produced in exactly the same way, except that /ð/ is voiced, which means

that the vocal cords vibrate. In both sounds, the tongue tip is between the upper and lower teeth. The sound is produced by forcing the air out through the opening between the tongue and the teeth.

Practice saying the following lists of words. Put your hand on your throat, and note that there is no vibration with /θ/.

| /θ/ | /ð/ |
| --- | --- |
| thin | then |
| thank | there |
| theme | them |
| thief | this |
| author | other |
| method | father |
| bath | bathe |
| cloth | clothe |
| breath | breathe |

2. Compare /l/ as in *led* to /r/ as in *red*. The /l/ sound is made by pressing the tongue against the gum ridge behind the upper front teeth; air flows out over the sides of your tongue while the vocal cords vibrate.

To make the /r/ sound, the tip of the tongue is raised but does not touch anything; the lips are slightly open as the air flows out over the tip of the tongue while the vocal cords vibrate.

Practice saying the following list of pronunciation contrasts.

| /l/ | /r/ |
| --- | --- |
| law | raw |
| lead | read |
| lust | rust |
| lice | rice |
| lock | rock |
| lot | rot |
| lest | rest |
| light | write |
| fly | fry |
| flee | free |
| ply | pry |
| all | or |
| tell | tear |

3. Compare /s/ as in *sad* and /z/ as in *zoo*. These sounds are made in the same way, but /s/ is voiceless, with no vibration of the vocal cords. The tongue is near the gum ridge but does not touch it, and the air stream is continuous. The vocal cords vibrate for /z/.

Read the following pairs of words to practice the distinction between these two sounds.

| /s/ | /z/ |
|-----|-----|
| sky | zoo |
| ski | zinc |
| seal | zeal |
| fast | lazy |
| pencil | easy |
| castle | puzzle |
| bus | his |
| yes | is |
| box | buzz |
| face | raise |

4. Compare /tʃ/ as in *church* and /ʃ/ as in *shoe*. The /ʃ/ sound is made by bringing the tip of the tongue near the upper gum ridge without touching it; the middle of the tongue is arched upward. The air is forced over the tongue and through the teeth while the lips are slightly rounded. The vocal cords do not vibrate.

The /tʃ/ sound is a combination of /t/ as in *ten* and /ʃ/ as in *shoe*. The tip of the tongue is pressed against the gum ridge, stopping the flow of air; then the tongue tip is quickly lowered while the air is forced out. The lips are slightly rounded, and the vocal cords do not vibrate.

Read the following pairs of pronunciation contrasts aloud to practice the distinction between these two sounds.

| /ʃ/ | /tʃ/ |
|-----|------|
| shin | chin |
| shill | chill |
| ship | chip |
| sheep | cheap |
| leash | leach |
| wash | watch |
| marsh | march |
| bash | batch |

**3** **Final note on pronunciation**

Much more could be said and illustrated about pronunciation in English. This is just a beginning. Remember to listen closely, use your dictionary, consult the following bibliography, and—most important—be patient with yourself.

## 16e  Pronunciation bibliography

R. Allen, V. F. Allen, and M. Shute. *English Sounds and Their Spellings*. New York: Crowell, 1968.

A. Bens. *Active English: Pronunciation and Speech*. Englewood Cliffs, N.J.: Prentice Hall, 1977.

M. E. Clarey and R. Dixson. *Pronunciation Exercises in English*. New York: Simon & Schuster, 1963.

P. Dale and L. Poms. *English Pronunciation for Spanish Speakers*: *Consonants*. Englewood Cliffs, N.J.: Prentice Hall, 1986.

P. Dale and L. Poms. *English Pronunciation for Spanish Speakers*: *Vowels*. Englewood Cliffs, N.J.: Prentice Hall, 1985.

English Language Services. *Drills and Exercises in English Pronunciation*. New York: Macmillan, 1977.

G. Esarey. *Pronunciation Exercises for Advanced Learners of English as a Second Language*. Pittsburgh, Pa.: University of Pittsburgh Press, 1977.

J. Gilbert. *Clear Speech and Listening*. Cambridge, England: Cambridge University Press, 1984.

H. G. Grate. *English Pronunciation Exercises for Japanese Students*. New York: Regents, 1974.

E. Hecht and G. Ryan. *Survival Pronunciation*. New York: Alemany Press, 1980.

J. Morley. *Improving Spoken English*. Ann Arbor: University of Michigan Press, 1979.

D. Nilsen and A. Nilsen. *Pronunciation Contrasts in English*. New York: Regents, 1973.

G. Orion. *Pronouncing American English*. Cambridge, Mass.: Newbury House, 1988.

C. Prator and B. Robinett. *Manual of American English Pronunciation*. Fort Worth: Holt, Rinehart and Winston, 1972.

E. C. Trager and S. C. Henderson. *Pronunciation Drills for Learners of English*. New York: English Language Services, 1956.

# Index

Page numbers in **bold** type indicate exercises.